THINK TO BETTER ACT

SPEECHES AT THE 1969 PAIGC CADRE SEMINAR

VOLUME 1

AMÍLCAR CABRAL

Published in February 2025 by
1804 Books, New York, NY

© Fundação Amílcar Cabral
Originally published by Fundação Amílcar Cabral as
Pensar para melhor agir: Intervenções no seminário de quadros, 1969
Other selections © 1804 Books, New York, NY

ISBN: 979-8-9910139-4-9
Library of Congress Control Number: 2024946608

Translated by Jethro Soutar
Introduction translated by Maria Otani
Edited by Desmond Fonseca
Cover by Rachel Domond & Vivek Venkatraman

TABLE OF CONTENTS

AMÍLCAR CABRAL AND THE PRACTICALITIES OF REVOLUTION

Amílcar Cabral (1924–1973) came to politics because of the condition of colonialism. The hideous structure of Portuguese domination over the land where he was born in western Africa framed the life of Cabral from his early consciousness to his last minutes. It was impossible for a bright person of his class to ignore the limits placed by European dominion upon him personally, and for a bright person of his commitments to see how colonialism deprived the Bissau-Guinean and the Caboverdean working class and peasantry of the necessary productive resources and benefits of their labor. What germinated as an anti-colonial awareness rapidly accelerated due to his own experiences into an anti-capitalist and anti-imperialist political consciousness. Amílcar Cabral became a national liberation Marxist through the grip of colonialism on his country and by the limits placed by capital on his country.

An agronomist by training, Cabral's intelligence forced him to acknowledge the "development of underdevelopment" in his country's agricultural zones. It was here that he began to advance his break with bourgeois liberal ideology and enter a consideration of national liberation and Marxism. For Cabral, deep in struggle, the main points of thought revolved around how to overcome the fragmentation of the population of Guinea-Bissau and Cabo Verde and how to identify the fighting sections that could be recruited first into a civic force and then eventually into a national liberation force and army. The practicalities of building such a movement detained Cabral, whose speeches and writings for the last ten years of his life (1963–1973) centered around these issues. It is important to register that these practicalities did not only mean the gun: fundamental to Cabral's movement was the building of cadre for the PAIGC [Partido Africano para a Independência da Guiné e Cabo Verde (African Party for the Independence of Guinea and Cape Verde)]—including through intensive political education—the building of health and education systems for the people in the liberated areas, and the building of new social relations in the production of agricultural goods in these zones. Cabral's experience as a commander of troops and a leader of a liberated area enabled him to think at many levels: political, military, administrative, and ideological, but above all in terms of the practicalities of life (the agronomist in Cabral continued to assert himself when it came to issues of the growing of crops). In many ways, Cabral embodied praxis, the unity of theory and practice.

In November 1969, Amílcar Cabral conducted a seminar for the cadres of the PAIGC in Conakry, Guinea. The lectures from this seminar form this volume, and they provide a vivid description of Cabral's praxis and his understanding that what the Portuguese colonialists fear more than anything else, even more than the guns, is the people's consciousness. "The fact is weapons make it possible to win wars and for a people to progress, but the decisive factor is the people themselves," he said in the opening lecture. If sharp political consciousness is crucial, then the slogan to best articulate that is "unity and struggle," a slogan that Cabral explains at some length in these lectures. To struggle, he says, you need unity, but at the same time to build unity you have to struggle. "And that means," Cabral says, "that the struggle is sometimes with ourselves. The significance of this is that our struggle is not only concerned with colonialism but with ourselves." The struggle, in other words, is for clarity and confidence amongst the people. "Everything else," Cabral said, "is just the application of this, our basic principle. Anyone who doesn't understand this needs to understand it, otherwise they won't have understood a thing about our struggle."

Three years previously, at the Tricontinental Conference in Havana, Cabral spoke of the "weapon of theory." The dialectical process of building unity and struggle provides the people with clarity—as they bring to the surface the structures of colonial power—and these struggles provide the people with confidence to build their power and to seize the state and control their own society. This is the process of revolution. What Cabral says in these lectures echoes what Ho Chi Minh said in his lectures delivered to the Vietnamese comrades in China and what Mao said in the caves in Yan'an. These comrades laid out the importance of political education for our struggles because they had to build their movements in places of great colonial deprivation, a situation that was the ground for national liberation Marxism.

This text forms part of our ongoing archive of national liberation Marxism, a tendency that has long been neglected in favor of the more obvious theorization that took place in the West after the collapse of the German revolution in 1919. This national liberation Marxism emerged in places of scarcity, amongst peasants, for direct confrontation with colonialism, and with the objective of having to build a revolution against colonialism and capitalism at the same time. The people who built these struggles—such as Cabral—had to be everything to them, including military strategists and political theorists. They did not have the luxury of specialization. They also had to develop a language, a way of talking about their complicated ideas to people with rudimentary education. This text carries all the weight of the tradition of national liberation Marxism, which focuses on the practicalities of revolution.

— Vijay Prashad
Director, Tricontinental: Institute for Social Research

INTRODUCTION TO THE NORTH AMERICAN EDITION

A MAGNIFICENT GIFT FOR THE AMÍLCAR CABRAL CENTENNIAL

This first English-language edition of Amílcar Cabral's work titled *Think to Better Act* is the most valuable gift that 1804 Books could give to his foundation, Fundação Amílcar Cabral (FAC), and its Board of Directors in the hundredth anniversary of Amílcar Cabral's birth. In fact, one of its principal objectives is precisely the promotion of study and the dissemination of his vast and important intellectual, political, and ethical legacy in order to expand the possibility of its access and use by contemporary social activists and civic organizations of oppressed peoples and societies in search of autonomy and political, social, and cultural emancipation.

At the Tricontinental Conference of 1966 in Havana, about three years following the beginning of the armed struggle, Amílcar Cabral studied and reflected on the issue of true liberation of the colonized African peoples, insisting that the success of this historic, political, and cultural project demanded a political vision (an ideology) and a strategy that would enable autonomy of decision, the successful implementation of an emancipating project, and the defense of the fundamental interests of the African people and societies seeking liberation.

From the perspective of Amílcar Cabral, the fight for liberation was and continues to be a complex and demanding phenomenon, one that does not conform itself with "voluntarism," improvisation, ignorance, nor disorganization, insofar as it produces an uncertain and evolving situation of successive contradictions between the liberation forces and the forces for colonial and imperialist domination, who are generally endowed with technical superiority and will do anything to ensure their position of dominance, privilege, and political supremacy.

This critical reality of permanent conflict makes the liberation struggle a much more complex and demanding one. Its demands were identified and detailed by Amílcar Cabral, who drew attention to the heavy responsibilities that fell upon liberation movements and their respective leaders, and who, furthermore, should not neglect their own political, social, cultural, and organizational weaknesses which restrict their abilities in the most diverse areas of action.

He understood that the priorities of liberation movements and their leaders should be in studying the society they sought to liberate, building a solid political organization with the necessary ideology, developing a motivated and capable leadership, and maintaining well-prepared human resources, sufficient both in numbers and motivation. In short, what was required was a political organization, a political project, an ideology and an intelligent and efficient strategy in the service of liberation.

He identified the threat of neocolonialism as the greatest risk of failure for a project of true national liberation for the African peoples. These threats came from the political, social, and ideological weaknesses of the newly independent states, the societies involved and their respective leadership, or from the will and strategy of permanent and active domination of former colonizers and their allies to ensure control over economic and physical resources, preserve their domination, and influence the political orientation of the formerly colonized Africans.

As this could not be a historical inevitability, where could one find the indispensable solutions and human resources necessary to anticipate this treacherous risk? In Amílcar Cabral's perspective, the correct path would be the transformation of a colonized and apathetic society into one that is alert, conscious, and active: a custodian and defender of the authentic values of the liberation struggle. In fact, his liberation pedagogy was based on the transformation of freedom fighters—both civilian and military—into historical subjects for national liberation: actors and guarantors of the political and social emancipation of the "plural" nation currently being built. As agents of national liberation, the liberation movements would be called on to drive the subsequent processes of political and institutional development; the promotion of social, cultural, and economic progress and the defense and consolidation of the sovereignty of the new state.

It has been more or less proven that historical processes are usually not peaceful nor equitable. In this respect, too, the processes of construction, consolidation, and international affirmation of newly formed, independent, and sovereign states has not been peaceful due to the aforementioned conflict—intense or mitigated—generated by clashes of interests, sometimes incompatible, between the young sovereign states and the dominant imperialist states. The very architecture of current global governance continues to be unfavorable towards the interests of the recently liberated peoples and nations, which are more fragile, less developed and less influential. This irrefutable, oppressive, and discriminatory reality means that national liberation struggles and liberation movements, in a broad sense, must continue to exist and fight for the liberation of peoples and societies oppressed and exploited by dominant finance capital.

In such circumstances, the unavoidable question arises of how liberation movements can circumvent neocolonialism upon coming to power. When confronted with this complex and intricate question, Amílcar Cabral proposed that while imperialism and its methods and interests of dominating more fragile peoples in nations existed, the political regimes established after formal independence must continue to think and act as "liberation movements in power." However, the dominating world powers did not appreciate the patriotic aims of this proposal that defended the total liberation of dominated peoples.

Nonetheless, by observing the evolving world power dynamics, we can see that the process of liberation would be a complex and long-term project, especially when we take into account the internal transformations in international relations that such a project requires. Assuredly, this heavily implicates the respective societies and surpasses the national, and even continental, political scope. It demands changes in dominant economic and financial models, in unequal international relations and, eventually, a redistribution of global power. This project would be highly complex and would bring about new political, economic, and financial rearrangements at a global scale, requiring the emergence of new cultural and ethical values.

Referring back to this work of Amílcar Cabral, it is worth noting the date upon which it was written. It took place in November of 1969, about six years following the beginning of the armed struggle for liberation, which constituted sufficient time to assess the progress made, gather lessons, and overcome weaknesses. These texts are the result of the transcription of lectures given in Creole by Amílcar Cabral at the aforementioned Seminário de Quadros (Cadre Seminar).

Six years had passed since the beginning of the armed struggle, and it was evident that this struggle would prolong itself further, turning into a long-term fight. With the political, ideological, and military objectives of preparing the cadres and militants to lead and effectuate a long-term struggle, Amílcar Cabral felt it necessary to conduct this larger meeting of cadres and leaders. In this context, it was necessary to provide the PAIGC with solid political orientations, a sharp vision of the development of the struggle, the clarification of their objectives, and the perfection of the necessary tools of action for victory. I believe that this explains the density and the breadth of the presentations made by Amílcar Cabral.

The title of this work fully fits within Amílcar Cabral's thinking and leadership style, which was founded on the binomial "think to better act, and act to better think." This is a virtuous intellectual and ethical attitude, one which bases itself on the fruitful interaction between theory and praxis, avoids empty speculations and the loss of meaning in either one. This makes this title especially "Cabral-ist."

The Cadre Seminar was primarily geared towards the preparation of the PAIGC as a collective to fight and overcome new and complex challenges. It took teachings and inspiration from past victories and accomplishments, as well as from its past insufficiencies, failures, and mistakes, all the while seeking to reinforce self-confidence in its abilities and its intrinsic resources needed to fight and defeat the enemy and its strategies. The seminar was equally intended for the individual development of Party leaders and its militants, providing them with clarity and knowledge on how to perfect their work and leadership methods to enhance their technical, political, and ethical capabilities, benefiting from the productive and functional style of learning through and for action. In fact, the concern with ethics, truth, and mutual respect within internal relations and within the population involved stands out among the list of the topics presented and debated.

The approach of problems and challenges as a method of leadership, as well as the study and dialogue of analyses and solutions, were highly beneficial to the extent in which they allowed for the perfection and harmonization of study, leadership, and work methods; the improvement of the organization's internal cohesion; and the efficacy of the command and leadership functions, including improvements in interpersonal relationships and their relationship with the peoples in the liberated regions.

The intended results were the consolidation of the PAIGC's organizational structures and strategies, as well as its military component: making it better prepared, more capable, stronger, and more involved, transforming constituents into a single cohesive and effective fighting tool, endowed with leaders and combatants that were more capable, active, and better prepared to fight and defeat Portuguese military, political, and secret services, and the harmful actions of the psychological warfare. Furthermore, it was indispensable to maintain the diverse nation's internal unity and cohesion and to defeat the enemy's instigations and maneuvers to divide and demotivate our combative forces and the population in general.

The enemy's side was undergoing a period of organizational changes: replacing military commands, transforming its structure, and adapting its military strategy to the new correlation of forces, introducing military innovations such as the "Africanization" of warfare and the modernization of aerial combat and troop transport resources with the goal of achieving higher mobility and effectiveness in its fighting units. On the political and sociocultural side, the enemy's leadership was seriously investing in perfecting a campaign to corrupt the population, engaging in deceptive psychosocial manipulation, and fostering ethnic divisions to demotivate the population, including the families of combatants.

It was necessary to understand and efficiently fight this new military strategy to defeat the psychosocial moves to infiltrate, divide, and demotivate the civic and military organizations of the fighting Party.

From my point of view, the Cadre Seminar was realized at an appropriate moment of struggle. It allowed for, in due time, better understanding of the ongoing fight and better preparation of the political and military leadership and rank-and-file to continue the struggle to neutralize and deconstruct the perverse sociopolitical maneuvers and to defeat the enemy's political and military endeavors.

I would also like to take this opportunity to greet future readers of the work, *Pensar para melhor agir*, or *Think to Better Act*, hoping that they can find in it some inspiration, whether it is to take on and defeat their day-to-day challenges or to realize their most utopian aspirations.

Finally, I would like to send my regards and thanks to the leadership of 1804 Books for their solidarity and this magnificent centenary gift to the Fundação Amílcar Cabral, which encourages us to continue the work of valuing and preserving our cultural and historical memory that we have worked so far to thus maintain.

— Pedro Pires
President of the Amílcar Cabral Foundation
Former Prime Minister of Cabo Verde
Former President of Cabo Verde
Former General Secretary of the PAIGC
Praia, January of 2024

EDITOR'S NOTE

Think to Better Act is the first complete English translation of Amílcar Cabral's contributions at the 1969 PAIGC seminar in Conakry, Guinea. This two-volume English edition is divided in a manner where the speeches which have been already published in English make up the first volume ("Party Principles and Political Practice" and "Analysis of Different Types of Resistance," with the exception of the "Welcome Address" which had not been previously available in English). Still, while the two longer sections had previously been translated into English, they had never been published together, and this juxtaposition allows for readers of Cabral to better contextualize the historical moment and political setting from which he sought to communicate lessons to Party cadre.

The second volume consists of speeches which have not previously been published in English: it is an entirely new collection, and features insights and analysis from Cabral which were previously unavailable to English readers. We at 1804 Books are incredibly grateful for the collaboration of the Amílcar Cabral Foundation and their decades of work in preserving the legacy of Amílcar Cabral for a new, international generation of thinkers and fighters, exemplified by the contribution of former president of Cabo Verde and Secretary General of the African Party for the Independence of Cape Verde (PAICV), Comandante Pedro Pires in his introduction to this two-volume collection.

LIST OF TERMS

badiu	Comes from the Portuguese *vadio* meaning "vagrant," which was what the Portuguese colonists called slaves who escaped into the interior of the islands. Similar to maroons in the Caribbean, "badius" were known to live in the mountains and retain their African culture. Today, "badiu" refers to the residents of Santiago, the most populated island in Cabo Verde, due to the historical and cultural history of maroonage.
badjuda	Creole term to refer to a Guinean woman
bi-group	A small, mobile military unit of two guerrilla groups under a joint military and political command within the PAIGC.
bubu	A long traditional African shirt
Cassacá Congress	The first party congress of the PAIGC where the party leadership, amongst other things, rectified certain excesses, notably patriarchal and tribal chauvinism practiced by certain military leaders, and reorganized elements of the party structure and political program following the start of the armed struggle.
cuntango	Plain rice
dênde	Palm oil

djambacosse	Traditional religious medical healer in Guinea
djarama	Thank you
djidiu	Storyteller/griot
djiula/djila	Traders
fado	Traditional folk Portuguese music characterized by slow, melancholic style. Caboverdean *morna* is related to *fado*.
grigri	Charm
irã	Spirit guide
kola	Seed of the cola fruit, major export of Guinea.
liceu	High school
M'pidi Palabra	Radio program of the PAIGC, translates to "ask me a question."
mandjuandade	"Tribalism"—referring to the organization of society based on tribal relations.
mezinho	Amulet
patchanga	How PAIGC members would pronounce the PKP "Pecheneg" machine gun in creole.
Pilot School	PAIGC youth school in Guinea-Conakry
polon	Also known as the kapok tree, the polon is a tall and wide tree found in Cabo Verde, Guinea and elsewhere in West Africa which featured widely in folkloric stories.
régulo	Tribal chief
sepoy	A native of India employed as a soldier by a European power
Tuga	Derogatory term used by Africans to refer to a Portuguese colonist.

LIST OF ABBREVIATIONS

ANC	African National Congress
CUF	Companhia União Fabril (Factory Union Company)
CONCP	Conferência das Organizações Nacionalistas das Colónias Portuguesas (Conference of Nationalist Organizations of the Portuguese Colonies)
FARP	Forças Armadas Revolucionárias do Povo (Revolutionary Armed Forces of the People)
FRELIMO	Frente de Libertação de Moçambique (Mozambique Liberation Front)
GDR	German Democratic Republic
MPLA	Movimento Popular de Libertação de Angola (Popular Movement for the Liberation of Angola)
OAU	Organization of African Unity
OSPAA	Organization of Solidarity with the Peoples of Asia and Africa
OSPAAL	Organization of Solidarity with the Peoples of Asia, Africa, and Latin America
PAIGC	Partido Africano para a Independência da Guiné e Cabo Verde (African Party for the Independence of Guinea and Cape Verde)
PDG	Parti Démocratique de Guinée (Democratic Party of Guinea)

PIDE	Polícia Internacional e de Defesa do Estado (International and State Defense Police)
SWANU	South West Africa National Union
SWAPO	South West Africa People's Organisation
UAR	United Arab Republic
UDENAMO	National Democratic Union of Mozambique
UDIB	Bissau International Sports Union
USSR	Union of Soviet Socialist Republics
UN	United Nations
UNAMO	African Union of Mozambique
ZAPU	Zimbabwe African People's Union

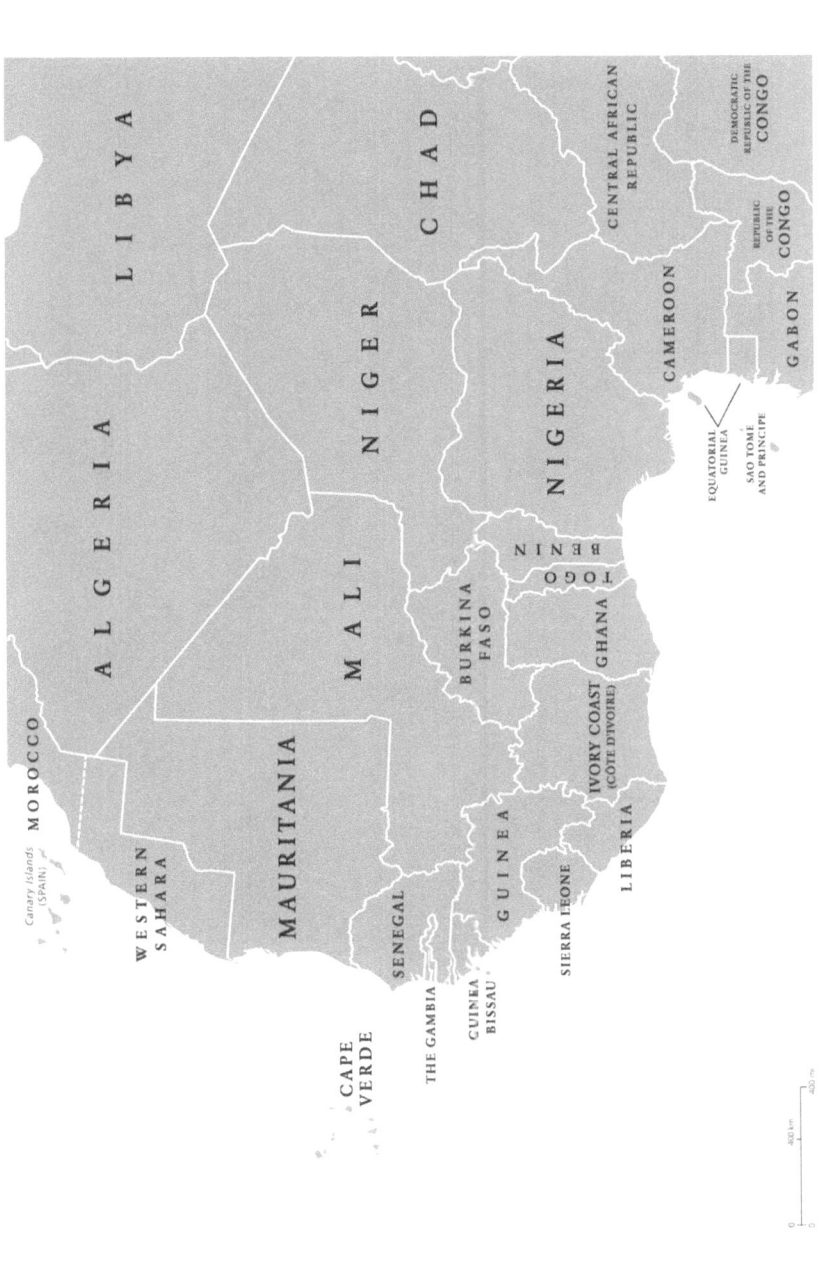

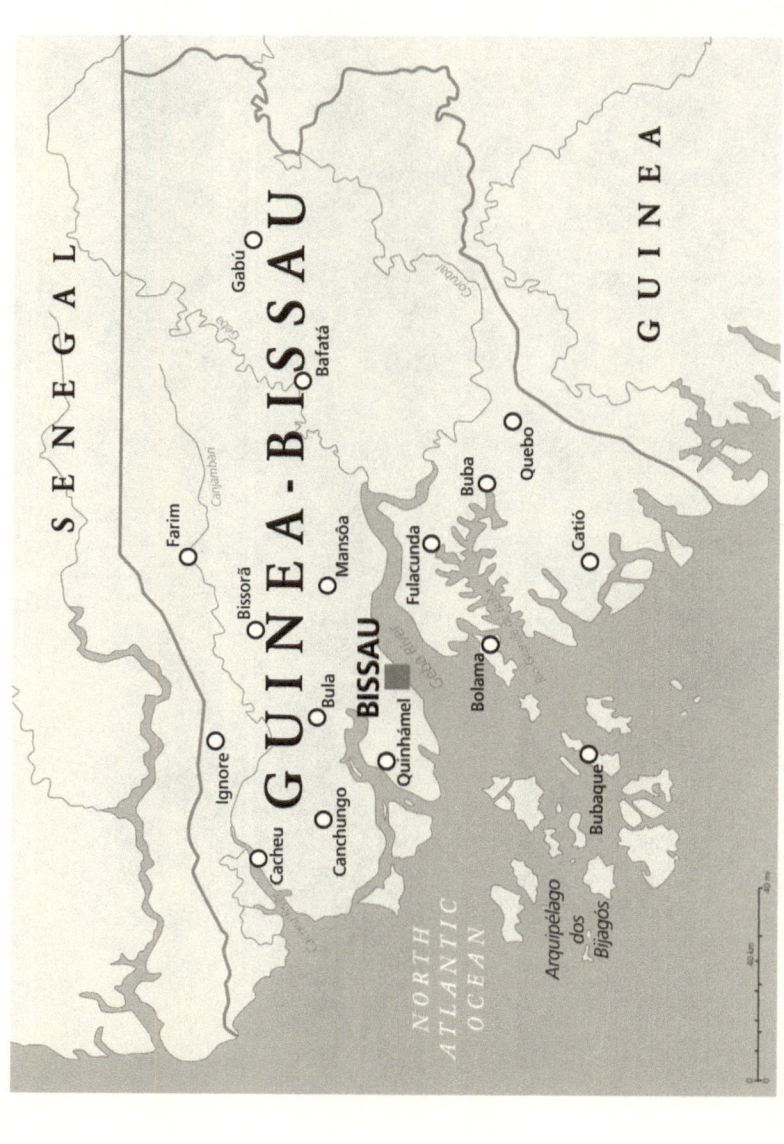

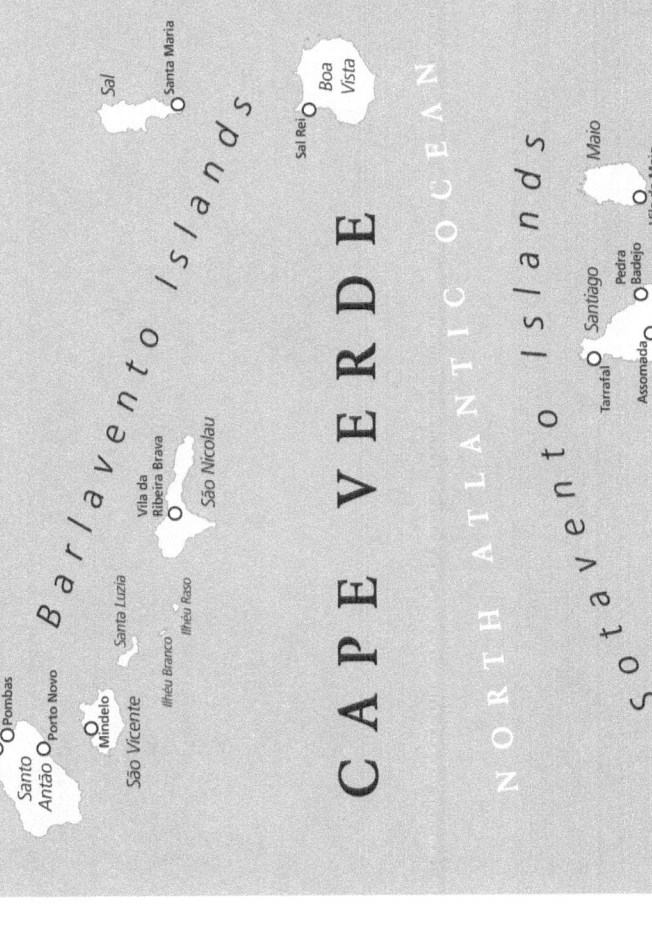

SECTION I:
WELCOME ADDRESS

The important thing is that everyone, those who have already put in a lot of work and those who have put in less, tries to give more of themselves each and every day, more of their intelligence, energy, effort, and sacrifice, to improve their knowledge, their understanding of the issues, and be ever more willing to put themselves completely at the service of the Party, and thus at the service of our people.

WELCOME ADDRESS

Comrades,

I had the opportunity to greet some of you yesterday, at the preparatory meeting for this seminar. Today, there are more comrades present and it gives me great pleasure to offer you all my warmest greetings. I do so on behalf of the Party leadership, as well as myself, and to reaffirm how vitally important we consider your presence here to be for the struggle in general, for the life and soul of the Party and its actions, and for every comrade's present and future, as militants, as soldiers, and as men and women capable of becoming ever more invaluable to the fight for liberation and progress for our people in Guinea and Cabo Verde.

It brings me great joy to hold a meeting with comrades who are, for the most part, young, but who already have responsibilities and whom we're counting on to advance our struggle, be it at the political or military level, or at any other level, in the liberated areas of our land. I hope every comrade present here is able to appreciate just how invaluable this seminar is, learn plenty of lessons, and generally get as much out of it as possible, even though we have so little time.

I regret that more Party leaders are not able to attend, but we cannot halt the struggle, neither inside nor outside our land, and so if I and other leaders are here, others must carry on doing their work so that the struggle is never halted.

Some comrades are abroad on missions that specifically had to be undertaken at this time. Others are heavily engaged in the armed struggle, whether that be striking the enemy with ever harder blows or advancing our front line ever closer to the enemy's rearguard, ensuring that supplies constantly reach all fronts, or attending to operational needs, at the internal and external level.

I'm sure these comrade leaders regret their not being here as much as we do, but I'm likewise sure that, given the documents that we'll produce, and which they'll all get to see, they too will benefit greatly from all this.

It's a shame that, whether through a lack of understanding, whether through delays caused by the difficulties we face in our life and struggle, some comrades who were invited to the seminar have not been able to get here. I believe this is due to difficulties inherent to our struggle. We regret that these comrades will miss out on the opportunity to have more direct contact with our ideas and principles, and address important issues relating to the struggle, things that would, no doubt, improve their work capabilities, in the service of the Party. Still, I hope the documents we produce during the seminar will likewise prove of benefit to them and that it will perhaps not be too long before we can hold another seminar that these comrades can attend.

Something else I regret is the fact that we have so few female comrades at the seminar. Our leadership made a mistake in primarily inviting cadres trained or working in fields that women aren't generally involved in or are but only in small numbers. In some areas, leaders did not show the initiative to include women in the groups of comrades they brought to the seminar. Thankfully, the North thought to send some and we have incorporated others. Nevertheless, there are too few here to represent, even remotely, the hugely important role that the women of our land, especially young women, militants, cadres, and Party workers, have played and will continue to play in the development of the struggle and our Party's eventual victory.

It gives me great pleasure to offer a special welcome to those comrades who have recently returned from studying abroad. They are Comrades Cruz Pinto, who graduated in international law in the German Democratic Republic, and Victor Vamaim, who completed a mechanical engineering course in the Soviet Union. I welcome them on behalf of all comrades and I wish them every success in their work as Party militants and as professionalized children of our people.

There are other comrades in this room who have also completed study programs and been back with us for a while now: Silvano

Rodrigues, a doctor, and Gil Fernandes, trained in sociology. I would like to welcome them on behalf of everyone here present and offer them our best wishes.

While we are here working at this seminar, other comrades are, at this very moment, armed with an array of different weapons and attacking the Portuguese colonialists in their barracks, their "ants' nests," as our radio calls them, thus combating the enemy's attempts to commit acts of terrorism against our people with their helicopters, their boats, and their criminal tricks. The colonialists fear our soldiers' operations, operations that are fundamental, indeed crucial, to the advance of our national liberation struggle. But I can assure you, comrades, if any of the Portuguese colonialists' leaders were to happen upon this room and see us sitting here at a seminar with the agenda we've just approved, I promise you it would fill them with even more fear than do our bazookas, guns, light weapons, and soldiers.

The Portuguese colonialists know very well what's happening. They may be stubborn but they're not stupid. They know you win wars with soldiers and weapons but that these things alone do not guarantee a people's freedom. Because the fact is weapons make it possible to win wars and for a people to progress, but the decisive factor is the people themselves! What counts is people's consciousness! The Portuguese colonialists know that the more conscious we are, the more clearly each one of us understands what we want, where we came from, and where we're going, the harder it is for them to continue to dominate us. And the easier, or the less difficult, it gets for us to win the national liberation war and ensure that our people lead lives made up of work, dignity, and justice, as the Party intends.

The Portuguese colonialists know—and, thankfully, we are each and every day more conscious of it ourselves—that a man or woman's worth is measured by the accumulation of ideas he or she has in his or her head, the strength of those ideas. And the enemy knows full well that a seminar like this will only strengthen our understanding of the path we are currently on, at this precise stage in our march for freedom, [of] where we are and where we're going.

Besides gaining a better understanding of the current situation in the struggle, the situation as regards our people, as regards Africa as a whole, and the world in general, and the situation regarding the enemy, the seminar will also fortify, in our heads and spirits, the decision we have all made to give our lives to the Party's cause. This, comrades, is something that makes the Portuguese colonialists very afraid. And they would be even more afraid if they could see the seriousness with which we are holding this meeting, the look of determination on people's faces, the will, evident in each and every comrade, to understand in order to better serve. Indeed, as I've said many times before, it's almost a shame we can't invite the Portuguese colonialists to come along to these meetings and see us working hard to improve our understanding.

We want you to consider this seminar as a significant moment in the evolution of our struggle, as a marker of how far we've come. We're not doing this just for fun. Nor are we doing it because we want to get to know our comrades better. We're doing it, and we'll go on doing it right until the end, to get maximum benefit out of it and because it's a necessary part of the struggle. This is the first in a series of seminars that we will need to hold over the coming months in order to perfect our struggle, make it even better than it already is and move it further forward, in the service of the Party and, therefore, in the service of our people, in Guinea and Cabo Verde.

So, who's taking part in this seminar?

We decided to invite to the seminar a number of comrades who have received instruction as soldiers or militants, from whatever branch of the Party structure, in order to strengthen their training in such a way that they may better serve our struggle, whether that be in political or military terms, or indeed some other form of activity. We have also summoned a few younger comrades, young people who have shown a good work ethic, a good understanding of the Party Guidelines and a willingness to fulfill them whenever possible. Then we have some older comrades taking part, the Party's leaders.

Almost all of you present here, sons and daughters of our people, of our land, had practically nothing before we began our struggle, before our Party took action. Young fellas from the cities, from Bissau, Bissorã, Mansôa, and Catió, young fellas from the bush, wherever you were in our land, your destinies were determined by Portuguese colonialist hands. Those of you here present from Cabo Verde, from the city or the countryside, from whatever island you were on and even when you were away from the islands, your destiny was likewise shaped by those same Portuguese colonialists, for they refused to allow the sons and daughters of Guinea and Cabo Verde to assert themselves and fulfill their potential, to serve their people's interests to the best of their abilities and seek progress and happiness, as is every people's right throughout the world.

Some of you went to school more than others, but generally speaking, you've all had very little schooling. Some of you began to better understand what you'd learned in school through the prism of our struggle, and therefore under the Party's flag. Nowadays, every one of you can ask: "Where do I come from? Who is my mother? Who is my father? Who is my grandmother?" Every one of you can reflect on the destiny that was mapped out for you yesterday and the destiny that awaits you today, one the Party has created for you through the struggle, at the cost of hard work and sacrifice.

Today, every man and woman holds their own destiny in the palm of their hand. They can scale the heights and prove themselves to be a valued child of our people, of Guinea and Cabo Verde, to better serve our people. But they can also take that destiny and punt it forward, like a boy playing football. We've been telling comrades for a long time now that, with our Party, every human being in Guinea and Cabo Verde has their own destiny in their own hands. A path has been opened up that anyone may advance down, one way or another, according to their will, according to their conscience, according to the work they put in. Everyone is free to choose to be a scoundrel or to be a man or woman of worth.

Nowadays, ever since our Party was created—and all of you here today are the concrete proof of this—it is no longer the case that everyone knows beforehand what a person born in our land will be by the age of fifteen, twenty, thirty, or even when they'll die. Many of you sitting here now will know what you would otherwise be doing if the Party did not exist. You would be tending rice fields, you'd be carpenters in the city, maids to Senhor Joaquim whatever, or sepoys at some administrative post—and that's if you'd been lucky. The Caboverdeans would be toiling away in São Tome or Angola as indentured workers, experiencing all manner of suffering in another peoples' land, though you'd maybe get to eat and dress well enough. Women would be leading wretched lives working in the bush and the fields, carrying rocks to build the Tugas' roads. At best, one or two of you might have been fortunate enough to get to study a bit, to advance a little. But this was very rare, comrades!

Not now! Everyone here has forged their own path in life and knows that, provided they don't stray from that path, they may go as far as their capabilities take them. People will no longer stand in your way. Simply by joining our Party, you won the right to be treated as a man or woman of dignity. The rest is up to you, your will to advance or to be left behind. And this is true for every child of our land, whether they're in the Party or still with the Tugas.

There are several twenty-something youngsters sitting here, leaders in our land. Some of you understand that no administrator or chief of post ever had as much authority in the eyes of our people as you do now. Those who still side with the Portuguese, assuming they do so out of choice, are scoundrels; they prefer servitude to being free men and women in a free land. They may yet change sides: people change sides as the struggle advances. But there are many others who remain on the Tugas' side not out of choice, but because they're trapped. The path to becoming free men and women remains open to them, as it does to all of us.

Several comrades present here have already made valuable contributions to the struggle. I want to tell them that the Party is very aware of the worth of those militants who are committed to their work, who earnestly strive to fulfill their mission.

Our struggle has to be the fruit of collective endeavor. In Guinea and Cabo Verde, inside and outside our land, the struggle will only progress through our hard work. And the struggle has progressed because we have, indeed, worked hard.

On the one hand, we have proved capable of reflecting on our struggle in order to find the best way to resolve issues. On the other, despite all the difficulties, obstacles, and sacrifices, several comrades, men and women, inside and outside our land, have been able to take the Party's lead and follow instructions, resolutions, and decisions taken by the Party leadership in order to advance the struggle.

In all struggles, in all forms of human enterprise, in every kind of work that mankind performs collectively, there are always some who work harder than others, some who do more than others. This is normal. There are, therefore, here at this seminar, some people who have done more work than others, for the Party, for the struggle, for our people. The important thing is that everyone, those who have already put in a lot of work in and those who have put less in, tries to give more of themselves each and every day, more of their intelligence, energy, effort, and sacrifice, to improve their knowledge, their understanding of the issues, and be ever more willing to put themselves completely at the service of the Party, and thus at the service of our people.

The Party places great trust in its comrades. Our trust is unlimited, so unlimited that there is no one in the Party, in our struggle, who, after making a mistake, has not been trusted in again, has not had a path opened up for them to continue along. Right since our foundation, the Party has based its relationship with militants on the following principle: trust us to trust you. This is our principle for any relationship between human beings in whatever enterprise we undertake. Trust first in order to earn another's trust. Here, now, I gladly say to all comrades present, whether you have earned it yet or not: we trust you. We trust that those of you who have already worked hard will prove capable of making even more of an effort, of becoming even better. For as our people like to say, if you've been up one palm tree, you can climb every palm tree.

As for those of you who haven't worked hard enough yet, who have not, for one reason or another, made the contribution you might have, we trust that you'll prove capable of improving, of recognizing that you haven't done enough and that others have taken up the struggle while you have merely pretended to. We trust that your consciousness will awaken, that you will put your hand on your heart, or as our poet Kauberdiano Dambará says, *"finca pé na tchon,"* and start to work properly, to truly fight for the people of our land.

It is a fundamental duty of the Party, and therefore of mine as the principal leader of our struggle, to open the way for our young people to move ahead.

Leaders who don't want anyone else to take their place are misguided, they lack consciousness in their duty to their people; leaders who fear the young and seek to hold on to their positions even when the hairs on their head and in their beards have gone gray, who block others from moving ahead when they themselves have grown old, are misguided. Leaders like this only serve their own interests, they do not serve their people.

Our duty is to open up a path so that others can move ahead of us and so that, above all else, young people can progress and become ever more capable of serving better, of performing to their full capabilities in order to lead the Party and our people in Guinea and Cabo Verde. Even more than liberating our land, even more than leading the struggle up to this point, our objective, the objective of the generation that created the Party, is to ensure that our land has a future, a future that lies in the hands of our own people, through their children, and a future for the Party that lies in the hands of our militants.

We have done our utmost to achieve this, and this seminar is, to a certain extent, an extension of our efforts to get young people in our Party, those here absorbing everything, to commit themselves to the struggle ever more each day in the certain knowledge that how far they progress is entirely up to them. Nobody will stand in their way. What we wish for, and what I personally wish for, is to see the young folk here today in the highest posts leading our Party and our people tomorrow. And that's because I remain convinced that, no matter the merits of our older cadres, it is, and must be, the young who guarantee our people's future.

We all recognize the merits of our older Party cadres. I'm not foolish or vain, but nor am I so modest as to be stupid: I know my own worth in all this, I'm well aware of it and I don't need anyone else to remind me. That's why there's no need for any cheering or applause, or for my name to be shouted from the rooftops. We're all well aware of the worth of our older Party comrades, whether they be gray-haired by now, like Aristides Pereira, Luís Cabral, and Vasco, or younger but veterans nevertheless, like Nino, Osvaldo, Chico, Bobô, and so many others. We know their worth as Party cadres, for they proved that worth yesterday and they go on proving it today. But this is of no use to anyone if we don't also bear in mind that they cannot live forever. This is why we need others to advance, why we need to open a path for our younger folk. And if we fail to do this, we'll have only been wasting our time and fooling ourselves.

We'll end up like a banana plantation that doesn't produce any new plants. The banana plant is very beautiful, it has big leaves, but unless a new stem is born underneath it, the plant simply produces a bunch of bananas and that's the end of it, for each banana stem only produces one bunch of bananas. If no new plant is born, no more bananas.

Our consciousness in this struggle is only of any value if we appreciate that the future of our Party, of our land and our people, belongs to our younger comrades, militants, and supervisors. Furthermore, it also becomes clearer and clearer by the day that our Party must belong to those sons and daughters of our land who as militants are truly capable of improving the Party each and every day. Every opportunity and possibility must forever be open to those militants who are sincere in their actions and seriously committed to the Party, rather than to their own petty interests; those who are honest and decent and true friends of our people; who fulfill their duties and respect the leadership but also respect themselves; who are courageous and who know how to use the authority that the Party has given them without abusing that authority. These are the people who, ever more by the day, must take charge of the Party.

We know that mistakes have been made in the past (and indeed present) of our struggle. Given how lagging we are in our land as a society and an economy, it's normal to do things wrong. It's acceptable in a struggle such as ours. Thankfully, there haven't been as many wrongs committed in our struggle as there have been in others.

Nevertheless, we need to be aware that these wrongs do exist. We've cut a lot of them out but there are still some. Principally at the supervisor level, at the leader level. We have to make a big effort so that our comrade leaders do not bring negative elements with them when they turn up in our land. This is the last thing we want!

But doubtless within the Party, perhaps even within this seminar, some comrades will end up left behind. In every march, in every hard struggle, just as in life, some people will always get left behind while others march on. It is the duty of our leadership, and my duty as principal leader, to be conscious of our situation and needs and to do everything we can to ensure that the number who march on gets bigger by the day, while the number who fall behind gets smaller. But we must also keep our eyes peeled and our guard up to make sure that no wolf in sheep's clothing moves ahead. This we cannot allow!

One thing is for sure, and this seminar will confirm it once more: only those who follow the Party line will march on with us. We have told comrades clearly and repeatedly, out loud and in writing, what it is that we want, what the Party's objectives are. No child of our land, no man or woman, will tomorrow be able to claim: I was left behind because I did not know. As the poet says, you can never say you weren't touched by the truth. You can ignore the truth perhaps, but you're always touched by it.

We want to make the following absolutely clear: we reject opportunism, we reject opportunists. Right from the start of our armed struggle, we have rejected opportunism of every kind, rejected it once and for all. Opportunism is taking advantage of favorable circumstances in order to get what you want, while forgetting the principles you work under. This we reject, comrades. We have made this very clear and expressed it openly, every which way. This is our Party, this is what we want, done in this way. Anyone who doesn't agree should leave, go and do something else.

This is the way it's been since the very beginning of our struggle. There are comrades here who attended numerous meetings then and know this. There have been people, whether from Guinea or Cabo Verde, who left the Party because they wanted to join me but they didn't want to join a common struggle. We said to them clearly: "You lot are from Guinea, you don't want us to fight together as Guinea and Cabo Verde, fine, go and create your own party just for Guinea; you lot are from Cabo Verde, you don't want us to fight together as Guinea and Cabo Verde, no problem, go and create your own party just for Cabo Verde and leave us alone." We have made this clear right from the start.

There are people in this Party (at least there were, and if there still are, we'll soon find out) for whom the liberation struggle consists of distrusting others. For example: in our lands, generally speaking, those who were a bit lighter-skinned, mulattoes and mestizos in general, had a better chance of getting an education, given the circumstances in our land. One or two people have become preoccupied with the idea of leaving all the mestizos behind, setting them to one side. We told these people very clearly that we will not tolerate racism in our Party. Here, anyone who serves our people well is a son and daughter of our people, even if he's white, like Zeca, for example. We will not accept any idiotic discrimination because of a person's color, because that is opportunism of the worst kind. Anyone who wants a party made up only of Black people can go and create their own party. Anyone who wants a mulattoes-only party can go and create one. We're not having any of that here because it's got nothing to do with the interests of our people. We're not fighting to serve people's petty interests; we want to serve our people.

There have also been some who said: "it would be best to put the Manjacos all together"; or; " . . . just the Pepels"; " . . . only the Mandingas"; "we're Mancanhas, we're all the same group"; "we're Beafadas, Beafada brothers." Others have said: "What about Cabral? We don't really know what he is. But fine, we'll make an exception for him."

No, comrades! We have been quite clear about this: here there is no Manjaco, no Pepel, no Mandinga, no Balanta, no Fula, no Susu, no Beafada, no son of a Caboverdean. Here there are only sons and daughters of the people of Guinea and Cabo Verde who want to serve. Serve what? Our Party. Anyone who serves our Party is serving our people.

We must respect the customs of the Manjacos, Mandingas, Pepels, the sons and daughters of Caboverdeans, in other words, of all ethnic groups. Anyone who dances, or usually dances, by holding their partner can dance like that; if they dance with their hips, they can dance like that; if it's the "N'hai" dance, they can dance like that; if it's a Mancanha dance, they can dance like that. Songs that come from here or there are different, each to their own, there's no argument about that. But in politics, in the struggle of our people, there is no "race." We don't want it! Anyone who wishes to defend racism or tribalism can go and join the opportunists in creating groups of Manjacos in Senegal or France. Anyone who accepts racism or tribalism in our land is destroying our people, playing into the hands of the imperialists and colonialists against our people.

There were some who joined me thinking the following: "I can read, I can write, I was even a chief of post, or I was a whatever. Cabral is surely not going to start with some nonsense about how people from the bush, indigenous people, are more important than me."

These people thought we were going to drive the Tugas out for our own benefit, so that those of us who got to study more and know how to tie a tie could take over ruling the land. They were utterly mistaken.

They soon realized that in this Party, if Bacar proves his worth, if Malan proves his worth, if N'Bana proves his worth, he takes the lead. If someone is more suited to a particular task, he leads it. Even if others have previously been chiefs of post, administrators, or doctors with degrees, he leads it. That's why some people left the Party and maybe others will leave in the future.

That's why some people think I defend ignorance over knowledge. I do not, this is a lie, I'm against ignorance. I'm not against the ignorant, but I am against ignorance.

But there are also those who didn't get to go to school very much and have a complex about it: "We don't want doctors with degrees here. They come here acting all doctorly."

If a person knows nothing today but proves their worth and can help us, then we welcome that help, but they'll have to catch up and learn, because the day will undoubtedly come when those who know nothing, those who haven't the least bit of understanding, will be left behind. That's why the Party is always urging everyone to make a big effort to study ever more each day, to improve their capabilities. That's why the Party is making a big effort to send people away to train in an array of different fields.

We reject opportunism no matter where it comes from and what form it takes. As you all know, we have always rejected opportunists. We all remember when people would accuse us of being the enemies of the children of the Guinean people, and of who knows what else besides. Today, those people are all with the Tugas, they've moved over to their side, become their toadies, PIDE [Polícia Internacional e de Defesa do Estado (International and State Defense Police)] agents in Guinea, Senegal, Gambia, sometimes even here.

Our struggle today clearly shows who really wants to fight for the people of our land. There was a time when anyone had the right to say: "I'm fighting for the people of my land. I love my people. Oh, my people, my people!"

It's very easy to talk about the people, comrades. But who are the people? If you stop and think about it, you'll see that those who talk about the people the most are those who think about their own petty interests the most.

After so many years of struggle, anything with a conscience in our land today knows one thing: that anyone wanting to fight for the people of our land must stand firm with the PAIGC. It is the PAIGC that represents the people of our land, because it is the PAIGC that is realizing, through struggle, sacrifice, and hard work, our people's aspirations for freedom, peace, and progress. Anyone who doesn't understand this today, or who denies it, is a colonialist agent. That's why nowadays, for us, PAIGC militants, just as for any child of our land who is a genuine patriot and a friend of the people of Guinea and Cabo Verde, there is one simple, concrete, clear, and genuine way of expressing our love for our people. That's to be able to say: I have a lot of love for the PAIGC!

Anyone who is against the PAIGC is against the interests of our people and in favor of the Tugas. Because there is no choice in our land today. Listen to the colonialists' radio. Do they speak of anyone else? No! They only speak of the PAIGC. Open a Portuguese newspaper and everywhere you look you'll see the PAIGC, the PAIGC, the PAIGC . . . There is no choice in our land, be it in Guinea or Cabo Verde. A few days ago, they put some of our compatriots on trial in Cabo Verde. "PAIGC Members Tried," ran the headlines in the Portuguese newspapers.

There is no choice, comrades, let us be under no illusions. Saying, "I love my people but I do not love the PAIGC" is a falsehood. Anyone making statements like this wants to side with the Tugas, like Seni Sane, those traitors who talk on Radio Bissau, and a handful of others, such as the one who deserted a few days ago and went on the radio to say: "I'm a true child of Guinea, that's why I want to be on the Portuguese side."

Am I making myself clear, comrades? We cannot afford to be under any illusions any more. We in the leadership cannot afford to be and neither can you. None of us should be under any illusions any more. The choice is between the PAIGC and the Portuguese colonialist criminals.

A number of Party militants here present among us have had the opportunity to go away and study, have completed higher education courses and other such things and returned. It brings me great pleasure to note that they have not come back with a complex of any kind, and nor is anyone else showing any kind of complex towards them. It also brings me great pleasure to sense that, though many of you sitting here now would also have liked to go away and study, you stuck firmly to your Party tasks, you accepted making the necessary sacrifices in the bush, whether as guerrillas, as members of the army, in the north, south, or east of our land, or as nurses, teachers, political activists, or members of the security forces. Whether you've been sent away for training or not, you've proved yourselves capable of sticking to your task in order to advance our struggle, while other comrades have been for their instruction.

But it's also a pleasure to know that those who went away to study did their duty. Studying is another aspect of our struggle. Having returned, they will enrich our ranks and bring their skills to bear so that we can advance evermore, while respecting the Party line and its Guidelines, pursuing its program, which is to achieve liberation, peace, progress, and happiness for our people.

To one or two of you, I must again emphasize the need to study the Party Guidelines, the documents and the books that the Party makes available to you, to study them ever more each day, thus improving your reading and writing skills while at the same time following the Party Guidelines. Any Party militant who is serious about serving our people must always find the time to study and progress.

Comrades must try to avoid wasting time with chitchat, fooling around, chasing women, living it up, and so on. Anyone involved in the struggle who has time to find themselves a wife and have children, though this be a natural thing, must also have time to improve their own capabilities. So I'm going to end my welcome address with the following message to comrades: whether it be on the battlefront or in education, health or security, in our political work, which is the most important aspect of our struggle, or simply performing tasks related to our work, which is important too, be it inside or outside our land, doing whatever job in the service of the struggle, every comrade must always make an effort to improve themselves each and every day.

I wish you all good health and good training, because one thing is certain: if a people wants to advance, its children, the militants of a party like ours, its supervisors, and its leaders, have to prove themselves capable of advancing more and more each day. The demands of the struggle grow by the day, a struggle that will not end once we've driven the Tugas out, will not end once we've taken control of our land. On the contrary, that's when the hard part of our struggle for the progress and happiness of our people will truly begin.

People like us cannot let a single day go by without learning, because the demands on us are so great. This, then, is my wish for you all, comrades: good health and good work! Learn from life, learn from theory, learn from the experience of others. This is very important to ensure that you and others like you successfully fulfill the role that the Party has marked out for you, so that you may take charge of the Party tomorrow. Those of most merit must take charge today and those of most merit must take charge tomorrow, so that our struggle progresses, under the glorious flag of our Party, and ensures not only our liberation but, more importantly, peace, progress, and happiness for our people in Guinea and Cabo Verde.

SECTION II: PARTY PRINCIPLES AND POLITICAL PRACTICE

Many people have principles but, when the moment to apply them comes, they forget them or aren't true to them. We must stay true to our principles, apply them every day, make no concessions to them, whether internally, in our inner lives, or externally, in our relationships with the outside world.

1. UNITY AND STRUGGLE

We are now going to continue our work by talking a bit to comrades about some of the principles of our Party and our struggle.

Comrades who are familiar with a document published under the name *General Guidelines of Our Party* in 1965 will recall a chapter at the end entitled "Putting Party Principles into Practice." Those Guidelines speak of a number of general principles and today we can speak of a few more. You all know this already, but what you may not appreciate is that what we're really talking about here is the very foundation, the basis, the guiding principle of our struggle, seen in purely political terms, which are its primary terms, for our struggle is political. Naturally, in order to define strategy, for example, and indeed discuss tactics devised for our armed liberation struggle, other principles have since been established, but principles relating to the armed struggle are simply our general principles applied to the field of armed struggle.

A first principle of our Party and our struggle is "Unity and Struggle"; it's one we all know well and is even the Party's slogan or, if you like, its motto.

Unity and Struggle! Of course, in order to properly study the meaning of this seemingly quite straightforward principle, we must first establish what unity is and what struggle is. We must then place issues of unity and struggle into a specific context, that is, give them a geographical perspective, and consider what kind of society exists— its social life, economy, etc.—wherever it is we wish to apply this principle of Unity and Struggle.

So, what is unity?

Unity can, of course, be considered in what we might call a static sense, that is as being no more than a matter of numbers. For example, if we think of all the bottles in the world, one bottle is a single unit. If we think of all the men in this room, comrade Daniel Barreto is a single unit. And so on. But is this the unity we speak of in our Party principles, the unity we wish to consider in our work?

It is and it isn't. It is insomuch as we want to transform a diverse collection of people into a well-defined collective seeking a path. And it isn't, because we mustn't forget that within this collection of people there is a diversity of individuals. Conversely, the sense of unity that can be seen in our Party principle is one in which, no matter what differences exist, we must act as one, as a single collective, in order to achieve our given objective. In other words, in our principle, unity exists in a dynamic sense, as something that moves.

Think of a football team, for example, which is made up of various individuals, eleven different people. Each person has his own particular job to do when the team plays. Each person is different from the other, with different temperaments, quite often with different levels of education; some don't know how to read or write while others are university graduates, doctors, and engineers, and with different religions—one might be a Muslim, another a Catholic, etc.; they might even be politically different, someone from one party, someone else from another. One of them might come from the status quo, like Portugal, for example, while another might come from the opposition. In other words, they are all different people, they all consider themselves to be different from the others, and yet they're in the same football team. And if that football team cannot manage to achieve unity among all its various members when it plays, then it will not manage to be a football team. Each individual can preserve his own personality, his own ideas, his own religion, his own personal problems, even his own way of playing to a degree, but they all have to submit to one thing: they must act collectively in order to score goals against whoever they're playing, that is, act according to a particular objective—scoring as many goals as possible against the opponent. They have to form a unit. Because if they don't, they're not a football team, they're nothing at all.

Let's say you see a person with a basket on their head selling fruit. You don't know what kind of fruit is in the basket, but you say to yourself: here comes someone with a basket of fruit. There may be mangoes, bananas, papayas, guavas, etc. in the basket. But in our mind, we see this collection of fruit as a unit, as a basket, a basket of fruit on someone's head. You know it's a unit, both in the numerical sense—one basket of fruit—as well as what's being sold, fruit, it's all the same thing even though there are various kinds of things in there: different fruits, like mangoes, bananas, papayas, etc., but the fundamental issue, that the person has come to sell fruit, turns them all into one single thing.

This is just to give comrades an idea of what unity is and to explain the basic principle that in order to have unity you must first have different things. If they're not different, there's no need for unity. There's no issue of unity.

What, then, does unity mean for us? If we're going to build unity in our land, what's the objective that we're going to build unity around? We're not a football team, of course, or a basket of fruit. We are a people, individuals within a people who, at a certain point in their history went down a particular path, raising certain issues in terms of their spirits and lives, pushing their activities in a particular direction, raising certain questions and seeking answers to those questions. It might have started with just one person, or with two, three, six . . . But at a certain point this issue appeared in our midst—Unity. And the Party understood this so well that it made it a fundamental principle, at the basis of everything we do and part of our motto— Unity and Struggle.

Now a question arises: Did this need for unity arise out of necessity, because our ideas were so different from a political point of view? No, we didn't have any political customs in our land, there wasn't a single political party. What's more, under foreign domination, as is the case for both Guinea and Cabo Verde, whereby there isn't all that much difference in most people's circumstances, though there is some inequality, as we'll see, it's hard for people's political objectives to differ all that much.

In other words, we did not have a problem of unity in terms of what was in people's heads, in terms of bringing together different people with different political points of view, programs, or objectives. Firstly, because in the very structure of our society, in the reality of our land, the differences are not so pronounced as to cause too many differences in terms of political objectives. Secondly, and primarily, because our land is under foreign domination and the formation of any kind of political party has always been, throughout our lives, totally forbidden, there were no different political parties to unite, there were no different political directions to set on a single path, to join together and make into a unity.

What was the problem of unity in our land then? Fundamentally, the problem of unity was this: firstly, as everyone knows, unity brings strength. From the moment the idea arose in the minds of certain sons and daughters of Guinea and Cabo Verde to force the foreigners who dominate us to leave our land, to put an end to colonialist rule, the problem of strength arose, the strength that would be required to oppose the strength of the colonialists. Therefore, the more that people unite, the more united that we can become, the more we are adhering to a principle known to all: unity brings strength. If I want to break a matchstick, I can just pick it up and snap it quite easily; if I put two together, it's not so easy; then three, four, five, six, until a point comes when I can't break them. But beyond the fact that unity brings strength—and we must also note that unity doesn't always bring strength, for certain kinds of unity can lead to weakness, it being one of the wonders of the world that all things have two sides, one positive, the other negative—those of us who came up with this idea of unity sought to instill it in the spirit and reality of our struggle, because we knew there was a lot of division in our midst.

There is division in Guinea just as there is in Cabo Verde, and in Crioulo the word "division" means conflict. In our society, for example, anyone who gives serious thought to our struggle knows that things would be a lot simpler if everyone was a Muslim or a Catholic or an animist. At least then no force, acting against the interests of our people, could try to divide us because of religion. But moving beyond that, let's look at Cabo Verde. In Cabo Verde there aren't many problems with religion, aside from the odd squabble between Protestants and Catholics leading their town lives, but there are other problems that divide people. For example, some families have land, others don't. If everyone had land or didn't have land, things would be simpler. The enemy, for example, the force that opposes us and from whom we seek to liberate ourselves, can try and turn those who have land against us by telling them that we want to take their land off them. Just like in Guinea where the enemy tries to turn the *régulos*[1] against us by telling them we want to take away their authority. If there were no *régulos*, things would be simpler. In other words, the problem of unity arises in our land, let me repeat this clearly, not because of a need to join together people with different ways of thinking politically, but because of the need to bring together people with different economic circumstances, though the difference is not as great as it is in other lands that have different social and cultural circumstances, religion being one of them. In other words, we have approached the issue of unity in our land, both in Guinea and Cabo Verde, in order to deny the enemy the opportunity of exploiting any areas of conflict that might exist among our people, in order not to weaken our strength in opposing the enemy's strength.

So, we can see how forming unity is something we need to do in order to be able to do something else. To put it another way, if we want to have a wash, whether it be with a faucet or in the river, then unless you're mad, you need to remove your clothes before getting under the water. You have to first undress in order to then wash. It's an action we take, a preparation we make so that we can bathe. Better still, if we want to hold a meeting in this room, with people sitting down, etc., we have to invite people, set up tables, get pencils, pens, etc. That is, we organize the means for us to be able to have a proper meeting.

Unity is, then, also a means. A means is not an end. We may have had to fight a bit to get unity, but achieving unity doesn't mean the struggle is over. There are many people in this struggle of the colonies against colonialism who are still, even today, fighting for unity. Unable to carry out the struggle, they end up thinking that fighting for unity is the struggle.

Unity is a means with which to fight and, as with any means, a certain amount of it is sufficient. You don't have to unite everyone in order for a country to fight. Can we ever be sure that everyone is united? No, it's enough to achieve a certain degree of unity. If we can get that, then we can fight. Because then the ideas in people's heads

---

1   Tribal chiefs

develop, advance, and become ever more useful in achieving the goal we've set our sights on.

So, comrades, you have now seen, more or less, what this fundamental idea entails, this principle of ours that is unity.

What, then, is struggle? Struggle is the normal condition of every living being in the world. Everyone is in a struggle, everyone struggles. For example, you're all sitting in chairs, I'm sitting on this chair; my entire body is forcing itself down towards the floor, through the stool it sits on top of, but if the floor didn't have the force to withstand me, I'd keep on going and bore through the floor, and if there was no force in the ground beneath either, I'd keep on going, boring into the earth and so on.

So, there's a silent struggle underway here between the force I exert on the floor and the force from the ground that holds me up, that won't let me pass through it. And as you all know, the earth is in constant movement. Maybe some of you still don't believe this, but the earth makes a rotational movement. If you set a plate spinning and place a coin on top of it, you'll see how the rotational force of the plate throws the coin off. Anyone who uses a sling to scare away crows or sparrows with a stone, as is done in Guinea and Cabo Verde, will know that when you put the stone in the sling and swing it round and round, you don't need to hurl it, you just let go of one end of the sling and the stone comes flying out with tremendous force. What you do need is good aim, to know when to let go. In other words: everything that spins develops a force that throws things out. So, all of us here on Earth, as it spins, are constantly being repelled by a force that pushes us away from the earth, from the center outwards, something called centrifugal force. But there is also another force that draws people to the earth, which is gravity. This means that Earth, as a magnetic force, draws in every body that is close enough to it, according to the distance to and mass of each body. We are here on Earth and not floating off up there because the force of gravity is so much greater than the centrifugal force that would throw us out. The problem of sending people to the moon, etc., the fundamental problem for scientists, is how to get bodies to overcome the force of gravity and be thrown out from Earth. And we now know that in order for a body to overcome the force of gravity and be thrown out from Earth, they have to be moving at eleven kilometers per second. If they're going fast enough to reach a speed of eleven kilometers per second, they'll overcome gravity. It therefore follows that any force exerted against anything else can only exist if there is an opposing force. You there, with your hand on your face, your hand doesn't push your face away because your face resists it. You don't feel it, but your face is pushing too, for weight alone is a form of pushing.

In our specific case, the struggle results from the Portuguese colonialists who have occupied our land, as foreigners and occupiers, exerting a force over our society, over our people, which has meant that they've taken hold of our destiny and halted our history, making it linked to Portugal's history like a carriage in Portugal's train, and they've created a series of conditions within our land: economic, social, cultural, etc.

To do this, they had to overcome a force. For almost fifty years, they waged a colonial war against our people: a war against Manjacos, Pepels, Fulas, Mandingas, Beafadas, Balantas, Felupes, against almost every ethnic group in our land, in Guinea. In Cabo Verde, the Portuguese colonialists, who found the place deserted when the great exploitation of Africans as slaves began, saw Cabo Verde's advantageous position in the middle of the Atlantic and decided to turn it into a slave warehouse. People brought from Africa, from Guinea in particular, were placed in Cabo Verde as slaves. But little by little, they grew in number, the laws of the world changed and the Portuguese had to stop trading in slaves. So, then they began to exert pressure on these people, a pressure similar to the one they'd exerted in Guinea, in other words, colonial force. There has always been resistance to this colonial force. If colonial force pushes one way, another force pushes back, a force of our own that manifests in all manner of ways: passive resistance, lying, taking off your hat, saying "yes sir," using every trick imaginable to deceive the Tugas. Because we couldn't oppose them face-to-face, we had to deceive them, but at the cost of great misery, suffering, death, disease, misfortune, and other consequences of a social nature, such as our falling behind in relation to other peoples of the world. Our struggle today is the result of a new force emerging, through the creation of our Party, to oppose the colonialist force. The problem is knowing if, in practice, this united force of our people can defeat the colonialist force. This is our struggle; this is what we call the struggle.

Now, taken together, "Unity and Struggle" means that to struggle you need unity, but to have unity you must struggle. And that means that the struggle is sometimes with ourselves. The significance of this is that our struggle is not only concerned with colonialism but with ourselves.

Unity and struggle: unity to struggle against colonialism and struggle to create unity, to then build our land as it ought to be.

Everything else, comrades, is just the application of this, our basic principle. Anyone who doesn't understand this needs to understand it, otherwise they won't have understood a thing about our struggle.

And we have to honor this principle on three fundamental levels: in Guinea, in Cabo Verde, and in Guinea and Cabo Verde. Everyone who has studied the Party's Guidelines knows this.

From what I've already said, you can see the conflicts we've had to overcome, and will continually have to overcome, in order to ensure the unity needed for the struggle in Guinea. The examples I've given you concerning Guinea will give you a rough idea of the conflicts we have had to, and will have to, overcome in Cabo Verde in order to ensure the unity needed for the struggle there. Comrades know how much the Tugas have divided us, and how we too have divided ourselves as a consequence of the evolution of our lives.

In Guinea, for example, you have town people on the one hand and bush people on the other, just for starters. In the towns there are whites and Blacks. Among the Africans, there are those in high-level employment and those in medium-level employment, people who feel sure that, come the end of the month, they will be duly paid. It might occur to them to buy a car, as I have done, for example, I have my own car, and to get a fridge, freezer, a pretty wife, children who will, of course, go to the Lyceum Lycee[2] and, eventually, if they study hard, to Lisbon. Then there are those in low-level employment, who have their bottle of red and plate of codfish every Saturday, who can afford to buy a transistor radio, own a few little things. Then there are the dock workers and car mechanics, and let's include drivers and other people like that who live a little bit better than the rest, salaried workers in general. And then there are those who have nothing to do, or who do odd jobs here and there, or who haven't a clue how to make a living,

---

2   Secondary school; most Caboverdeans and Guineans did not go to secondary school.

or who live loose, as prostitutes, as beggars, as crooks and thieves, etc. This is society in the towns.

But if you look carefully, you'll see that all these descendants of Guineans or Caboverdeans who are doing okay in life are only interested in one thing and have a common interest: they all cling to the Tugas, they pretend to be Portuguese as much as possible, they even forbid their children from speaking any language other than Portuguese at home, you all know what I'm talking about. If we look at another group, they're interested in more or less the same thing. The Zé Marias, the João Vazes, and others like them, were, of course, staff workers. Some of you, for example, were staff workers, but you're nationalists, are you not? But anyway, their interests are more or less the same, they exist in the same sphere, in the same social group.

Just like the dock workers, boat workers, porters, etc., they comprise another group. You might meet them, talk to them, etc., but you're not going to sit down at the same table with them and eat. The same goes for the Tugas as a group, for example, the governor's family, the bank manager's family, the director of the Treasury's family, etc., you never see them with a Tuga metalworker or a laborer's wife. Not unless the laborer happens to have a beautiful daughter who everyone likes the look of and who sometimes gets to go to upper-class dances. But the mother who can't read or write doesn't go, she walks her daughter to the door and takes her leave. You'll recall cases like this in Bissau.

Society in Cabo Verde is similar, with the same type of society in the towns. But in Cabo Verde, Africans of means have long comprised a larger group than in Guinea, both in terms of the numbers of public functionaries and proprietors, that is people who own land. Their land will be in the countryside, although they live in the towns. And the division in the towns is more or less this: public functionaries or staff of a particular distinction; lower-level public functionaries and staff; workers who might be fired at any moment; and those who have nothing to do. The number of whites in Guinea and Cabo Verde has always been small. In Guinea, there have never been more than three thousand whites, and in Cabo Verde it doesn't seem like there has ever been more than one thousand civilian whites, leading normal lives as public functionaries, technicians, shopkeepers, staff, etc. This is urban society, both in Guinea and Cabo Verde.

Naturally, we have to look at urban society in relation to our struggle to create unity. Because we want to have people even from the white group fighting on our side against the Portuguese colonialists, if they want to, because there may be some whites who are in favor of colonialism and others who are anti-colonialists. If the latter want to join us, then great, it gives us more strength against the colonialists. Besides, as you know, this is something we've exploited a lot. If Comrade Luís Cabral managed to escape, for example, it's because some white people took him out of Bissau, through Ensalma and to the border. It was two white men, as you all know. A Portuguese woman had a big influence on our Party's work in Bissau.[3] Only people who aren't in the Party don't know that. She was the first person to teach Osvaldo things about the struggle, not me. I didn't even know Osvaldo back then.

In other words, we should welcome all the forces we can join together in our struggle against the colonialist enemy. We should welcome them, but not blindly. We need to know what each person's position is in relation to the colonialists.

In the towns, it's plain to see that very few whites have done anything against the colonialists. Firstly, because they are the colonial class, the ones who most represent colonialism in our land; secondly, because most of them aren't interested, they have their own lives to worry about, they just want to make some money and leave, they don't want to complicate things; and lastly, because the whites, the Tugas who live in our land, generally don't have enough of a political education to adopt an openly concrete stance against any regime anywhere.

What about us Africans? Among the groups of what we might call the petite bourgeoisie, people who enjoy a certain quality of life, whether they be descendants of Guineans or Caboverdeans, there are always three subgroups. Firstly, a small but powerful group who are in favor of the colonialists, who won't even hear of a fight against the Tugas. These are the people who came to my house in Pessubé, like big men, with their good jobs, who eat well, drink well, go away on holiday, etc., and they sat down and said: "Now, we want to talk to you. You, son of so-and-so, we know you well, our advice to you is that you're making trouble for yourself, you're ruining your career

---

3   Cabral is referring to Sofia Pomba Guerra.

as an engineer, because we've got nothing against the Tugas, we're all Portuguese." This group is a lost cause.

But the vast majority of people in the African petite bourgeoisie were undecided and no doubt remain so today, because they think: "Cabral comes along with all these things, with his people, and it would in fact be good if we drove the Tugas out, but . . . " These are the people who suffer most at the hands of the Tugas, these towns-folk. The Tugas are all over them every day, hassling them in Mansoa, Bissau, Bissorã, Praia, and São Vicente. The whites come along as trainees or clerks and, whenever there's an opening, they go straight to the front. Cruz Pinto's father, for example, was repeatedly passed over for promotion, as were the fathers of others sitting here today. These townspeople suffer from colonialism directly every single day, while, say, a man living in the bush, in deepest Oio, or Foreá, might go to his grave without ever seeing a white man. I remember, for example, when a Portuguese agronomist came with me to visit certain areas in Oio, the children would come up to him and rub his arm to see why he was white like that. Some of them even asked him: "Why are you like that?" They had never seen a white person before, while those who live in the towns see white people every day. To continue, then, this is a group of people, a large group of petite bourgeois Africans who get paid at the end of the month and do want the Tugas to leave, but are afraid because they're not sure if we can actually win: "Cabral comes along with all his people and his big ideas, but what if we lose? We'll lose our fridge freezer, our monthly salary, our transistor radio, our dream of going on holiday to Portugal." Going on holiday to Portugal just to come back and "strut" around. All of this leaves them sitting on the fence, undecided.

But there is a smaller group that, right from the start, rose up as soon as they heard of the idea to fight, of fighting against Portuguese colonialism, a group that's prepared to die, if necessary, in order to fight Portuguese colonialism. And it is from this group that people emerged and aligned themselves with the Party. Because if you look carefully, you'll see that most of the people who created the Party didn't pay taxes, didn't suffer beatings, didn't even lack for a job; on the contrary, they led reasonable lives. That's the situation with our petite bourgeoisie in terms of the struggle, both in Guinea and Cabo Verde.

What about salaried workers? The majority are in favor of the struggle, at least they were at the start. We're talking about the start here. The majority—carpenters, bricklayers, sailors, mechanics, drivers—workers who were really hit hard by exploitation and earned a miserable wage. Because when a man works as a bricklayer and earns one hundred dollars and a white man earns eight thousand dollars, if not eighty thousand, then naturally he feels like he's being exploited terribly in life. But within this same group there are also those who do not want to fight and who are in favor of colonialism.

As for those who don't have anything to do, who have no work, you don't generally find people who want to fight in that group. Some of them are reasonable enough, but generally speaking, this is the group that the PIDE recruits many of its agents from.

In the case of Guinea, specifically, we need to take note of a particular group of people positioned somewhere between the petite bourgeoisie and the salaried workers, I'm not quite sure what to call them. There are a lot of young fellas who don't have a fixed job, who can read and write, do a bit of work here and there, who often live off some uncle who lives in a town (we have a lot of this in our land), but who come into constant contact with colonialism: footballers, say, who quite admire the Tugas but who also somehow sense that, great players though they are, they will never get into the UDIB [Bissau International Sports Union] dance, for example. These young men joined the fight very quickly and played an important role in it because, though they were, on the one hand, from the towns, they were also connected to the bush. They had nothing to lose aside from a game of football or some small job (tailor, carpenter), a job they almost didn't want because it wasn't worth enough to allow them to "strut" about alongside the Tugas. Because they want to "strut" about alongside the Tugas but they want Africa too. They are people who learned in the town how nice it is to have nice things, but who, because of the humiliations they suffered, feel the Tugas are simply too much. And the Party has helped these people to raise their consciousness in this regard.

And what about in the bush? In the bush, it depends: if it's in our Balanta society, there's no problem. Balanta society is what's called a horizontal society; in other words, it doesn't have classes one above the other. The Balantas don't have big chiefs, it was the Tugas who fixed them up with chiefs. Among the Balantas, every family, every compound, has its own autonomy and if there's a problem, the council of elders resolves it. But there's no state, no authority that rules over everyone. If there have been chiefs in our time (because you're young), then this is because the Tugas installed them. There have been Mandingas appointed as Balanta chiefs, former sepoys installed as chiefs. Can't they resist, do something about it? People accept having these chiefs but pay them no attention. Each person rules his own household and people get on fine, they plant together, etc. but there isn't much conversation. There might be two compounds in Balanta society, one right beside the other, but they don't get on, because of the land or some other issue from the past. They refuse to have anything to do with each other. But these things are ancient customs, we'd have to look into their origins and don't really have the time. Things from the past, blood, marriage, beliefs, etc. In Balanta society, it's like this: the more land you plant, the richer you become, but wealth isn't for saving, it's for spending, because you shouldn't become very much richer than anyone else. This is the principle in Balanta society, as it is in other societies in our land.

As for the Fulas, Manjacos, etc., they do have chiefs, not because the Tugas installed them but because of the evolution of their own history. Of course, we should explain to comrades that some of the different peoples in Guinea, not least the Fula and Mandinga, came to Guinea from outside. Most Fulas and Mandingas were originally old folk from our land who became Fulas or Mandingas. It's good to know this in order to understand certain things, because if you compare the Fula way of life in our land to real Fulas in other parts of Africa, you'll see quite a few differences. Even in Fouta-Djalon it's different.

Lots of people became Fulas in our land: the ancient Mandingas became Fulas. The original Mandingas came and conquered the Mansoa region, "Mandingafied" all the people and turned them into Mandingas. The Balantas resisted and many people say that the word "balanta" itself means those who resist. A Balanta is someone who will not be persuaded, who refuses. But they didn't refuse quite that much, because there are the Balanta-Mané and the Mansoanca. People were always appearing in dribs and drabs who gradually accepted becoming Muslims.

The Balantas, Pepels, Mancanhas, etc., were all people from the interior of Africa whom the Mandingas drove towards the sea. The

Sussus of the Republic of Guinea, for example, come from Fouta-Djalon, and it was the Mandingas and the Fulas who drove them out. The Mandingas drove them out and then the Fulas came along and drove out the Mandingas.

As we've said, the Fula and the Manjaca have class-based societies. But the Balanta don't; anyone who raises their head too high above everyone else is considered a good-for-nothing, to be acting white, etc. For example, if you grow a lot of rice, you have to hold a big party to get rid of it. The Fulas and the Manjacos have other rules, with some people more important than others. That is to say, the Manjacas and Fulas are what we call vertical societies. There's the chief at the top, then the religious figures, the big men of religion who form a class with the chiefs. They are followed by professionals of different guises (cobblers, blacksmiths, goldsmiths), who don't have the same rights as those at the top in any society anywhere. In ancient customs, it was even shameful to be a goldsmith. And even more shameful to be a *djidiu*.[4] So there's a scale with a series of professions, one below the other. A blacksmith is treated differently to a cobbler, a cobbler's treated differently to a goldsmith, etc. Everyone has their profession. Then comes the great mass of people who farm the land. They farm the land for the chiefs, as is the custom. That's how Fula and Manjaca societies work, with all the theories that are required to back this up, such as how a given chief is linked to God. Among the Manjacos, for example, if someone is a farmer, they're not allowed to farm the land without the chief's authorization, because the chief must give God's word for him to proceed.

Everyone is free to believe whatever they want. But why was this entire system created? For those on top to ensure that those down below couldn't rise up against them. Nevertheless, among the Fula, those down below have risen up several times and fought those up above. There have been several large-scale peasant revolts. There is the case of Mussa Molo, for example, who overthrew the *régulo* and took his place. But he ended up simply taking his place, adopting the same old laws, because they suited him, and keeping everything just the way it was, because that suited him just fine. He soon forgot where he'd come from. This is what a lot of people want to do, unfortunately.

---

4   Storyteller/griot

In terms of our bush society, a large number of Balantas have taken up the fight and this is not by chance; it's not because the Balantas are necessarily better people than others. It's because of the type of society they have, a horizontal society of free men, men who wish to be free and who have no one above them oppressing them, no one except for the Tugas, that is. For a Balanta man, it's just him and then the Tugas above him, because the "chief" there, Mamadu, knows full well he isn't really their chief, for it was the Tugas who installed him. So it's in our Balanta man's interest to put an end to this situation so that he can have his absolute freedom back. This is also why, if a Balanta is wronged by a member of the Party, he takes great exception and angers very quickly, much more quickly than with any other group.

It's not like that with the Fulas and Manjacos. The great mass of people who really suffer are those at the bottom, the workers of the land, the peasants. But there are a lot of people in between them and the Tugas. The peasants have become used to suffering under their own people, they're accustomed to oppression. Because anyone who farms land has to work not just for one chief but for all the chiefs, as well as the chief of post. And so it was proved that, once they properly understood it, vast numbers of peasants joined the struggle, most of them in fact, except the odd group here and there who we didn't do a very good job with. As for those above them, the professionals, the artisans, some have taken up the fight and others haven't though they're all very self-interested, they work mostly for themselves. Very few of their religious figures and chiefs have joined the Party because they fear losing their privileges, even if it is for the good of the struggle.

In these class-based societies, there is a group that plays a special role and that is those who take goods from one place to another, to sell or to trade (inside or outside the land). They trade goods, lend money to the chiefs, etc. They are the *djilas*.[5] They form a special group within the framework of our society.

These societies have classes: the ruling class, the artisan class, the peasant class. We had to unite the strength of these different classes as much as we could, combine different elements of society in order to carry out the struggle in our land.

---

5   Traders

You don't have to unite everyone, as I said, but you do need to have a certain degree of unity. But this is looking at society only in terms of its social structure, in the classic, typical sense. Because in our society there are various ethnic groups, that is groups with different cultures and customs and, according to their own beliefs, different origins: Fulas, Mandingas, Pepels, Balantas, Manjacos, Mancanhas, etc., and this also includes the descendants of Caboverdeans in Guinea.

In Cabo Verde, it's complicated in the countryside because there are landowners (large and small), tenant farmers (generally linked to large landowners), and partners who farm land that doesn't belong to them and share the harvest with whoever it does belong to. The tenant farmers tend the land but have to pay rent to the landowner. And there are some agricultural laborers too, but not many, not enough to form a class. They work on other people's properties. Fortunately, in one sense, and unfortunately in another, because many calamitous things happened in the crises that befell Cabo Verde due to a lack of rain, but mainly due to Portuguese mismanagement, the big landowners lost a lot of land. The landowners had to mortgage their land so that the bank would give them money, but then they couldn't pay up afterwards and lost their land. So today, the central bank and the savings bank, the Caixa Económica, are the biggest landowners around.

There are still a few small landowners. But tenant farmers rent their land from the Central Bank or the Caixa Económica, or the odd big landowner who still exists. In other words, they are a group of people who have no land. In Guinea we can't really say to anyone, "Let's fight to get land," but in Cabo Verde we can say to the tenant farmers, "Let's fight because everyone who fights will get their own bit of land to farm." This is the fundamental difference between the Guinean bush and the Caboverdean countryside. This whole group, if we make a good job of it, will be in favor of the struggle. The big landowners will undoubtedly be against the struggle. Among the small landowners, there will be some who are for and others against, because they're comparable to the petite bourgeoisie. Some will be for it, others against it, and others undecided: some will be against it because they think we want to seize their land and put an end to property ownership; some will be for it because they think that if we seize land, it'll be a free-for-all and they'll be able to convert their own small plot into a large plot; others will be hesitant and filled with doubt, not really knowing what our aims are, whether they stand to lose or gain, and because they're still more or less okay with the Tugas.

But there are other conflicts to consider, for example, in Guinea. There are ethnic groups, so-called tribes, which we call races. We know there have been conflicts between them in the past, the not-so-distant past sometimes, for example, in Bissau in the 1930s, in the Bissalanca area, in Chão dos Manjacos. In Oio, in 1954, I myself witnessed a major conflict between Balantas and Oincas. All because of ancient ideas that still exist in some people's heads, or because of concrete interests, practical matters: they stole our cows, they took our *badjudas*,[6] they farmed land that didn't belong to them, etc., things the Tugas can and do exploit to provoke conflicts among our people. These are the kinds of conflicts we wish to explain to comrades.

In both Guinea and Cabo Verde, our aim has been to eliminate these conflicts the best way possible, which is to get everyone to come together with a common goal: to drive out the colonialists.

And what about within the framework of Guinea and Cabo Verde, considered collectively, is there a conflict there? Everyone has their own thoughts and views on this. The conflict that existed, or seemed to exist, derived from the fact that many colonial employees and officials in Guinea were Caboverdeans, several chiefs of post were Caboverdeans, and given how education was more developed in Cabo Verde, there were more opportunities for Caboverdeans to get jobs in Guinea than there were for the sons and daughters of Guinea itself; the Caboverdeans were the winners in all this. This made it seem like the interests of the Guinean people lay in Caboverdean hands.

But if you look properly, some sons and daughters of Guinea are in the same position as the Caboverdeans and there has never been any conflict between these people in the towns and our people in the bush. It's in the towns where there's a conflict. Conflict between who? Between descendants of Guineans who want to have the same life the Caboverdeans enjoyed as chiefs of posts, even though chiefs of posts are colonial agents who act against our people, and even though people are exploited in Cabo Verde just as they are in Guinea, and in some regards even worse, through hunger and through men being

---

6   Creole term to refer to Guinean women

exported to São Tomé and Angola as indentured laborers, practically like animals.

So any conflict that there might be between Guineans and Caboverdeans is the conflict of competing for jobs, for good positions. For example, a person who completed second or third grade in Guinea sees a Caboverdean come along and take up a chief of post position, feasting on chicken and goat, people doffing their hats to him, etc. The Guinean cannot attain the same things and so a certain something is born within him. But if we study the problem properly, we'll see that the general trend is for the Guinean petite bourgeoisie to live just as well as the Caboverdean petite bourgeoisie. The general trend is for both groups to reach some kind of consensus with the Tugas. And there's never any conflict between Caboverdeans and Guineans in the bush, for example. Nothing comparable to the deep-rooted conflicts that sometimes break out between certain races in Guinea. This is clear for most comrades to see.

So if we stop and analyze the difficulties we, the PAIGC, have had in uniting Guinea and Cabo Verde around the central objective of our struggle, we'll see that we haven't had as many as we've had in maintaining unity within Guinea or within Cabo Verde. Take Guinea alone, there are numerous conflicts within it. Take Cabo Verde alone, there are numerous conflicts within it. But take them together and the number of conflicts diminishes. They're confined to the petite bourgeoisie, where there is some conflict, and it is precisely from within this petite bourgeoisie group that the opportunists fighting the PAIGC have emerged, opportunists who, when they first set up their movement, had already made themselves ministers of this and that, seeking to boost their own career and status, no more than that.

Naturally, this issue of uniting Guinea and Cabo Verde isn't the result of some whim, it's not because Cabral was born in Bafatá the son of a Caboverdean, so he's full of love for the Guinean people but he's also full of love for the Caboverdean people. This may well be true, I am, but that's not why we're doing it.

I've seen people die of hunger in Cabo Verde and I've seen people flogged to death in Guinea, I've seen people be slapped, kicked, taken away for forced labor, you understand? That's the reason for my revolt.

But the basic reason for the struggle for unity between Guinea and Cabo Verde lies in the very nature of Guinea and Cabo Verde. We did it because it was in both Guinea and Cabo Verde's interest for us to do so. You'd have to be ignorant to study the matter seriously, to grasp the history of the different races in our land, both in Guinea and Cabo Verde, and colonial history in general, and not come down in favor of unity between Guinea and Cabo Verde, not if you are genuinely interested in seeing our people advance. Furthermore, given the specific possibilities for carrying out a struggle in our land, in Guinea and Cabo Verde, it would not be possible to undertake a struggle in Guinea without us doing it together, united as the PAIGC. It would not be possible to undertake a struggle in Cabo Verde without us doing it together, united as the PAIGC.

And do you know what the concrete proof of this is, comrades? It's that there is no movement that has declared itself to be "just for us, the children of Guinea" and advanced. Does anyone know of one? In Cabo Verde, there is no movement just for the sons and daughters of Cabo Verde that has advanced, no such thing exists. This means that we were right in our analysis, that we were fair, especially if we consider our prospects as a viable economic and political entity in Africa, one capable of genuinely bringing about a new way of life. No wonder everyone fighting for African unity sees us as the only true example, along with Tanzania, which resulted from the union of Tanganyika and Zanzibar, of a force genuinely fighting for African unity. But struggling for unity between Guinea and Cabo Verde really ought not to be a problem because by our very nature, by our history, our geography, our economic trends, our everything, even our blood, Guinea and Cabo Verde are one. You'd have to be ignorant not to understand this.

The Tugas understand it perfectly well. Carreira, after all the abuse he committed in Guinea, understood it well.[7] They pretend not to understand in order to divide us. Their hope was that, were Cabo Verde to take up the fight, they would be able to mobilize Guineans to fight against Caboverdeans, those good-for-nothings who were only in Guinea as chiefs of post. And if Guineans were to take up the fight, they'd mobilize Caboverdeans, both in Guinea and Cabo

---

7   Cabral is referring to Antonio Carreira, a Caboverdean historian who also served as an administrator in Guinea. There, he oversaw the Pidjiguiti massacre of August 3, 1959, which launched the PAIGC's drive toward armed struggle.

Verde, to fight back hard against the Guineans and prevent them from rising up, prevent them from becoming free. But our Party gave them quite a shock. The Tugas had never had such a shock in their lives as when, in that first batch of people they sent to jail, they saw there were Guineans and Caboverdeans acting together. And if you think about it carefully, you'll see there are lots of people in Bissau who could go on the radio to rubbish us, to do good radio spots on the Tugas' radio, but who don't. Does that not seem strange to you? There's only Alfa Umaro, Malan Ndjai, and I don't know who else on their radio, or some crook who fled the Republic of Guinea or Senegal and winds up in Bissau talking French.

Have you noticed this? Why is it that none of our fellow country-men, be they from Guinea or Cabo Verde, go on the radio in Guinea when plenty of them went to school and have things to say? But they don't because the Party gave the Tugas a good shock back then. The Tugas no longer trust these people and they no longer trust the Tugas, they don't want to get involved because they don't know what might happen. But not so long ago, just after the armed struggle began, the Tugas were still proclaiming in Portuguese and even in Crioulo: "Children of Guinea and Cabo Verde, you are one, under the flag of Portugal." Remember hearing that? But at the same time, they were saying in Mandinga that the Caboverdeans were useless. That was to see if they couldn't still sow some division. They've gradually stopped doing this nowadays. Every now and then, they get someone to say "I'm a full son of Guinea, I'm not a foreigner's son like others born here" to see if they can't keep a certain sense of division going, just like how at the beginning of the struggle they would say "Fulas, we're going to win this war with you, because you're the best sons of Guinea," etc. They say the same thing when they speak in Manjaco, they say it's the Pepels who are harming the Fulas, it's the Fulas who are harming the Pepels, and so on, in order to divide. But they've seen how this doesn't work. No one in our Party seeks to divide; on the contrary, we unite more by the day. There are no Pepels, Fulas, and Mandingas here, no children of Caboverdeans, none of that. There is the PAIGC and it is marching forward.

The Tugas are desperate because now they're the ones who are, for example, publishing big articles in their magazines, like the one called "Ultramar," studying the issue of Guinea and Cabo Verde, and writing "Guinea and the Cabo Verde Islands—their historic and demographic unity." And do you know who wrote that article? Carreira. He really does know a lot of historical facts. For this article, he gathered together all the documents in the Tugas' archives and studied where the sons and daughters of Guinea went when they were sent to Cabo Verde. To Santiago island? Balantas, Mandingas, Beafadas, etc. To São Vicente island? The Fulas, etc., complete with reports about their arrival. They said they were against it at first, but they have always known we are the same people in Guinea and Cabo Verde.

In other words, whether it be out of historical knowledge, the reality of our past lives, an understanding of our people's and Africa's interests, or as a matter of simple fighting strategy, anyone giving serious thought to the struggle knows that there can be no independence for Guinea without independence for Cabo Verde, nor can there be independence for the Republic of Guinea, or for Senegal or Mauritania, not if they really want to be proper countries—do you hear what I'm saying? There just cannot be. Only someone with no understanding of strategy can think that Africa can be independent while Cabo Verde is occupied by the colonialists. It isn't possible. Just as, vice versa, there cannot be real independence for Cabo Verde without real independence for Guinea and real independence for Africa. Anyone who places the interests of their people above their own interests and who values serious analysis above their own pretensions and ambitions can only come to one conclusion, which is the following: the best thing that the PAIGC ever did, that the group of people who created the PAIGC ever did, was to establish Unity and Struggle as a basic principle—unity in Guinea, unity in Cabo Verde, and unity of Guinea and Cabo Verde.

Anyone who can't see this yet will see it later. But many Africans have already begun to see it. Many forces friendly to us have begun to see it, but so too have our enemies begun to see it. The imperialists' main concern today is the following: "Would Cabral accept Guinean independence without Caboverdean independence or not?"

That's their biggest concern: "Would the PAIGC accept Guinean independence without Caboverdean independence?" That's what the imperialists want to know and they ask me this directly. I reply: "Get the Portuguese to ask, you're not Portuguese." They know very well how important our unity is.

One day, an African leader said to us: "You're clever." We asked him why and he said: "I know your people in Guinea and your people in Cabo Verde. If you really achieve what you're aiming for, even though you're a small country, you'll be a strong country in Africa."

Let's see, we said.

Comrades, let us move forward then, fortified by the knowledge that we were right: creating the PAIGC based on the principle I have just explained was our people's greatest achievement in our quest, which is to bring freedom to and build progress and happiness, in Guinea and Cabo Verde.

2. STARTING WITH THE REALITY OF OUR LAND. BEING REALISTS.

Reality

Another issue we will discuss is the following Party principle: We began our struggle convinced of the reality in our land, with our feet planted firmly on the ground. That is to say that we believed, given our circumstances, that it wouldn't be possible to fight for the independence of our people, nor carry out an armed struggle such as the one we needed to undertake in our land, unless we thoroughly understood our own reality and began the struggle genuinely based on that reality.

So what is our reality?

Our reality, like all other realities, has positive aspects and negative aspects, strengths and weaknesses.

No matter where our heads may be, our feet are planted firmly on the ground of our land, in Guinea and Cabo Verde, in the concrete reality of our land, which is the main factor that should guide our Party's work.

Some people of the world think that reality depends on how we interpret it. Reality, things that are seen, touched, felt, the world that surrounds every human being, is, according to these people, the result of what humans have in their heads. There are others who think that reality simply exists and mankind is part of that reality. It's not what a given man has in his head that determines reality; rather, it is reality itself that determines that man. He is part of reality; he exists within that reality and whatever he has in his head does not determine that reality. On the contrary, it is the reality in which the man exists that determines the things he has in his head.

Comrades may ask: What is our position, in the PAIGC, in relation to these two opinions?

Our opinion is that mankind is part of reality. Reality exists independently of any man's will and a man, as he becomes aware of reality and as reality influences his awareness, nurtures his awareness and can gain the power to transform reality, bit by bit. This is our opinion, our Party's principle, let's say, as regards the relationship between mankind and reality.

It is very important in a national liberation struggle that the people leading the struggle never confuse what they have in their heads with reality. Quite the opposite, they must have many things in their heads, ranging from the reality of their own land to the reality of other lands, but they must weigh everything up and make plans based on reality and not what they have in their heads. This is very important and the fact that it has been ignored has caused countless problems in peoples' liberation struggles everywhere, especially in Africa.

I can have my own opinion on various matters, on how to organize the struggle, on how to organize a party, resulting from things I've learned, for example, in Europe, in Asia, in other African countries even, in books I've read, documents, people who've influenced me. But I cannot seek to organize a party, organize a struggle, according to what I have in my head, it has to be done according to the concrete reality of the land.

We can provide many examples of this. We cannot seek, for example, to organize our Party the same way parties do in France or any other country in Europe or even in Asia. We started off a bit like that, but we gradually had to change in order to adapt to the concrete reality of our land. Another example: at the beginning of the struggle, we were convinced that if we mobilized the workers of Bissau, Bolama, and Bafatá to go on strike, to protest in the streets and make demands of the administration, the Tugas would change their stance and give us independence.

But that wasn't true. First of all, in our land, workers do not have as much strength as in other lands. They do not represent such a great force from an economic point of view, because in our land the greater economic force essentially resides in the countryside. But it was practically impossible to organize strikes in the countryside, given the political circumstances of our people, their lack of a political consciousness and even their immediate interests. It was impossible to get our people to stop cultivating the products the colonialists were exploiting. Moreover, our colonialist enemy is not like us, for we have some respect for certain things. The Tugas would respond to strikes and demonstrations by coming down hard on us, by killing us in order to put a stop to everything. We therefore had to adapt our struggle to suit different conditions, those of our land, and not do as had been done in other lands.

Many other things besides clearly show just how necessary it is to consider the concrete reality of our land in order to fight. Even on the question of mobilization, preparing people, etc., we had to consider the issue in Guinea one way and in Cabo Verde another. In the case of Guinea, we can come and go from either the Republic of Guinea or Senegal. With Cabo Verde it's more difficult because it's in the middle of the sea; we have to find another, better way to back the struggle up, so that there's no need for a lot of coming and going. And, later, when the struggle evolves, when we begin the armed struggle in Cabo Verde, it will have to be conducted differently to the struggle in Guinea, because we cannot consider the issue the same way we did, for example, in 1962, in our land, when our comrades were under attack in the bush—we didn't have any weapons then—and we gave orders for all the cadres to withdraw. And more than two hundred cadres withdrew to avoid considerable disaster, until we came back again and advanced with the struggle. But in Cabo Verde, we cannot quickly withdraw a lot of people.

We have to consider the concrete reality of every concrete case. Even in Guinea, for example, we made a serious mistake in our analysis before the struggle, even though we took into account the living conditions of the Balanta people, the Fula people, the Mandinga people, the Pepel people, and their positions in the struggle. We considered the petite bourgeoisie, the salaried workers, the shop workers, the port workers, the descendants of Caboverdeans, and their positions in the struggle. We took all of this into account, but we made a big mistake. We didn't sufficiently take into account the situation of the traditional chiefs, the *régulos*, especially among the Fulas and Manjacos. We didn't take them into account sufficiently because we assumed that, because their ancestors had fought against the Tugas in the past and been defeated, they would want to fight again. This was a mistake. We were wrong.

We must consider the way we learn how to conduct the struggle as we advance along its path. The struggle is one thing along the coast, another thing among the Manjacos, and yet another thing in Oio. There are numerous differences. For example, we have to look at the way we deal with the Mandinga "big men," which is different from the way that we deal with the Balanta "big men." But in Gabú, we have to conduct the struggle in a totally different way. If we compare the struggle in Gabú with the struggle in the South, it's like we're talking about two entirely different lands.

We need to be realistic, to consider concrete reality, even when it comes to those things that are advancing, bit by bit. At the beginning, men didn't want to have meetings with women present. We took things step by step, we didn't force things, and women joined meetings straight away in other areas without any problem. But we have to be aware of reality, not just the general reality of our land, but the particular reality of each different thing, so that we can orientate the struggle accordingly. Those supervisors and leaders who take this idea of reality into account, who don't think that truth means whatever they have in their own heads, that it is in fact what lies outside their heads; they are the ones properly orchestrating their work as militants, as supervisors, doing it the way it must be done in a struggle such as ours. Unfortunately, we must recognize that many comrades have taken on responsibilities in this struggle without considering this point, though we have always emphasized it.

But reality isn't something that exists in isolation. For example, Comrade Manuel Nandigna is a reality; he's real and that's a fact. But he cannot exist on his own; he is nothing by himself, a reality is never isolated from other realities. Whatever reality we're considering in the world or in life, no matter how small or large, it's always part of another reality, influenced by other realities, which are themselves influenced by and have an influence on other realities. Our land, Guinea and Cabo Verde, and our struggle are both part of a larger reality; they're influenced by and have an influence on other realities elsewhere in the world. For example, if we consider the reality of Guinea and the reality of Cabo Verde, first of all, there is already a bigger reality, Guinea and Cabo Verde. But that reality is part of the reality of West Africa and with the reality of our two nearest neighboring countries; we can extend it a little further with our two neighboring countries first, West Africa next, and then the reality of Africa as a whole and the reality of the whole world, though all of these things have other realities within them too.

All of which is to say that, for us, our reality is at the center of a complex reality, because it is the reality that interests us the most. It's different for other people because they're elsewhere and their central reality is their own reality. But even if we consider our reality to be at the center, it still doesn't exist in isolation. With many of the things we must do, we have to think about how we are integrated into other realities. This is very important so that we don't make mistakes.

Let's imagine the position of one of our army corps somewhere. It cannot ever act as if its own reality existed in isolation. It has to always act as part of the PAIGC army, as part of the struggle of the people of Guinea and Cabo Verde. If it acts like that, it's acting well; if it doesn't act like this, it's acting wrong. A political commissar in Quínara or wherever, let's say São João, must always act as part of Quínara, but not only as part of Quínara; rather, also as part of the South, the whole South; and not only that, as part of the whole of Guinea; and not only that, as part of Guinea and Cabo Verde together. We have to keep in mind, at all times, the parts and the whole. Only then will we act well. Unfortunately, the tendency among many comrades is to act as though their own reality is the only reality that exists, forgetting all others. This happens to such an extent that it is possible to come across comrades in one area, for example, who know that comrades in another area are out of ammunition and yet they prove themselves incapable of mobilizing to supply their comrades with ammunition. This shows a lack of consciousness, of not being able to see how our own reality is integrated into a bigger reality, one we ourselves have created and yet are still not fully conscious of.

Besides this, we also have to contend with the reality of others. In the interior of our country, for example, a political commissar might be doing a great job in, say, Sara. But if the political work being done in Oio, Biambi, or the Bafatá area isn't very good, the work in Sara won't progress much. An army corps might fight hard and attack the Tugas every day in, let's say, Canchungo or the Nhacra area, for example. But if our units in other areas don't fight very hard, the great sacrifices and victories in Nhacra or Canchungo lose their worth. But for us there's even more to it than that: if the struggle in Guinea advances a lot but the struggle in Cabo Verde doesn't advance at all, then sooner or later the lack of progress there will hinder our struggle in Guinea.

Suffice to say that, from a strategic point of view, there cannot be peace in Guinea so long as the Tugas have air bases in Cabo Verde. It's impossible. If we completely liberate Guinea, for example, they can still bomb us from their airbases in Cabo Verde. They can get plenty more planes: South Africa, for example, which has a number of interests in Cabo Verde, can supply them with planes in large quantities. We have to study how we can move these two realities forward at the same time, as a combined reality, a single reality.

But even then, if we fight hard in Guinea and Cabo Verde but people in Angola and Mozambique don't fight at all, the Tugas could then take all their troops out of Angola and Mozambique and send them to fight in our land. I can't imagine when we would gain our independence then because the colonialists would inhabit every one of our villages. There would be so many of them that they could occupy every single village and cultivate rice. We can therefore see how the reality of our struggle is part of the reality of the struggle of the other Portuguese colonies whether we like it or not; it's not a matter of wanting it—I didn't decide it, nor did the Party's Political Bureau, none of you decided it. But whether we like it or not, that's the way it is.

Such is the power of reality. It's all about us being conscious of this, working to ensure that we march forward together, as we should. This is the only explanation for our Party's policy, our Party's stubbornness towards the CONCP [Conferência das Organizações Nacionalistas das Colónias Portuguesas (Conference of Nationalist Organizations of the Portuguese Colonies)], that is, towards the group of movements from the Portuguese colonies, as a collective. Because we understand the reality of things. We ourselves had a big influence on the creation of FRELIMO [Frente de Libertação de Moçambique (Mozambique Liberation Front)], the movement in Mozambique, because there was a need to fight in Mozambique and quickly.

And yet, we might fight in all the Portuguese colonies and we might even win, win our independence, but if racism still holds in South Africa, if the colonialists remain in charge, directly or indirectly, in several other African countries, then we cannot really believe that Africa is truly independent. Misfortune will befall us once more, sooner or later. So we are part of a concrete reality that is Africa, fighting against imperialism, racism, and colonialism. If we're not sufficiently conscious of this we're liable to make a lot of mistakes.

And even in our part of the earth, with Cabo Verde in the middle of the sea, across from Mauritania, Senegal, and Guinea, we constitute a collective in which all the parts depend on each other. For example, our struggle is highly dependent on the Republic of Guinea and Senegal. We understood right from the start how important the Republic of Guinea and Senegal would be to us. We have geared our entire struggle towards advancing alongside them, to creating favorable conditions so that we may benefit from the consequences of this reality. But we must be aware that both the Republic of Guinea and Senegal are also aware that our reality is important to their reality, and that this awareness determines the greater or lesser degree of help they give us. Because they'll both be thinking: "Who is going to rule that land tomorrow? Does this affect us, is it in our interest or against our interest?" This is a big issue in itself.

But the Tugas also have a clear sense of this. Just a few days ago, for example, I went to Mauritania and radio stations all over the world reported that I'd had talks with President Ould Daddah, that I'd been very well received, etc. The Portuguese immediately launched a campaign on their radio stations, and South Africa launched their own campaign too, saying that I went to Mauritania to set up a base to attack Cabo Verde and that they'd been saying for a long time now that our ultimate aim was to undermine the Atlantic Pact. So you can see how all these realities are related. But all of us here in Africa are part of a bigger reality, that of the world, which has all the problems that it has and, whether we like it or not, we're implicated in those problems.

Today, a man can walk on the moon and gather bits of the moon's surface to bring back to Earth. Now it might seem that this has nothing to do with us, we sons and daughters of Guinea and Cabo Verde. We're still up to our knees in mud trying to drive the Tugas out of our land. But it has a lot to do with us, our cause, as of tomorrow, and if we weren't in the middle of this difficult struggle, we ought to throw a big party to celebrate the fact that mankind has reached the moon. This is very important for the future of humanity, for our Earth, for this, the planet we live on.

Other people's reality is, then, of great interest to us. So is the experience of others. If I know that one of you went down a certain path, tripped up several times, hurt yourself, and reached the other end in pieces, I'll be extremely careful if I have to go down that same path because someone else already knows the reality of that path and I know of their experience. If there's another path, a better path, I'll take that one instead, but if there isn't, then I'll have to go carefully, feel my way, drag myself along on the ground if necessary.

Other people's experience is of huge importance to anyone experiencing anything. Other people's reality is of huge importance to everyone's own reality. A lot of people don't understand this, they fixate on their own reality and some wild notion that they're going to invent things for themselves: "I don't want to do the same thing others have done, I don't want anything others have already done." This just shows great ignorance. For in reality, if we really want to do something, we first have to look at who's already done the same thing, who's done something similar, who's done the opposite, so that we can take something from their experience, not copy them totally, because each reality has its own problems and requires solutions appropriate to those problems.

But there are lots of things that belong to lots of realities at once. Other people's experience needs to be useful to us and we need to be able to take away the bits that we can adapt to suit our own circumstances so that we can avoid unnecessary effort and sacrifice. This is very important.

Naturally, it's the same thing with our struggle. A good political commissar, for example, is working and another political commissar is standing right beside him, but the latter doesn't show any interest in the former's way of working, doesn't try to learn from his experience or understand why he's doing a good job. He just turns his back and goes off to do his own work by himself. A commander is in an area and there are other commanders in the same area, who are of a lower rank. Yet they prove themselves incapable of exchanging thoughts with the senior commander, let alone asking for his advice on how to solve certain problems. He's been engaged in the struggle for longer and has more experience than them. But they don't want to know. People like this are destroying the struggle.

Geographic Reality

Of course, in a struggle such as ours, we have to connect reality to the development of the struggle. Yesterday, we talked a fair bit about certain conflicts that exist in our land, both in Guinea and Cabo Verde, at the social level.

To develop our struggle, we had to consider the geographical reality of our land, its historical reality, its ethnic reality—that's to say the different races, cultures—the economic, social, and cultural reality. And we had to consider how all of this is wrapped up in the larger reality of our land, in terms of the struggle, and that is our political reality, in other words, the fact that, both in Guinea and in Cabo Verde, we are under Portuguese colonial domination.

Comrades will know, in general terms, the geographic reality of our land. We are a small territory, about forty thousand square kilometers in total, including Guinea and Cabo Verde, with Guinea being nine times larger than Cabo Verde, which is itself comprised of ten islands off the West Coast of Africa. Guinea is wedged between two African countries (Guinea and Senegal) and Cabo Verde, which lies about four hundred miles off the coast. Our reality is, therefore, that we have a continental part and an insular or island part, made up of the Bijagós islets and the Cabo Verde islands, which in total amount to over one hundred islands and islets.

Many people, perhaps even today, still don't appreciate how important this is. But it is very important to everything in our land, from defense to our economics and riches, the very strength of our land. Our geographical reality is also that Guinea has practically no mountains, except for a few hills in the Boé region, the highest being three hundred meters, and Cabo Verde is a series of volcanic and mountainous islands.

Even in this aspect we can see how one completes the other. One land has no mountains and the other is all mountains. This is also of great importance, not only in terms of the economy, but also in the social, cultural, etc. life that we find within our people.

In Guinea, the land is cut through by arms of the sea that we call rivers, though they aren't really rivers: the Farim is only a river beyond

Candjambari; the Geba is only a river from Bambadinca upwards and there's sometimes saltwater even past Bambadinca; the Mansoa is only a river beyond Mansoa, towards Sara, near Caroalo; the Buba is not a river anywhere, because it is saltwater all the way up until we reach dry land; Cumbidjã and Tombali are all sea arms, except in the upper part where there is a bit of freshwater in the rainy season, especially the Bedanda river, which gets fresh water from Balama. The only genuine river in our land is the Corubal. This reality is very important for us, because if, on the one hand, we have a lot of ports we can enter with boats, on the other hand, it's easy to see the risks this brings. If our land were landlocked, given the way the struggle has been going, the Tugas would be getting very desperate by now because there wouldn't be any food in their barracks. But as they have boats and our people don't attack their boats enough, they can use the sea arms to deliver food and supplies to barracks deep in the interior.

Meanwhile, from an economic point of view, it's very important to have navigable rivers or sea arms. I'm talking about from the future point of view of our land. For the struggle, specifically, you can see how important it is for us to consider all these things in order to be able to develop our struggle. If, at the start of the struggle it was very useful to have so many rivers, so many sea arms, streams, etc., it was because it allowed us to isolate ourselves, defend ourselves from the Tugas by making it hard for them with wet terrain, forcing them to cross rivers; today, it makes things a bit more difficult for us, because if Bissau were on the mainland, if it weren't on an island, if it weren't for the Corubal river on one side and the Mansoa river on the other, we'd be in Bissau by now. We fire upon Bissau every day as we do in Mansoa, for example. But the circumstances now favor the Tugas, just as the Buba River also favors them as they can use it for their boats. It's the same in Farim. You can see, then, how important it is to consider such simple things as geographic reality.

Anyone who has read books on guerrilla warfare will no doubt remember the statement that a guerrilla force's best weapon is its mountains. But there are no mountains in Guinea. If we hadn't paid attention to our own reality, analyzed it, and come to conclusions on how best to act, we might have simply said that you can't fight a guerrilla war in Guinea because there are no mountains. Cabo Verde has mountains, this is very important, but what kind of mountains? You have to take this into account too, mountains alone are not enough.

It's not the mountains that do the shooting, it's people, and they need to be mobilized. In Guinea, for example, we have the Bijagós islands. Why didn't we begin the struggle on those islands, why did we do it across the water on terra firma? Because of another reality, the economic reality.

We have a serious problem in Cabo Verde. If Cabo Verde were just one island, like Cyprus or Cuba, it would be easier, but there are ten islands. And so we have to think about which island to start the armed struggle on, so that the struggle is one of real significance. And even in terms of mobilization, which island or islands should we start on? All of this was and is extremely important. The problem of getting communications from wherever we are to the islands, between the islands, etc. All this is a consequence of the geographical reality of our land.

Economic Reality

Another reality we have to consider is the economic one. Our principle economic reality is that we are Portuguese colonies because, when all is said and done, the political situation is a consequence of our economic situation.

We, in Guinea and Cabo Verde, are a people exploited by the Portuguese colonialists, our labor is exploited by them. That's what's important. This is the economic reality.

But are we a developed land?

No. We are economically backward, with almost no development at all in Guinea or Cabo Verde. There is no real industry, our agriculture is behind, our agricultural methods date back to the time of our grandparents. The riches of our land were basically extracted through man's labor. But the Portuguese did nothing to develop any of the riches of our land, absolutely nothing. Our ports are pathetic, Bissau and São Vicente. The Portuguese could have made good ports but they made pathetic little quaysides instead. When you look at the port of Dakar or even the port of Conakry, which are both good ports, or even better, the ports of Abidjan and Lagos in Nigeria, you can see how the French and the British built great ports where twenty or so ships can dock. And you can see how much time the Tugas wasted, using us, taking from us, leading us along, and messing us around. They've done nothing for our land.

So this is our economic reality and, whether it's in peace or war, whether in Guinea or Cabo Verde, we are an economically behind people, a people whose main way of life is agriculture. That is, cultivating the land to cover our food needs, or not cover them, as happens in Cabo Verde. Even in Guinea, if there isn't much rain, there are always shortages in some areas, at least when the "deep" does not mature.

Despite the presence of the Tugas for all these years, the situation has always been the same: we are still economically behind. There isn't even any real industry to speak of, in Guinea or Cabo Verde. In Guinea, we have the so-called rice husk oil factory, which is not a factory at all but a large pestle, the little rubber preparation factory and a small fish flour factory in Bijagós. In Cabo Verde there are three fish canning factories, where the Tugas work whatever hours they want, line their pockets with money, close the factory, and go home to rest. To give you a better idea of their shamelessness, I remember when I was in high school, my mother went to Cabo Verde and worked in the fish cannery, because sewing wasn't bringing anything in. Do you know how much she earned an hour? Five *tostões,* and if there was a lot of fish, she might work eight hours a day, earning four *pesos* (*escudos*). But if there wasn't much fish (and you had to walk a long way to get to the factory), she would just work for an hour and earn five *tostões.*

So our economy is backward. This is very important in a war. Look: we're a people who don't have factories so we cannot take factories from the Tugas and make things in them. Today, we have vast areas of liberated land; it would be great if there were factories in that land, because then maybe we could make textiles, maybe we could make soap in large quantities, instead of Comrade Vasco's modest little soaps. We could make other things if we had mines and there would be a lot more people wanting to help us; friends and enemies would want to help us if we had working mines, in the knowledge that there would be lots of bauxite, lots of oil. They would all come running. If oil from our land had already started being exported, maybe we'd even have Standard Oil itself on our side against the Tugas. Maybe the American government would be on our side against the Tugas. Maybe they would even have the courage to say: "Either you stop and give Guinea independence right now or we'll take away all your aid and attack you in the UN." Why? Because it would be in their interest. But because nothing has been developed in our land, they think we're just a corridor between the Republics of Guinea and Senegal, a mere passing place.

More important from the point of view of the war, as I told you, is how backward our economy is, and indeed the uncertainty that surround our riches. Everything would be different if our people already had a fair knowledge of how to work iron in order to make weapons. In other places carrying out armed struggle, some people fight at the front while others make weapons at the rear. We cannot do that, we can only make "long ones," though such rifles are ineffective. If we're going to win a war against the Tugas, or against any other colonialists, by relying on long ones, our struggle will be a long one . . .

But if our economy were developed, our people would also be culturally stronger from a modern point of view, with more primary schools, more secondary schools, [and] the capacity to work with mortars, cannons, and even airplanes. Our commanders would be better able to understand issues of strategy and tactics, and they would all be able to work with maps. So we see the significance of fighting in an economically backward country.

Social Reality

You all know the social reality of our land, the disaster of colonialist exploitation.

But let's not blame everything on the colonialists. The disaster is also the exploitation of our people by our people, as you saw when I talked about our social structure.

We are absolutely exploited by the colonialists in our land, in Guinea and Cabo Verde. Commercially, both in Cabo Verde and Guinea, it's always the colonialists who make the most money at every step of the way, because in Cabo Verde, for example, there isn't a single commercial company that isn't linked to a company in Portugal. The same goes for Guinea where Gouveia and Ultramarino—linked to the banks, all of them owned by the Tugas—have a monopoly on all our trade (I say ours—theirs!). But, comrades, we have to be honest with ourselves. A lot of people in Cabo Verde suffered because they were exploited by Caboverdean landowners, just as a good deal of our people's suffering in Guinea came at the hands of our own people. We must make sure not to forget this, in order to know what we must do in the future.

There is, then, a concrete reality to this.

In Cabo Verde, our people live in poverty. In the years when it rains a lot, there's plenty, you eat well, you fill your belly and you can even lie down and get some rest; but most of the time, when there isn't enough rain, there is hunger. Over the last fifty years, more people have died of hunger in Cabo Verde than live there today. Then, when contracted to go and work in São Tomé or sent to Angola, Caboverdeans were transported like animals in the hold and, if they died, thrown overboard into the sea.

In Guinea, as you know, the colonialists performed all kinds of exploitation: forced labor on the roads, all manners of abuse, insults, and humiliations. Portuguese doctors sent to study the situation in Cabo Verde said that, in their capacity as scientists, they had no doubt about one thing: that everyone was living in a state of hunger. And if it's not absolute hunger, it's specific hunger, in other words, a lack of certain things that are necessary for the human body to live well. This kind of specific hunger also exists in Guinea. In Guinea, almost everyone has malaria, if we were to examine all the comrades here right now, we'd find almost everyone has parasites in their stomachs. There's a huge amount of leprosy, diseases of every kind.

This social disaster has made our people weak from a scientific point of view, in health terms. A man who eats pretty much only rice cannot hope to have the same resistance as a man who eats rice, meat, milk, eggs . . . It's true that when a foreigner comes to our land and walks with our comrades in the bush, he gets left behind. That's a different thing. But from the point of view of being resistant in life, we know that in our land someone who's thirty years old is already starting to age. It's unusual to find old people with gray hair and beards. The average lifespan in our land, in Guinea or Cabo Verde, is thirty years. Our life expectancy is thirty; anyone who makes it past thirty is lucky. Now, life expectancy in other countries, where they eat well and drink well (I'm not talking about getting drunk), is sixty, sixty-seven, and every year the figure goes up. That's much nicer, whatever way you look at it. If, when you're born, you know that you're going to live to be seventy, you have time to do things. But what can you do in thirty years? This is due to a lack of food, poor hygiene and medical care, poverty. That's the social condition of our land. Abused by the Tugas, abused by certain sons and daughters of our land, poverty, suffering, illness, hunger and a short life on top of everything else. Difficult conditions, very difficult.

Cultural Reality

While it's true that, from a cultural point of view, conditions in Cabo Verde are a little bit better than in Guinea—because given the conditions in which the population has developed, being indigenous or nonindigenous has never really been an issue and so, in theory, any child from Cabo Verde could go to an official school—it's also true that there were far fewer schools overall than in Guinea.

There are certain things that comrades will not know and this may confuse them but, although it's true that more people learned to read and write in Cabo Verde than they did in Guinea in the time of the colonialists, illiteracy in Cabo Verde stands at 85 percent, never mind what some vain Caboverdeans who think they know everything might claim. The Tugas boast that there's no illiteracy in Cabo Verde. This isn't true! Because among those who can supposedly read, as I found out in 1949 when I went there on holiday, there are people who finished second grade maybe four or five years ago, this is in the countryside, in Godim or Santa Catarina, who, if you give them the newspaper today, cannot read it. They are illiterate people who know their ABCs. There are a lot of people like this in the world, some doctors with degrees, even. But we need to let go of certain illusions.

In Guinea, 99 percent of the population could not go to school. School was only for the assimilated or the children of the assimilated, you all know the story, there's no need for me to go over it again. But it's disastrous for our land that the Tugas did not allow our children to advance, to learn, to understand the reality of their lives, their land, their society, to understand the reality of Africa, of the world today. This is a major obstacle we must overcome, a huge hurdle in developing our struggle. Only today I told you about how the people emigrated within Africa, how the Mandinga people did it and what happened, and many of you did not know this, just as many comrades won't know, a Beafada comrade who calls himself Malam something, for example, probably won't know that in ancient times the names Malam, Braima and others were not Beafada names. What happened to the Beafadas happens to a lot of people in our land. For example, take Vasco Salvador Correia. In the old days, his people weren't called Vasco or Salvador, much less Correia. In other words, when the Mandingas dominated the people of our land, they brought in assimilation (the Tugas weren't the first to try and assimilate people in our land) and the dominated people ended up adopting Mandinga names. Just as today's Mandingas don't have the same names as they did back then. The old names of the Fulas didn't include anything like Mamadut. That's copied from the Arabic: Mamadu means Mohammed, Iussufe means Joseph, Mariama is Mary, these are Semitic names.

The cultural reality of our land in Cabo Verde is the result of the fact that the colonialists let Caboverdeans study, because they needed to train people as colonial agents, the same way the Indians were used. Just as the English used the Indians in colonialism and the French used the Dahomeans, so the Portuguese used the Caboverdeans, educating a certain number. But at a particular point they stopped and blocked their path for good: no more than a certain number of primary schools, no more than one secondary school, which, incidentally, Vieira Machado, the former Minister for Overseas Territories, wanted to turn into a school for fishermen and carpenters at the time when I started there. I couldn't go for three months because they shut it down. As far as they were concerned, they'd done enough, they didn't need any more. From then on, there would only be schools for fishermen and carpenters. The population rose up and protested and the secondary school started up again.

The reality of our own land in Cabo Verde is, then, the reality of an African culture being transplanted to the islands and coming into contact with other, outside cultures, from Portugal and elsewhere. Lots of people think that Cabo Verde is Praia or São Vincente. But anyone who knows the Caboverdean countryside senses that Cabo Verde, in reality, beats with a pulse as African as any other part of Africa. The culture among the people is extremely African. The beliefs are the same—there is a *polon*[1] in Santiago, which some people still consider a sacred tree. There aren't many *polons* because of the droughts, but nobody touches the ones that do exist. Furthermore, witchcraft, "souls" that appear at night, people who can fly, who do strange things, things that just happen, this form of interpreting the reality of life is exactly the same as in Africa. Not to mention "casting lots" . . .

In Cabo Verde, there was a coming together of various ethnic groups and a fusion of their cultures, but up until the 1940s there were still certain groups that preserved certain characteristics of their own. For example, groups that settled around Praia, in Santiago, had their own villages, which lent their name to whatever festivities they had, and behaved a certain way, while elsewhere, Achada de Santo António, for example, there was another kind of village, and then there were the people of Santa Catarina, the Picos, etc.

In Guinea, the culture of our people is a product of many different African cultures. Each ethnic group has its own culture but they all have the same cultural background, their means of interpreting the world and organizing societal relationships. And we know that, although there are Muslim populations, even they, at heart, are also animists, like the Balantas and others. They believe in Allah but they also believe in *irãs*[2] and *djambacosses*.[3] They have the Koran but they also have their *grigri*[4] on their arm and other things. And the success of Islam in our land, as with Africa in general, has to do with Islam being able to appreciate this and accept other people's culture, whereas Catholicism always wants to put an immediate stop to such things and have people believe only in the Virgin Mary, Our Lady of Fatima, and Almighty God Our Lord Jesus Christ.

That's the cultural reality of our land. But we must think about our culture carefully: a lot of it is dictated by our economic condition, by our circumstances of economic underdevelopment. We should certainly like our African culture and indeed we love it very much, our dances and songs, our way of making statues, canoes, and cloths, all

---

1   Also known as the kapok tree, the *polon* is a tall and wide tree found in Cabo Verde, Guinea and elsewhere in West Africa which featured widely in folkloric stories.
2   Spirit guides
3   Traditional religious medical healers in Guinea
4   Charm

this is wonderful. But if we hope to clothe all our people in only our own clothes then we're going about things the wrong way. We have to be realistic. Our land is very lovely, but if we're not fighting to also change our land, then we're going about things the wrong way.

A lot of people think that being African means being able to sit on the ground and eat with your hands. It's true, this is certainly African, but all the peoples of the world have sat on the ground and eaten with their hands at some point. A lot of people seem to think that it's only here in Africa that people eat with their hands. This isn't true: all the Arabs of North Africa, even before they came to Africa, ate with their hands, sitting on the ground. We have to be conscious about our things, we have to respect what's valuable about our things, what's good for the future of our land, for our people to advance.

But no one should think that they're more African than someone else, even a white man who defends Africa's interests, just because they're better at eating with their hands, better at making a rice ball with their hands and chucking it in their mouth. The Tugas, when they were still Visigoths, or the Swedes, who are now helping us, back when they were still Vikings, also ate with their hands.

If you watch a film about the Vikings in ancient times, you'll see they went to war wearing big horns on their heads and with charms fastened to their arms. They wouldn't dare go to war without their big horns on their heads. No one should think that being African means wearing horns around your chest, or having charms around your waist. People who think that way haven't yet fully understood the relationship between man and nature. The Tugas did it, the French did it when they were Franks and Normans, etc., the English did it when they were Angles and Saxons, traveling the seas in canoes, big canoes like those of the Bijagós.

We have to have the courage to state these things clearly. No one should think that African culture, what's truly African and what must therefore be preserved forever so that we can go on being African, means being powerless before nature. All the peoples of the world, in whatever state, have already experienced this powerlessness or will experience it. There are peoples who haven't even got that far yet: they spend their lives climbing trees, eating and sleeping, and that's it. And what a lot of beliefs they have!

We mustn't allow ourselves to be persuaded that being African means thinking lightning is a result of God's fury. We mustn't believe that being African means thinking that man cannot stop the river from flooding. Anyone who leads a struggle like ours, anyone who is responsible for a struggle like ours, has to understand this, bit by bit, for this is the concrete reality.

Our struggle is based on our culture, because culture is the product of history and it is a strength. But our culture is replete with our powerlessness before nature. We need to understand this.

We might say more. For example, there are certain dances we do that show man's relationship with the forest, in which people appear dressed in straw looking like birds, with a big beak, and people run away in fear. We can do these dances and many others that are similar, but we also have to move beyond them, not just stop there. We can preserve the memory of all these things in order to develop our art, our culture, as we present it to others. Because we've moved beyond this, we now know that in the forest, in the bush, we rule, mankind does, not some animal, not some spirit in there. This is very important.

But this is the cultural reality of our land. Many comrades sitting here have a *mezinho*[5] at their waist, convinced as they are that this might stop them from being shot by the Tugas. But no one can tell me that those comrades who have died in the struggle weren't also wearing charms at their waists. They all were. We've had to respect this belief because when we began our struggle this was our reality and there was no way we could tell comrades to take their charms off, we would have been treating them as if they were Germans. Years ago, Germans never went to war without a charm. Some still carry an image of Our Lady of Fatima inside a little book, that's their charm; the Bible is their *mezinho* and they cross themselves before going into battle. The Tugas go about with their big crosses at their chests and they kiss them as soon as the fighting starts, that's their *mezinho*. And yet people still believe in the power of our own charms.

This is our cultural level in relation to the concrete reality of war. That's why we allow it, but don't for a second think that the leader-

5   Amulet

ship of this struggle believes that if you wear a *mezinho* at your waist, you won't die. You won't die in a war if you don't fight in a war but nor will you die if you don't attack the enemy from a position of weakness. If you make mistakes, from a position of weakness, you'll die for sure, there's no getting around that.

Now you might tell me about a number of cases you have in your heads: "Cabral doesn't understand, but we've seen cases in which charms saved comrades from death, the bullets came ricocheting back." You can say this, but I for one hope that our children's children, when they hear such things, will be pleased that the PAIGC was able to fight according to the reality of the land but will say: "Our parents fought hard but they believed in strange things."

This conversation may come too soon for some of you, I'm talking about in the future. But I'm sure most of you understand what I'm saying and know that I'm right.

The *mezinho* is typical of Africa. I even know lawyers from other African countries who wear a *mezinho* around their waist and put on an extra big one when they go to defend a case in court, because they think: "You never know, it might help me win." But because our struggle has advanced so much here, comrades fighting in another Portuguese colony even sent word to ask us if there were any good *grigri* we could send them.

I'm just bringing this to comrades' attention to show that, while on the one hand this is a strength, on the other hand it is a weakness. It's a strength because a comrade who puts a charm on believes in something; beyond the Party's words, it gives him extra courage and we mustn't forget that. But it's a weakness because he might make a lot of mistakes by trusting in it too much.

There have been comrades of ours who have died the following way: an airplane comes, everyone throws themselves to the ground, the plane drops bombs, but nothing happens. A comrade suddenly remembers that he doesn't have his charm, so he gets up, runs home, gets his charm and then he's machine-gunned down on the way back and dies with his charm in his hand. Some of you may know of other cases like this. But how many of you are capable of asking yourself: "What kind of joke is this, how can this be?"

The fact is the struggle, for us, has its strong and weak sides. A lot of us thought we shouldn't install ourselves in certain parts of the bush because the *irã* was there. Nowadays, thanks to there being so many *irãs* in our land, our people have realized, as has the *irã*, that mankind controls the bush and no one is afraid of it anymore. In Cobiana, even, where we'd been in the bush without any problems, it turned out that the *irã* was a nationalist. He clearly "said" that the Tugas must leave, that they have no business being in our land.

But comrades have to understand that all this is also an obstacle in our struggle. A lot of comrades who took up this life and committed themselves to the struggle right from the start, comrades who I hold in high esteem and have spent a lot of time with, if I'd said to them back then, "Go into the interior and focus on mobilizing the people," but then Secuna Baio or some other "Moor" had said to them, "Don't go, I cast lots and foresaw very bad things for you if you go into the interior," then they'd have rather died of shame in front of Cabral than go. There have been comrades who've refused to carry out ambushes because a "Moor" told them not to, having foreseen that someone was going to die. Indeed, some comrades had got so used to the big men ordering them around, making decisions for them about the war, that the big men themselves came to see me later to complain: "Cabral, what's going on? The young fellas no longer obey us, they go and perform an attack without even consulting us." I replied to one of them: "Look, big man, if the young fellas never used to do an attack without first consulting you, I never said anything, and I'm not going to say anything now either But I never appointed you as a commander, they're the commanders. If they used to consult you, that's up to them, and if they no longer want to, it's still their business not mine." The big man was a bit annoyed but he's not stupid, he is, of course, very clever—after all, the big men were the intellectuals in our society, our true, authentic society, the ones who saw things clearly and understood everything, our strengths and weaknesses—so he soon changed tune and adjusted to the new situation.

The Party has, in cultural terms, tried to get the best out of our cultural reality, whether that be by not forbidding things it was possible to let go without jeopardizing the struggle, or by coming up with new ideas that comrades could instill in their spirits, new ways of seeing reality, or by making the most of those comrades who'd had a bit more schooling, having them lead the struggle itself and sending them to study and prepare cadres for the future.

It may seem like this is very simple, but it's difficult, it's very complicated to reach a solution like this.

Political Reality

The political reality of our land is that bigger reality we know only too well, the fact of our having been a Portuguese colony. Our people could not rule over themselves, either in Guinea or Cabo Verde. The Tugas ruled even if they put a Black administrator in place, which Honório Barreto alone had the luck or misfortune to be.

But the fact is the Tugas have ruled our land, Portuguese colonialism. This bigger reality is that which has created the conflict between us, the exploitation of our people, under cover of Portuguese policy. This, essentially, is what prompted our struggle.

Our struggle has grown so much that we now need to take advantage and transform geographical reality itself, at least as much as we can. It might not seem like it, but the fact is that when we build dams, bridges, etc., we will have changed the geographical landscape of our land and we will thus create a new human geography, this is what we're creating in our land. When we've completely transformed the Bijagós islets, when we've turned Cabo Verde into a magnificent center of world tourism, for example, we will have created a new geographical reality. The boats we now see passing in the distance will stop off in Cabo Verde. But we first have to transform, through our struggle, the economic reality of our land. We're going to end the Tugas' exploitation but we're also going to end the exploitation of our people by our people. And we have to develop our land, and make it advance as much as possible. This is our struggle: social reality, cultural reality, everything is going to change. And there is a new political reality that has emerged in our land, which is that we will rule over ourselves.

Of course, our reality has its strengths and weaknesses, as I've already demonstrated. Because, for example, the fact that we don't have much economic development is a big weakness, but it's also a strength, because if our land had big mines, big factories, etc., the imperialists would have entered the war harder and faster. Perhaps we wouldn't only be fighting the Tugas but other imperialists as well. This way, at least, things are a bit more calm, it's just bush and desert.

But we cannot sleep on the job. The social reality of our land does not, of course, feature big bourgeois capitalists, and this is good for our struggle, because we don't have the problem of having to fight those who exploit our people too much. But it's also a weakness because, in some countries, a number of national capitalists have joined the struggle, with all their means, all their money, and they've helped a lot, like in Cuba, in China and other countries, where many local capitalists have joined the revolution in earnest. Some leaders are even the children of big capitalists.

Another advantage is that in our land there aren't many class differences and the wealthier classes, who have more means, are small in number. This avoids a lot of issues concerning division, from a social point of view. But in the social reality of our land, as we've discussed, there's the question of ethnic groups, which is a great weakness, because even in this room there may be people who still think: "I'm Pepel" or "I'm Mancanha and a Mancanha always looks after his own" or "I'm Mandinga." This is a great weakness in our struggle. And it would be very bad if we allowed this to continue, if we were not capable of, in fact, eradicating this during our struggle.

I want to draw comrades' attention to this and for you all to think carefully about what happens in Africa whenever there are problems between tribes, so-called tribalism, wars between ethnic groups, etc. It's not people themselves who come up with these things, they don't remember such things, because people are very realistic in their pursuit of reality and in defending their own interests. The fact of the matter is this: the time of tribes is over in Africa. There was a time when tribes fought each other over land, to take over land on which to graze their cattle, to find better land, or because of children or women, or in order to be able to impose their strength, etc., but that time has passed.

Ever since we Africans have managed to establish states, states of a military kind even, ever since we've managed to bring people together from different tribes to do a particular job, to serve a particular class, tribes began to come to an end.

When the Tugas and other colonialists came, they put an end to tribalism once and for all, but they tried to preserve the upper echelon, those who ruled over tribes or groups, to serve as intermediaries and help them to rule. Nowadays, our people, Balanta or otherwise, may still have old memories in their heads like "actually, we never got along very well with the Mandingas," but if there's no one to incite them, they no longer pursue such things. It's the same with the Ibos and Yorubas in Nigeria, or the Bakongos and other people in the Congo. Someone has to incite them, someone has to say: "Right, come on then, they're full of themselves but the Mandingas will show them."

There are even people who disown their tribes, people who no longer want to have anything to do with them, who studied at universities, in Lisbon or Oxford, or the capital of their own land even, but who today, given the access Africa has to independence, want to rule, want to become president of the republic, want to be a minister, in order to exploit their own people. And when this isn't possible for whatever reason, they suddenly remember: "I am Lunda, son of Lundas, descendant of the Lunda king. Rise up Lunda people because the Bakongos want to eat us."

But it's got nothing to do with the Lundas or Bakongos, it's just because some man wants to become president, to have all the diamonds, all the gold, get hold of all the lovely things so that he can do whatever he wants, live well, have all the women he wants, in Africa or Europe, be able to travel around Europe, be received as president, dress expensively, in tuxedos or big *bubus*,[6] pretend he's African. This is a lie, these kinds of people are not Africans at all. They're no more than the whites' lackeys or puppy dogs.

It's the same thing in Nigeria and the same with us. No matter how it may seem to us, these people are only out to serve their own political ambitions. In other words, we have to recognize that the only argument in defense of division, no matter what form that division may take, is personal ambition. For example: the Tugas have done us a lot of harm but we cannot consider every white person to be a Tuga. Only someone with personal ambitions can claim: "We can't accept help from that fella in Bissau because he's white, or from that fella in Catió because he's white." What? This cannot be. If we want to serve our land, our Party, our people, we have to accept help from everyone. Oh, but he's a friend, a comrade. When someone's only interested in serving their own belly, in sorting themselves out with a good job, we wait to see if he's dumb or smart: "Maybe we can accept him, but only if we can walk all over him. Otherwise he'd better be on his way, I don't want him taking my place. No way."

---

6   Long traditional African shirts

This is why we need to know the reality of our land, in all ways and in every aspect, in order to be able to orient the struggle in general terms and specific terms. And we have to recognize that, in the concrete circumstances that are the reality of our land, in Guinea and Cabo Verde, it takes a good deal of courage to answer the following question in the affirmative: "Can we really wage a war like this?"

We can, of course, answer with a yes, because we are doing. But it was difficult at the start. There was that man who asked: "But how are we going to fight the Tugas if we don't even have proper clothes, if we can't even read or write? The Tugas wage war with commanders, majors, etc., trained at university, at the highest academies, how can we fight against them? We have nothing, how are we going to assemble the means to fight, how is it possible?"

This is where we have to put our heads together in order to be able to answer with a yes. We have to place our own reality before the reality of the modern world. Then we'll be able to say we were divided, each group on its own, but faced with the reality of the modern world, a number of us in our land were able to rally our people and make them understand that we, Balantas, Pepels, Mandingas, the children of Caboverdeans, etc., can be united, can advance together, without losing our heads. And we've proven that it really is possible. And in the reality of the modern world, a new Africa has emerged primed for independence, for progress, and we must take this into account. There is also a socialist camp that has emerged since the October Revolution that defends self-determination for all peoples, in other words, that all peoples everywhere should get to choose their own futures, hold destiny in their own hands. There are also international laws established at the United Nations.

We have to reckon with all this, with the reality of the whole world, the reality of the wars that have taken place elsewhere in the world, all the problems they brought, to give us courage to advance the struggle in our land. Because if we focus on one single reality, the reality of our own village, and try to think about how to fight colonialism based on that, it will be impossible.

So, you can see how important it is for us to know our own reality and to know all the other realities besides, in order to know where ours fits in with the others, in order to be able to know what our overall strengths are, what our overall weaknesses are.

Only then are we able to see that we might fight hard, carry out our struggle, make lots of sacrifices, rely only ourselves and our own means, and it still wouldn't be enough. It wouldn't be enough for us to win. We have to be capable, as a party, of taking advantage of what favorable conditions exist elsewhere in the world and in Africa in order to advance our struggle. And we have been taking advantage of them, we take advantage of them more and more each day. This is why we've been able to get weapons, ammunition, clothing, medicine, hospitals, etc., which we couldn't have got from within our land, by being demanding in terms of our own sacrifice and effort but also by relying on the reality of the modern world, forces that may come from outside. This is how important the help we get from other countries is, help we accept with only one condition: that there are no conditions. And we guarantee that all the help we receive is put to the service of our Party and our people.

And we might even say that there isn't a liberation movement anywhere in the world that has benefited more from outside help than ours. We all know how much admiration we inspire whenever anyone comes to see what we're doing, inside and outside our land, and when they see that we really do put absolutely everything we're given to the service of the struggle, to the service of our people. We have sought to put all our comrades' capabilities at the service of the Party. If comrades don't give their all, it's because they don't want to. It's not through a lack of example or encouragement. We have sought to improve comrades' capabilities ever more each day through the direct use of the help we receive in training up cadres.

In order to transform our reality, we therefore need to use our own experience, our own strength, our own sacrifice and effort, but we also need to use other people's experience, get other people's help, and use that help properly.

By combining our strength with the strength that may come to us from outside, we can really transform the reality of our land, and we have already transformed it a lot, because nowadays the Tugas no longer rule over most parts of our land. The Tugas are hurting in Guinea because they're engaged in a colonial war they know is lost, and in Cabo Verde things are already coming to the boil, they're starting to hurt there too, to the point that they're calling upon friends to come and help, because for them the loss of Cabo Verde would be the end of Portuguese domination in Africa. So we know that we are capable of transforming this reality, and the mere fact that we're holding this meeting is further clear proof that we've created a new reality in our land. In the reality of our land yesterday, a reality in which, for example, Cruz Pinto left to study in Portugal or Bobô left when he went to do a politics course, a meeting of comrades like this would have been simply impossible, whether inside or outside our land. When, at a certain point in Bissau, I called my closest friends to my house and said: "Comrades, you're my mother's very good friends, you're my friends too, you come to my house, we eat, we mess around, but the time for messing around is over, let's start to have a few little conversations." They replied, "yes, sir." We had those conversations and scheduled a meeting. But only one or two of them came. The others didn't come because they thought it was madness.

If we compare that moment with this moment now, we can see that, in fact, the creation of the PAIGC was the starting point for creating a new reality in our land, in Guinea and Cabo Verde. And we have to keep on creating that new reality and develop it more and more each day in order to better serve the interests of our people, primarily, but also the interests of Africa and human progress in general.

3. OUR PARTY AND STRUGGLE MUST BE LED BY THE BEST SONS AND DAUGHTERS OF OUR PEOPLE

Our struggle is not just talk: it's a real struggle, we have to seriously fight. Comrades will remember that in the early sixties many people were convinced that the struggle consisted of merely talking on the radio. Great "victories" were won on the radio in Dakar or Conakry, against the PAIGC even, but not against Portuguese colonialism, because the opportunists never did anything against the colonialists. Those were the days when people raced each other to see who would be the first to speak on the radio! As if that's what the struggle was!

In our Party, we have always believed it to be basic and correct that the struggle is not mere talk or words, whether they be written or spoken; the struggle is everyday action, against us and against the enemy, action that transforms and grows with each passing day until it has developed into all the forms necessary to drive the Portuguese colonialists out of our land.

And we must carry out this struggle wherever it's necessary. Firstly, within our land, because you cook rice inside, not outside the pot. But we should never forget that a struggle such as ours must also be waged outside, not only against our enemies but alongside our friends in order to obtain the necessary means for our struggle and to establish every possibility for sustaining it within our land.

The fact that the PAIGC made it a principle that the struggle must be undertaken for real and that everyone, no matter who they may be, must fight, caused many people to distance themselves from the Party. This is because some people approached the PAIGC, and even joined the PAIGC, convinced that it was just going to be a matter of carrying out the fight on the radio today and then taking up a ministerial post tomorrow. When they sensed that for the PAIGC, carrying out the struggle meant being inside or outside the country, depending on what the leadership decides, some left and some even went back to join the Tugas, to benefit a little from the last traces of colonialism. This is one of the main reasons why, for example, the opportunists in Dakar are fighting our Party. Some of them have a huge desire to join the Party but they don't have the courage because they know that the Party might say to them, "Brace yourself, we're going in," when all they want to do is go straight to Bissau from Dakar and take up a seat in the cabinet.

Everyone has to fight, that's another absolute certainty built into the Party framework. And, little by little, we've reached a situation whereby, in our minds and in reality, there's no difference between being inside or outside the land in terms of our struggle. At the beginning of the struggle there were some who got a bit big-headed because they were inside the land. Others, being outside, were fearful and didn't do much because they were outside. Anyone in a struggle like ours who still has such notions, vanity complexes, or fears because they are inside or outside the land, has not understood our struggle at all.

The same goes for anyone who has never left the bush, who has endured seven years of struggle but doesn't understand how important our outside work is to the struggle inside—they haven't grasped anything either. And anyone who is outside, sitting in a "bureau" or wherever, who isn't capable of appreciating the value of those inside the country doing the shooting, doing political work, or whatever else, likewise hasn't grasped a thing.

Our Party, without having to discuss it much, without too much talk, adopted the following stance: these days we all know that there is no inside or outside, because any one of us might be inside or outside the land.

Of course, we mustn't confuse other people's land, the Republic of Guinea or Senegal, with our land, Guinea and Cabo Verde. We know rice is cooked in the pot, but we also know that firewood and other important things are needed to cook rice.

Some Party comrades thought that, because they'd gone into the bush to fight, they were kings and could walk all over anyone else. They were wrong. Today we know this isn't true, that that's not how it works.

We've known it isn't true since the Cassacá Congress.[1] If someone goes into the bush to command the guerrillas, to fight, but doesn't follow the Party's Guidelines as they should, then they'd best brace themselves because we'll leave the Tugas be for a while and fight them instead. Others acquire vices while doing their work abroad, they come back and think they can't possibly get their feet muddy or be bitten by mosquitoes, that they can't go through what our soldiers, leaders and supervisors have been going through in the interior. They are wrong!

These are people who haven't actually seriously engaged in the fight. Maybe we were wrong to make them Party leaders, but sooner or later they'll come to realize that's not the way it works.

Our Party operates under circumstances whereby no one is inside or outside, everyone is inside and outside, depending on the Party's needs. And the leaders of the struggle and of the Party must always be aware of everything that's happening inside and outside our land, in terms of the type of work they do in the Party. Over the last few years, we can say that there isn't a leader or supervisor who hasn't been on missions outside the country, and there isn't a leader among us who hasn't also worked in the interior.

Of course, there are some militants and even leaders who have been outside more than they have been inside, and there are those who are always asking to go into the interior. It's nice to hear this, but you have to ask yourself if your work, your training, requires you to be inside or outside the land. That's what's important, because we'll do a little tourism later. There are also people in the interior who ask if they can be sent to Europe. But even if they don't get to go now, if they aren't sent on a mission, then afterwards, once we've taken back our land, if they work hard, they'll be able to fill their pockets, travel all over Europe, and come back.

Our people are moved around, inside and outside our land, according to the needs of the struggle. This is fundamental for us. In my case, as leader, I have to personally answer the needs of the struggle at conferences, at meetings with heads of state or with leaders of other parties around the world, and this requires of me, as it does the other comrades who work with me, a lot of effort, but effort that is decisive to our struggle. But another thing that gives me strength is knowing

---

1   The first party congress of the PAIGC, held in Cassacá, Guinea, 1964.

for certain that there isn't a single important operation in our war, nor an important bit of political work, that I don't personally know about, that I haven't studied. No serious changes to our work at the political level or relating to the armed struggle are made without first passing through my hands. It's just a shame that man has his limitations; I cannot be everywhere at once, alas, but I have spent as much time as possible alongside our soldiers and militants.

Another Party principle linked to the one I've just mentioned states that we should fight without rushing, fight in stages, develop the struggle gradually without taking giant leaps.

If you look carefully, you'll see that many struggles begin by creating a political bureau, a general staff, etc. A lot of struggles start with the immediate creation of a national liberation army.

We didn't start like that. We started our struggle the way you sow a seed in the ground. You sow the seed, a tiny plant grows, which grows and grows until it bears flowers and fruit. This is the way of our struggle, step by step, stage by stage, gradually, without making any giant leaps. Besides, each new stage also brings greater demands in terms of our work.

Some comrades, even some of you sitting in this room, have a tendency to get more comfortable the more your responsibilities grow. There are comrades who, it seems, spend several years waiting to be given responsibilities only to then make the exact same mistakes others made before them in that role. We have to have the courage to combat this, because the struggle is demanding, our Party is more demanding each and every day. Anyone who fails to understand this will have to be set to one side, no matter how much it pains us to do so. We cannot allow, as the struggle progresses, as our people sacrifice themselves more and more, as countless comrades are killed and others are wounded or maimed, as we rapidly age having given our whole lives to the struggle, when so many people have pinned their hopes on us, inside and outside our land, we cannot then allow certain comrades, militants or supervisors, to lead an easy life and commit acts unbefitting of their responsibilities, right in front of our eyes, right in front of our people, right in front of Africa and the rest of the world.

A lot of people think this is Cabral's backyard, it's up to him to fix the things that spoil or that someone has spoiled. They're wrong. It's up to each and every one of us to fix these things, to try and correct them, because if we don't, nothing can save us, no matter how many victories we manage to achieve. That's why our struggle is like a sifter separating the clean rice from the bran, like a sieve with pounded flour, separating the fine flour from the coarse flour and so on.

The struggle unites but it also separates people. The struggle shows who's useful and who's useless.

Each comrade must be vigilant of themselves, because the struggle is selective, it exposes us before everyone, shows us as we really are. This is one of the great advantages of having the people undertake a struggle, especially an armed struggle to liberate themselves.

There was a "big man," who's still involved in the struggle, who said to me three years ago: "Cabral, every day I pray that Salazar does not die." "And why is that, big man?" "So that the struggle goes on a little longer, so that while he stubbornly holds on we can get to know each other better."

This is a great truth: today we know each other well, we know who's useful and who isn't. We make an effort to get the useless to improve, but we know who is and who isn't ultimately of use, we even know who is and isn't capable of lying. There are some people we still don't know very well. But comrades know me well, you know the other Party leaders, who we respect a lot because they are and will always be of use, right until the end, you all know this very well. There are others that some people are afraid of because they know that they are of use only because they wield power. Some of you have seen Party leaders make serious mistakes but you carry on obeying them because you're afraid of them.

Today, we know each other well. Some of you have seen Party supervisors wrong other people and you know, in your conscience, that this is not fair, but you keep quiet, you hide it. And yet you remain convinced that they are not good leaders, that they are not good supervisors, that they do wrong, that they stray from the Party line, and that they do all this convinced that the Party leadership will never find out.

Everyone who's here with their supervisor or leader has their own particular idea about that man or woman. The struggle has allowed us to get to know each other very well and this is very important. Some have been able to improve more and more each day, while others have gone backwards by the day, despite all the help we've tried to give everyone to move forward, with their heads held high, in the service of the Party, to serve our people as they ought to.

But whether we like it or not, the struggle is selective and, gradually, some people will pass through the sieve while others will get caught in it, because we've made a firm decision that, for as long as we are here as leaders of this Party, the following will apply: only those who really want to fight seriously will move forward; only those who have really understood that the struggle advances in stages, that it becomes more demanding with each passing day, and that it requires more responsibility from us; only those who are willing to give their all and demand nothing back except respect, dignity, and the opportunity to advance in the service of our people.

I would like to remind you, in regards to the struggle advancing in stages, that many comrades thought things would progress more quickly and that we'd be straight into Bissau. It doesn't work like this, it has to be in stages, we have to be prepared for a long struggle. As things stand, our independence could come tomorrow, the day after tomorrow or in six months' time, because the Tugas are in a desperate position in our land and, if we hold out, they will become more desperate by the day. But we have to be prepared in spirit for a long struggle, and we have to prepare new people to carry the struggle on, if necessary.

And you, the young people sitting here today, must be prepared to shoulder that responsibility and properly understand the following: if this struggle ends tomorrow, you must be ready, as the younger generation, to protect our people's work, to build the progress our Party craves. But if it lasts for another ten years, you young people here will have to replace us older ones when we can no longer continue, and you'll have to train other young people and prepare them to, in time, replace you and continue the struggle.

The Vietnamese say that they will undoubtedly win the war because if the Americans are prepared to fight for ten years, they're prepared to fight for ten-and-a-half years; if the Americans are prepared to fight for twenty years, they're prepared to fight for twenty-and-a-half years. That is the consciousness of a people who know their own rights in their own land, for the land is theirs and they have young people and adults who are truly prepared to properly serve their people.

Clearly a struggle like ours, a Party like ours, requires a secure leadership, a united leadership, a conscious leadership, and for our own reality to determine the leadership's consciousness. We need consciousness because, to the extent that man is conscious of a reality, he creates the conditions to change and transform that reality for the better. And within this framework, the most conscious men and women, in other words, those who have the clearest sense of our reality and the reality that our Party wants to create, are the ones who must move forward to lead, no matter their origins, wherever they come from. We do not care where you've come from, who you are or who your parents are, but we do care whether you understand who we are, whether you understand what our land is and what our Party wants to do in it.

Do you seriously want to do this, under the flag of our Party? Then step forward and take the lead. The people who lead will be the people who are the most conscious of this. We may be fooled today, we may be fooled tomorrow, but the best proof of what's really true is reality; practice shows who is of use and who isn't.

Therefore, our principle is this: the best sons and daughters of our land should lead our Party and our people.

Does this mean we've always put the best people forward to lead? Some have proved themselves ultimately to be of no use, but that's part of the experiment we're undertaking.

The fact is we've always given people the opportunity to improve, we've given everyone in the Party the opportunity to advance, to be capable of leading. There are comrades sitting here now who three years ago were simple recruits at our military preparation camps. Today, they are members of our Interregional Committees or leaders of our Armed Forces. This shows how much our Party has been able to open up a path wide enough for comrades to advance upon, those who are most conscious, of most use, to move forward and take the lead.

Our struggle demands a conscious leadership and we have said that the best sons and daughters of our land must lead. At first, it's difficult to know who the best people are but, in accordance with a principle we talked about right at the beginning—trust in order to be trusted— as comrades begin to demonstrate their capabilities, we move them forward to see if they truly are the best or not, to see if they further improve or get worse.

No one can truly say that everyone in this Party hasn't had the chance to lead. Everyone has had a path opened up for them to advance upon and we have always believed that the more people we have capable of leading the better, because then we can choose the best of the best as leaders. We have done everything we can to improve our training of comrades, to get them to think more about our problems, to show more initiative, more enthusiasm, more dedication, to advance. And we've done our utmost to be fair, to make sure that those who advance deserve to do so because of their work and not because they have a pretty face or act like a servant to others.

We have done our utmost in the Party to avoid anything that involves subjecting some people to others, having people become servants of some kind to others. I've said the following right from the start: we don't want servants, we don't want attendants, we don't want boys at our beck and call. We want men and women, conscious comrades, our comrades, capable of raising their heads to speak to us and discuss things, with all due respect. We want conscious men and women who hold their heads up high, and we have fought hard against any tendency on the part of leaders or supervisors to have boys following them around, to have other supervisors taking orders like errand boys. And we've also fought the tendency some comrades have within their own spirits of always letting others take responsibility.

Of course, there has been some resistance to this. For example, there has sometimes been deaf, or silent resistance, particularly towards the presence of women among those who lead. Some comrades do their utmost to prevent women from leading, even when there are women who are better qualified to lead than they are. Unfortunately, some of our female comrades have not managed to uphold the respect and dignity required to defend their status as leaders. They've proved unable to avoid certain temptations or, at least, incapable of assuming certain responsibilities without developing a complex.

Some male comrades refuse to understand that freedom for our people means freedom for our women too, that sovereignty for our people means that women must participate too and that the strength of our Party is all the greater the more that women commit to leading, alongside the men. A lot of people think putting women in charge is just one of Cabral's quirks: "Let him do it, we can just sabotage it behind his back." These people haven't understood a thing yet. They can sabotage it today, they can sabotage it tomorrow, but sooner or later it'll come back to haunt them.

Something else that met with a lot of resistance within the Party for a while was this: we have been made up of this many leaders and now no one else can become a leader. Several of our comrades, good, capable soldiers, were ignored, blocked in their progress, because someone in charge denied them the opportunity to advance. This is killing the Party, it's like drowning it. Because while the oldest among us still have enough air to breathe, we're moving forward, but when we run out of air there will be no one to replace us. Our Party can only really be said to be strong if we, as leaders, are capable of paving the way for young people to move forward, young people like you, and other young people who are a bit further behind you for now, hundreds, thousands of young people who can take over and put the best people forward to lead.

We in the Party leadership, and me in particular, have done everything to support everyone who shows a willingness to work hard. The biggest joy for me is seeing a comrade, male or female, fulfill their duty with conscience, with goodwill, without being pushed, because we so often have to give people a push just to do what they're supposed to be doing. So seeing people independently performing their duty fills us with great encouragement, it makes us feel certain that we are capable of winning this struggle, of achieving what our Party wants to achieve. Everyone in the Party knows the sense of friendship, esteem, respect, and affection we have for those who prove capable of doing their duty. Each person we see working enthusiastically is like a piece of us, a new piece that guarantees the future of our Party and the victory of our people. That's why it's been our job to nurture, to try to develop in the spirit of everyone, men and women, starting with the youngest, the will to commit, to understand the Party's business and advance. That should be the job of every leader, of every supervisor in our Party.

But the tendency of some comrades is that, for example, a political commissar sees a boy proving himself to be a good militant and, instead of taking the time to help him learn more in order to advance, instead of encouraging him, he makes him his errand boy, because the kid's smart, learns fast, moves quickly; or else, instead of trying to increase the boy's worth to our land, he gives him a sack of clothes to look after, because the kid can be trusted. An intelligent girl comes along, who's quite pretty, and instead of assisting her, giving her a helping hand to advance, to become a nurse, a teacher, to go away and study, to become a good militiawoman, or whatever else, he makes her his lover because she's very pretty and he thinks he has the right to control her. We have to put a stop to this.

We don't want to ban people from having servants, from having girlfriends, *badjudas*, or from having children, that's not it. What we have to put a stop to is spoiling the future of our Party. Anyone who wants a servant must wait until tomorrow and have one in our independent land. They'll have to work hard and, if they earn the means, they can get a servant, assuming there are people who want to be servants. But they must not take advantage of the Party's authority, which the Party has placed in their hands, to get themselves a servant. Anyone who wants a *badjuda*, today or tomorrow, can get one, win her over, marry her, but don't use the Party's authority to have as many women as you want. So long as this kind of thing exists, we're only fooling ourselves and providing the Tugas and all our other enemies with justifications for the way they behave towards our people.

We have to be conscious of this. You, young people, Party militants and supervisors, must be conscious of this. Your job isn't to look to have children today, it's to serve the Party and raise its flag up high, to help the sons and daughters of our land to rise up, men, women, and girls of our land, and not to chase after tergal pants from Senegal or go around wheeling and dealing, because doing so means you've roundly failed in your historic mission, which is to be responsible for this Party in your early twenties.

Some of you who have been outside our land have seen the respect our Party inspires, how admired it is and how much hope it has inspired in people all over the world, including in Africa. Comrades often forget this, when they're out in the bush they completely forget about their responsibility as leaders. Some have tried to take advantage of the authority the Party has given them to serve their own bellies, satisfy vices, do whatever suits them. This has to stop. And you yourselves have to put a stop to it, at all levels.

This is precisely why we have to be vigilant against opportunists. It's not only those in Senegal trying out their "little maneuvers" who are opportunists. There are opportunists within our midst too, people who, knowing that our leadership wants the best sons and daughters of our land to lead, pretend to be the best, or do everything to satisfy their supervisors as much as possible, so that they put them forward to become leaders or supervisors.

We have to be careful about this, we have to unmask such people, combat them. Comrades have to understand that the only good leader, the only good supervisor, is one able to call out, face-to-face, another's mistakes. Many supervisor comrades, at all levels, have made a grave error in covering up other people's mistakes: "my lips are sealed," "if Cabral finds out, fine, if he doesn't . . . patience." This kind of thing undoes all the good work that supervisor himself has done, all the sacrifices he's made, because it is building with one hand and ruining things with the other. We have to take care and unmask all the opportunists in our midst, all the liars, all the cowards, anyone who doesn't follow the Party line. We have to have the courage to shoulder our responsibilities, each and every one of us, young supervisors and Party leaders alike. We have to have the courage to look each other in the eye, because our Party can only be led by men and women who don't lower their gaze to anyone.

Another important aspect the Party leadership must defend, and we've already made this clear in the published Guidelines, is that our Party is led collectively; it isn't for just one person to lead. At every level, in our political activities and in the Armed Forces, in security and education, wherever we may be, there is always collective leadership, at various levels. Yet some comrades have the tendency to monopolize the leadership and hog it for themselves. They decide on everything and never ask those around them for their opinions. We cannot have this, because two heads are always better than one, even if one head is smart and the other one dumb.

On this subject, comrades have to take the conversation we had about collective leadership seriously. But I would remind comrades that collective leadership (to lead as a group) does not mean that everyone has to lead to the point that there is no longer any authority. Some people think: "If we have to lead, then let's lead, even if we know nothing, just to pretend that everyone's leading." This is nonsense. I said a long time ago that, although you don't have to be a doctor with a degree to lead our Party, we must not forget that there are some tasks that those who can't read or write cannot do. Otherwise we're only fooling ourselves, and we must never fool ourselves. There are certain jobs that, depending on your level of schooling, you can or cannot do. Besides this, we have to remember that there is a hierarchy in the Party, that's to say a scale of people who lead and must be respected, truly respected, because this has not always been properly observed.

In the specific conditions of our struggle and our land, given the demands that history has placed on our people at this precise moment, our Party must have well-defined leaders, so that everyone knows who's who and there's no confusion. It doesn't matter what leadership level, whether it be the Politburo or any other organization, they must have the following in their heads: Here's a boss, who doesn't feel the need to remind everyone that he's the boss, who blends in with everyone and doesn't have any pretensions. That's how a boss should be, he doesn't get big-headed and show off to everyone that he's in charge, but nor does he ever forget he's the boss, and if others forget, he makes sure to remind them.

The leadership of our Party is the strength of our people, it is responsible for everything that our militants, supervisors and soldiers do. Our leadership must be one, united, we cannot allow any division within our ranks. And if we're talking about the Party's top leadership, I'm also talking about the leadership at any level, whether it's the Interregional Committee or the Party's Zone Committees.

Nobody should ever turn their back on a comrade. If anyone doesn't understand this then they're jeopardizing everything. For example, in the leadership of the Armed Forces, there have been several cases where political commissars don't get along with commanders. This is criminal, not getting along with one another when you have the Tugas right there in front of you to fight. We've had to swap comrades around because they develop personal ambitions and start bickering with colleagues.

We can't allow this to happen any longer. The time has come to demote anyone who can't get along with anyone else. They're no longer going to get transferred, they'll get demoted, become simple foot-soldiers or militants. Because we're way past having to teach comrades about the importance of getting along with one another, that the colonialists are our enemy and no one else.

Even in this room there are comrades who have worked together but haven't been able to get along with one another. How shameful!

And why is this? Because people are too busy looking after their own bellies, their own ambitions, instead of serving the interests of the Party. It's the result of a mentality focused on petty personal ambitions and pretensions. Instead of focusing on the struggle, the work of the Party, they spend their time looking at who has more things than them, who has fewer things, they focus on gossip, tittle-tattle . . . Deep down it's a lack of courage, it's cowardice.

We can't have it. The time has come to put a stop to this. In the bush or out of the bush, the time has come for everyone to get a grip of their conscience, put aside their pretensions and get down to some serious work, so as not to trip up along the way. And we must remind all comrades, but especially those in the zones, of the important role the local leadership plays in maintaining enthusiasm among the people. We cannot allow a comrade who has been political commissar of an area for one, two or three years to end up without any authority, everyone just doing their own thing, disregarding the leadership. This amounts to total failure on the comrade's part. And it should be noted that some local leaderships, which worked very well at first, only started to work badly and make mistakes when leaders began to look after their own bellies, deciding that their area was independent now so they'd move on to looking after themselves.

There's a film I'll never forget because it served as a great lesson to me. It was about a young boy who was educated in a seminary school and fervently believed in miracles. He didn't know anything about life because he'd spent his entire life at the seminary, until he left there as a man, twenty-one years old. All the injustices he then saw were simply evil; he didn't understand that there was poverty, and people suffering on the one hand and rich people on the other.

But he came across a dove that could perform miracles. And so, because his thoughts were so linked to the suffering of others, he decided to do everything he could to help others, so that nobody would go hungry, nobody would be cold, everybody would have a house to live in and everybody could fulfill their dreams; he didn't think about himself, he just asked the dove to perform miracles for others. The dove would appear and sit on his hand. He would say: "Dove, give houses to those poor people," and houses would appear with everything you might want inside. "Give food to those hungry people," and food would appear, nice food. He would even call people over to ask them what they wanted and then ask the dove to give it to them.

Then one day he got himself a girlfriend and sat down with her. She asked him for something and he got it for her. Other people came and asked for things too, but he didn't have time for them anymore, now it was all about his girlfriend.

Suddenly, the dove took off and flew away. There were no more miracles and everything that had earlier appeared by miracle disappeared again. Even when he got the dove back in his hand, the miracles stopped. He could no longer do anything for other people because all he could think about was his *badjuda*, his own belly.

This is a great lesson to us all.

Only to the extent that we are able to think about our communal problems, the problems of our people, of the masses, and afford them due importance, sacrificing our own personal interests if necessary, will we be able to perform miracles.

This is how all the leaders, supervisors, and militants of our great Party must behave, in the service of liberty and progress for our people.

4. STRUGGLE OF THE PEOPLE, BY THE PEOPLE, FOR THE PEOPLE

A fundamental principle of our struggle is that it is our people's struggle. Our people must carry it out themselves and the rewards must be for them.

By now comrades understand who our people are. The question we now ask is this: Who are our people fighting against?

Naturally, a people's struggle is only truly of the people when the reason for the struggle is rooted in the aspirations and dreams, the desire for justice and progress of the people themselves and not the aspirations, dreams, and ambitions of half-a-dozen or some larger group whose interests clash with the interests of the people.

Who must our people fight against? We've been clear about this right from the start: in Guinea and Cabo Verde, as colonies of Portugal, we are dominated by foreigners, but not all foreigners dominate us and, when it comes to Portugal, not all the Portuguese dominate us.

The force, the oppression that is being exerted on us, comes from the ruling class in Portugal, the Portuguese capitalist bourgeoisie, which exploits the people of Portugal just as it exploits our people. And, as we know very well, the ruling class of Portugal, the colonialist class of Portugal, is linked to dominant classes in other countries across the world, and collectively they enforce imperialist domination. This collective is in turn linked to capitalist forces all over the world that, already dominant in their own countries, have a vital need to dominate other peoples too, other countries, in order to get raw materials for their industries and new markets to sell their products in.

This is why we are dominated by the Portuguese colonialist capitalist class, in conjunction with world imperialism.

Our people are, therefore, fighting against the Portuguese colonial capitalist class and, by fighting them, they are, implicitly, fighting against imperialism, because the Portuguese colonial capitalist class is a part, albeit a small and even somewhat rotten part, of imperialism. So now we know who we're fighting against.

But we're faced with the issue not only of liberation but of progress for our people. And on that basis it follows that our struggle cannot be carried out against foreigners alone, it has to be carried out against some of our own people too. Our people must, therefore, fight the enemy without and within.

Who are the enemy within? They are all the social strata or classes in our land that don't want our people to progress and who defend only their own interests and the interests of their own family and people. That's why we say that our people's struggle is against everything that stands in the way of our people's freedom and independence, but also against everything that stands in the way of their progress and happiness.

The struggle in our land must be carried out by our people. We cannot think, even for a minute, of liberating our land, bringing peace and progress to our land, by calling on people from outside to come and fight for us. We're the ones who have to fight, in Guinea and Cabo Verde, and use every means available to us to fight. And that is, in fact, what has happened.

It's normal nowadays to hear the following conversation: "Are you of the people?" and someone answers: "No, I'm in the army," or "No, I'm in the militia," or "No, I'm a supervisor." This has become a typical conversation for us, but it's not only civilians who make up the people. You only have to look at where our soldiers, supervisors and leaders come from to realize that they are all people of our land. As is normal, in the armed struggle in Guinea, most of the people are from Guinea and, in the struggle in Cabo Verde, most of the people are from Cabo Verde, because Guinea and Cabo Verde are separated by the sea and it's not easy to transfer large units between them.

But there can be no doubt at all that the struggle is being fought by our people, through their sons and daughters, militants, leaders, soldiers, militiamen, etc. Our fundamental force is our people, it is they themselves. Our people or, if you prefer, people connected to the Party's work, who have been mobilized and organized by our Party and who, right from the beginning, have powered our struggle and endured sacrifices, have been the main force of our struggle. It would not have been possible for us to carry out the struggle, in clandestine times, if our people hadn't let us live among them like fish in water.

The enemy knows that our own people have taken up the struggle, and so they are trying to separate the part of our people that is the Party from the part of our people that is the civilian population, in order to take away the primary force of our liberation struggle, which is the support of the popular masses. It might be said that our struggle has more chance of victory the more we are able to keep the popular support of the masses on our side. The Tugas know this, which is why they are doing everything in their power to take that support away from us.

Our struggle is for our people, because our struggle's aim is to fulfill their aspirations, dreams, and desires: to have a dignified, decent life, as all peoples of the world desire, to have peace in order to build progress in their land and happiness for their children. We want everything we achieve in this struggle to belong to them, and we have to do our utmost to create an organization in which, even if some of us try and channel the struggle's achievements towards our own interests, the people will not allow it. This is very important.

Today, the people really feel that the struggle is theirs, not only because it's their sons and daughters with weapons in hands, not only because it's their sons and daughters who are being sent away to study to become cadres, nurses, doctors, engineers, technicians, etc., not only because it's their sons and daughters who are leading, but also because, even in the villages, militiamen or the local population have taken up the one thing that symbolizes our struggle: arms. It's not by chance or any other reason that the leadership of the Party has increasingly given weapons to the population. It's precisely so that no one gets the idea in their heads that the only people really fighting to get results are those who've taken up arms in the people's army or guerrilla forces. The more we put arms in the hands of our people, the more our population and our people know that the struggle is really theirs and the less our soldiers and leaders can be under any illusion that the struggle is theirs alone.

We are fighting for progress in our land and we must make every sacrifice to achieve this in Guinea and Cabo Verde. We have to put an end to all the injustices, all the poverty, all the suffering. We must guarantee for every child born in our land, today and tomorrow, that no wall will be placed before them. They must advance, according to their ability, so that they can give their all to making our people and our land ever better, serving not only our own interests but also the interests of Africa, the interests of the whole of humanity. That's why, right from the start, our Party has pursued the best way to achieve this: organization based on the mobilization of our people, the mobilization of the people of our land, to fight against Portuguese colonialism.

Our Party trained the sons and daughters of our land to mobilize the people. That work was no joke. Many of you who are here today, young folk who are now Party supervisors, would find it hard to imagine how difficult that work was. At the same time, we organized, within the framework of our Party, vast swaths of the population. This was and is the main political strength of our struggle, the reason why our struggle has advanced as much as it has. And we have to prepare ourselves, we have to prepare our people, our Party leaders and militants, our soldiers who are sacrificing themselves right now, prepare everyone to defend the conquests that the people have achieved through their struggle, no matter what the cost.

Nowadays our sons and daughters of the bush, who yesterday had no opinion whatsoever about their own lives and destiny, can offer their opinion, can help decide things through the Party committees or even the people's courts, where they have shown their ability to judge errors, crimes, and other wrongs perpetrated by sons and daughters of our land. This is further clear proof that this is a struggle of our people, by our people and for our people.

But some comrades in our Party, from senior supervisors to rank-and-file soldiers, have not understood this very well. They have tried to shape the struggle a little bit in their own interest, because they believe that, ultimately, they are the people, that the struggle is of our people, by our people, but . . . for themselves!

This is one of the most serious mistakes you can make in a struggle like ours. We cannot, in any way whatsoever, allow our Armed Forces, our militants, or our supervisors to forget, even for a moment, that the greatest consideration, the greatest respect, the greatest commitment must be shown to the people of our land, our local populations, especially in the liberated areas. Anyone who is prepared to be shot dead in this war but not capable of showing respect for the children of our people, for the people of the villages, for the civilian population, will die without even realizing why, or else die very much mistaken.

Anything we can do in our land to boost the morale of our people, to give them more courage, more enthusiasm for the Party, helps the present and future of our people, helps our Party. Anything we do that lessens the population's trust in us, whether it be by punishing people, being inconsiderate towards them, stealing their things, abusing their sons and daughters, men and women, constitutes a crime, the biggest crime a comrade-in-arms or supervisor can do, for it jeopardizes our Party, it jeopardizes the future and present of our land.

It's better to be fewer in number but incapable of causing the population of our land any harm, than to be large in number but with people in our ranks capable of doing harm. Because anyone in our midst who makes our people turn against our Party, lose trust in the Party, lose confidence in the Party, is a first-order servant of the Tugas. He might not realize it, but he's the best servant the Tugas could ever hope for. And you all know (for what I'm saying hasn't simply been dreamed up) that there are comrades who have done our population wrong. Things have thankfully improved a lot, because the Party has been vigilant about this.

And this requires us to be courageous in our fight against the Portuguese colonialist criminals and highly vigilant of imperialist agents, but also to continuously and decisively combat those who, even if they are Party militants, supervisors or leaders, do things that may jeopardize our people's conquest of and march towards dignity, freedom, and progress.

5. INDEPENDENCE OF THOUGHT AND ACTION

Another important Party principle is our independence of thought and action.

We are fighting for the independence of our land, for the independence of our people. The first proviso for doing this is that our Party and its leadership must be independent, in terms of the way we think about problems and solve them, and in terms of how we act inside and outside our land. This has always been our Party's line.

All the decisions we make within the framework of our Party, in relation to our work inside and outside our land, at an African or international level, are taken with absolute independence in terms of how we think and act. This is a sacred principle for us, one we must defend at all costs.

But we must also be aware that independence is always relative. For example, with many of the things we must decide, we have to somewhat orient ourselves according to the interests of our neighboring countries, if we wish to advance. For a lot of the decisions we make at the African or international level, we orient ourselves according to the interests of Angola and Mozambique too, and indeed some of the positions we adopt, some of our decisions relating to war materials and even operations, depend not only on us but on the friends who help us. Yet none of this stops this principle from being true.

The PAIGC leadership has always acted on the basis of independence of thought and action. We have been capable, and we must become ever more capable each day, of thinking a lot about our problems so that we carry out the proper actions, and carrying out a lot of actions so that we improve our thinking. Many comrades have not done this to the degree that their level of responsibility requires. Some have limited themselves to acting without thinking, while others have a lot of ideas but never actually do anything. We have to be capable of combining these two fundamental elements: thought and action, action and thought. This independence of thought and action is relative, of course, because even in our thinking we are influenced by the thinking of others and we are not the first people to carry out an armed national liberation struggle or to lead a revolution; others have done it before, there are other experiences of this, we did not invent guerrilla warfare, we only invented it in our land. But within the framework of this relative independence, we have to realize that no struggle can be carried out without alliances, without allies. In all struggles we have to decide on an option, that is, we have to choose one path or another. We cannot embark on a struggle without knowing which path we're taking. To decide this, we must first be conscious of who our allies are in Africa and the rest of the world.

We have spoken a lot about Africa, but in our Party we must remember that, while we are Africans, we are first and foremost men and women, human beings who belong to the world as a whole, and so we mustn't allow anything that is in our people's interests to be limited or jeopardized by our condition of being Africans. We must put the interests of our people above that, within the framework of the interests of humanity in general, and then place them within the framework of Africa's interests in general.

In Africa, our allies are the governments, parties or states, individuals or organizations, that truly want independence for Africa, that want genuine independence for their people, economic independence so that their people can take their history and wealth back into their own hands, in order to advance and build a better life. But in concrete, immediate terms, anyone who is openly against Portuguese colonialism in Africa is our ally. As you know, there are some Africans who are not against Portuguese colonialism. Anyone who is openly against Portuguese colonialism is our ally and anyone who doesn't only say this but actually helps us is an even bigger ally. It's not enough for someone to say "I'm from Africa" for us to consider them an ally; they may be telling stories, talking the talk. We have to ask them clearly: "Do you really want independence for your people? Do you want to work for it? Do you really want independence for our land? Are you really against Portuguese colonialism? Will you help us? If so, then you're our ally."

We are also part of the wider world. Who are our allies in the wider world? These days it's not hard to tell. All our people know. How? Because we have concrete proof. Who's helping us? Everyone who's helping us is our ally.

So who is helping us?

In the wider world, it's first and foremost the socialist countries. But some socialist countries have betrayed their duty to help us in our struggle, to be our allies, by putting their own state interests, their own fixations and ideas, above the interests of our struggle. They might sometimes even try to divide us, in a disguised way, in order to defend their own ideas rather than the interests of our struggle. So even among socialists we must ask: "Are you really helping us? Are you really not doing anything to act against us? Are you providing us with the help you can and should be giving to one of the world's vanguard movements? If so, then you are indeed fulfilling your duty as our ally."

There are other men and women in the wider world who are our allies. In capitalist countries, there are people who are against Portuguese colonialism; they are our allies. We have a criterion for distinguishing between our friends and the Tugas' friends: anyone who's against Portuguese colonialism is our friend, our ally; anyone who's in favor of Portuguese colonialism is our enemy, the Tugas' ally.

But in the wider world, whether it be as men or as Africans, we are clearly positioned as a group fighting imperialism, and it's not just us—there are other peoples doing it too. That's why we have to be consistent: if we demand solidarity from others towards us, we have to show solidarity towards others too, solidarity to all the peoples of Africa who are fighting for the true independence of their land, for the freedom, progress, and happiness of their people, especially those who are fighting against white-colonialist racism in southern Africa. First and foremost, there are our comrades in Angola and Mozambique, comrades-in-arms. We must show them as much solidarity as we possibly can, because their struggle is our struggle too.

We must show solidarity to the peoples of Asia who are fighting against imperialism, particularly in Vietnam, Laos, and Korea, where they are fighting against US imperialism. We must show solidarity to those peoples of Latin America who are fighting against imperialism, especially the people of Cuba, who have proved capable of defeating the imperialists and the reactionaries in their land in order to establish a just regime, while being surrounded by and threatened by imperialists. We must show the utmost solidarity towards them and towards all liberation movements in Latin America.

In North America, we must show serious solidarity to the descendants of African slaves who are now part of the population of North America and are themselves Americans. We must support them in their struggle with courage, but without any pretension that we're going to do their fighting for them.

Our obligation is to carry out the struggle in our own land. We are not going to fight other people's battles in Africa or anywhere else, we're going to fight our own battle in our own land. That's hard enough on its own, never mind trying to fight for others.

We have to understand how to show solidarity with socialist countries at all times. Many people think socialists are simply obliged to give us things, that they don't need anything in return, not even a thank you. This isn't right. If the GDR [German Democratic Republic] helps us, if the Soviet Union helps us more than anyone else, if other countries help us, that help doesn't just fall from the sky; it is the work of the sons and daughters of those lands, it is the work of the workers there, the sweat of each and every one of them. The only things that fall from the sky there are rain and snow, while here it's just rain. We have to have the conscience and courage to thank them and, if someone confronts them, we have to join them in solidarity, to be on their side, because they are our comrades-in-arms and they help us.

Often a comrade goes to study in these peoples' lands and, instead of showing solidarity towards them, as our friends, simply lives there and comes back angry at them. Such comrades have no conscience, just their own complexes and pretensions. A lot of Africans do this, they go there, knowing full well how much these people have sacrificed in order to assist us, and yet they fail to develop any friendships or show any appreciation. This is not the Party line. Our Party knows how to be grateful, knows how to show solidarity to those who help us. Fortunately, a lot of comrades do understand this and have acted admirably.

In terms of our allies, we must hail the name of the Republic of Guinea as our foremost ally, our dearest brothers, the people who help us the most. In overall terms, they have helped us more than anyone, by making all kinds of facilities available to us, and by accepting the sacrifices their own people have had to make with bombings of their villages. We must also hail the name of Senegal, just not as much as Guinea, while at the same time recognizing that it has not been easy for us, and that they still, unfortunately, cause us a lot of problems. For example, our people can no longer walk around Senegal dressed in uniform, why not? This is good for the Tugas, it's no good for us. For a long time, they didn't want us to enter Senegal armed, now they don't want us to enter wearing uniform. Why the reproach? Nevertheless, it must be said that Senegal has helped us somewhat. We need to be aware that their help has been invaluable to our struggle, even though, and I repeat, it has not been easy for us and we're beginning to tire of just how difficult it can sometimes be.

With regard to Guinea, we must hail the name of the PDG [Parti Démocratique de Guinée (Democratic Party of Guinea)]. It's our people's good fortune that there's a party like the PDG in Guinea, led by a man like Sékou Touré and by truly patriotic people who have a genuine interest in Africa. Because if we had people like the ones causing us so many problems in Senegal on both sides of our land, we'd be in a bad way. We must be aware of this. Guinea didn't lack for people who wanted to cause us problems too, and there are still people who want to do so today; but the PDG leaders and party have always been in favor of the liberation of our people. When they saw that we, the PAIGC, were truly fighting for it, they gave us their utmost support.

Within the framework of the general struggle against imperialism, we can also count on the support of various workers movements in countries across Europe, America, and the capitalist countries of Asia, but in Europe and America particularly. They are also our allies because they are fighting against imperialism too, against the forces that dominate our land. We must be aware of this and develop relationships of friendship and solidarity with these movements.

6. NOT EVERYONE IS OF THE PARTY

The Leadership's Work

Let's talk about another Party principle: Our struggle is based, fundamentally, on the work of our Party, the PAIGC.

Comrades know what the struggle is. By now you understand that struggle is the normal condition of any nonstatic reality. There is struggle within anything that moves, which is everything, because everything is in a state of motion whereby opposing forces act against each other. Every force that pushes in one direction meets another force pushing in the opposite direction.

Let's take a tree as an example. For a tree to grow, live, bear fruit, seed, or produce another tree, is a tremendous struggle. The first big struggle is between the tree's roots and the resistance of the ground, as the roots push through the soil seeking food in the earth. The tree then needs a certain capability, a certain strength, to extract food from the wet soil and have it enter the plant's roots. After it's been extracted, it then has to be pushed to other parts of the plant. So it's always a case of resistance coming up against resistance. But there's also resistance against rain and storms, with the plant having a major disadvantage in that it cannot leave wherever it is.

Plants and animals (and even a piece of wood or iron) contain a struggle inside them, thousands of struggles maybe. But the fundamental struggle is between a capacity for self-preservation and the ravages of time. Iron rusts, wood rots, time leaves its mark on things, from humans to the most insignificant of items. All of these external signs translate into internal struggle. But the struggle is clearer, more evident, when one thing forces itself on another, when it's waged between two different things.

Our struggle is the result of the pressure (or oppression) that the Portuguese colonialists exert on our society. Anyone who has acquired a certain amount of consciousness, or has been witness to a particular incident, or has any interest in Portuguese colonialism, might take up the following position: fight your own fight or don't fight at all. There have been a lot of people who fought in our land, both in Guinea and Cabo Verde, sometimes by writing verses or other things that are signs of struggle, like closing your windows and doors, shutting yourself away in the bedroom and insulting the Tugas. They can't hear you, but it's a form of struggle. In Canhabaque, a Bijagó woman comes along with water to sell. The Tuga chief of post tells her: "I'm not paying one *peso*, have five *tostões*," and he gives her the five *tostões*, but then she spills the water on the ground—this is a form of struggle, of fighting. Subservience (the act of accepting humiliation) can often also be a form of struggle. But other forms of struggle are revolts. Something I've never forgotten since I heard about it occurred on a farm in Angola. I used to think of the indentured laborers as poor old devils who accept their lot, but no, they revolt, each in turn, so you rarely sense they're revolting, but each person rebels in his own way. Some go around pretending to be mad and then take their machetes and cut down all the new palm trees the colonialists have planted. It's a form of struggle. But when one, two, three, or four people get together and unite their interests, they can carry out a revolt. How many revolts have there been in Guinea that were hushed up and maybe no one ever saw? How many revolts have there been in Cabo Verde, on the islands of São Vicente, Santo Antão, and Santiago, in the fight against Portuguese colonialism?

But in order for a struggle to seriously advance, it has to be organized, and it can only be seriously organized by a vanguard leadership. Fighting to liberate a people, starting from nothing, as we did, can be compared to, for example, man's struggle with distance. One of man's great problems in ancient times was that he was restricted by distance, by rivers, by seas. He wanted to travel but it was difficult because he lacked the means to do so. Then one day, maybe a man was sitting by a river and he saw a tree trunk float by and it occurred to him, for the first time, that maybe he could get on top of that trunk floating down the river. If this is what happened, then it was the moment when the first boat was born, or so the legend goes. But man, in order to overcome distance, to cross rivers and seas, and then to cross through the air, in order to conquer, in order to gain distance, had to create the means to do so. Small and weak means at first, which slowly developed, using all the means available—water currents, winds, sea currents—until he began to use energy that he himself had discovered, steam power, electric power and, nowadays, atomic power. Look how extraordinary man's struggle against distance has been, to the extent that, while it used to take years to travel round the world, even at a time of great progress, these days mankind can travel around the world in a satellite in eighty minutes, even less if he wants to. In Jules Verne's book, it took eighty days, and he was a visionary who foresaw the future.

Party

Fighting colonialism also requires means. An instrument must first be created to carry out the struggle. That instrument is our Party. Comrades might say that the Party is the base instrument, the mother instrument, if you like, the principal means that creates other means that are linked to it. The Party is the root and the trunk and it produces other branches for the struggle to develop.

The first question we might then ask is this: Why did we create a party when others created movements?

Others created movements, fronts, etc. If you look carefully, you'll see we are the only ones to have created a party, an organization with party in the name. There may have been others, but in any case, we are a party, even though there had never been a party in our land before. This didn't happen by chance, it's not because we like the word "party," rather it was with a clear sense of what was required, today and tomorrow. Because in our view, party is a lot more defined, a lot clearer as an organization. Party is everything encompassed by a given idea, a given thing, a given path; movement is a rather vague term. Our Party may well be, in reality, more of a movement today, but it is our job to make it more of a party by the day. We called ourselves a party right from the start so that everyone knew that we had very clear ideas about what path we had to follow, about what we wanted to do, in the service of our land and our people, in Guinea and Cabo

Verde, and in the service of Africa and humanity in general, to the extent that we can make a contribution.

Party, because we understood that, in order to lead a people towards liberation and progress, there was a fundamental need for a vanguard of people, those best equipped to lead and capable of showing this in practice. Lots of people try to be deceptive, but in a liberation struggle you do eventually have to define yourself as clearly being of the vanguard, a collective formed by the best sons and daughters of our people in Guinea and Cabo Verde.

We know that our Party was created in clandestinity. I'm not going to tell you the whole story, for it has already been written in numerous books that you'll be able to read if our comrades in the Ideological Commission do a good job. But anyway, it was created in clandestinity. In the beginning it really was a party, we were very few people, a small party, but we were of one mind and had deep trust in the line we'd drawn, like someone given the opportunity to trace his or her own path in life. The Party grew and grew, until it became more of a general national liberation movement. But it was a movement not in name, more as a concrete fact within the struggle, as a collective of people moving against Portuguese colonialism.

Objective

We are, I repeat, a party. Our case can be summed up as follows: those of us fighting in Guinea and Cabo Verde against Portuguese colonialism are all part of a national liberation movement, the "Party" is everyone. But the only people who can join the Party are those who share one idea, one thought, who only want one thing, and they must behave in a certain way in their private and social lives.

What idea, what thing, what form of behavior? Our Party is made up only of those people who really want to realize our Party's Program. We are the PAIGC, Guinea, and Cabo Verde. There's no racism, there's no tribalism, we're not fighting just to have a flag, a national anthem and a minister, perhaps we won't even have ministers in our land. We're not going to sit in the governor's palace, our aim isn't to take over the palace and install Cabral and one or two others. We are fighting to free our people, not just from colonialism, but from exploitation of every kind.

We don't want anyone else exploiting our people, whites or Blacks, because whites aren't the only ones who exploit people, there are Blacks who want to exploit people even more than the whites have done. We want our people to rise up and move forward, and if we want our people to rise up, then it's not just the men, because women are our people too. Those who understand that women have the right to advance, to be educated, to go to school like any other human being, to do any job, so long as they're capable of doing it; those who properly understand that a man, so long as he has three or four wives, will never be a real man, and that nowhere in the world can a people hope to advance while their men have four wives; those who understand that if you have a daughter you cannot sell her, the same way you cannot sell your mother, for a daughter is not some sort of slave; those who understand that children are the only living beings we should afford privileges to in our land, for they are the flowers of our lives, every sacrifice we make is for their sake, so that they may lead happy lives; those who do the jobs the Party has assigned them properly, in the service of our people; this is our Party's membership and these are the people who must rule our land.

I do not lead because I'm an engineer or a doctor, but because I'm serious about my work, for having qualifications doesn't make anyone better than anyone else. No one position in the Party is better than another. The only people who are deemed better than others are those who work harder, who produce the most. Anyone who understands our Party's Program as it ought to be understood, whether they're from Guinea or Cabo Verde, can join our Party. But they must be prepared to give their lives for the cause we're fighting for, at any given moment.

But while some people join the Party, others will perhaps leave; they may not even sense it, but they leave. Why? Because they don't do some or all of these things, or because they prove unable to understand or unwilling to understand them. For example, there are still some people in our Party who don't particularly agree with unity between Guinea and Cabo Verde but they're waiting to see what happens; some people from Cabo Verde and others from Guinea don't agree with it very much at all, they have their doubts but they'll wait and see. These people are mistaken, maybe they'll end up joining another party, but they'll certainly end up leaving ours, that's for sure.

Members

I have spoken quite clearly to comrades about our work. Only honest, seriously committed people enter the Party, and anyone dishonest, or who wishes to take advantage of the Party in order to serve their own personal interests, must leave. They may fool us today, but they'll be on their way tomorrow for sure. Anyone who lies, anyone who only wants to serve themselves, so that they can have tergal trousers and nice shirts, or who takes advantage of our young ladies or goes around abusing the people of our land, must leave. Anyone who lacks respect for the people of our land, who pretends to respect them in front of Party leaders but out in the areas they oversee, behind Party leaders' backs, behaves like some colonialist chief of post or administrator, must leave. Anyone who thinks they're fighting in this struggle and sacrificing themselves today so that they can act like chiefs of post and abuse people tomorrow, must leave. The time has come to speak clearly about this, because some comrades are making a lot of sacrifices in the belief that they will benefit from it tomorrow by getting a nice car, a few servants, several wives, etc. They are mistaken. They are not of our Party and will surely soon discover this.

Our Party is open to the best sons and daughters of our land. Today the "Party" is all of us but bit by bit the Party nucleus is becoming defined. Anyone who is genuinely of the Party is already in or will enter that nucleus; those who are not of the Party will leave. We can only really achieve what we want to achieve in our land if we are a strong group of men and women, capable of being honest with our comrades, never deceiving or lying to them, capable of looking comrades in the eye, and prepared to believe that the young will be the masters of our land tomorrow, in Guinea and Cabo Verde.

So we have to fulfill our duties as best we can, give ourselves every chance of advancing. Anyone in our Party who has ambitions to act like a *régulo* will sooner or later have to leave. Anyone who hasn't learned to respect their colleagues, men and women, as they ought to, will sooner or later have to leave. Anyone who thinks that our policies of tomorrow will serve some foreign nation or other will sooner or later have to leave, because we're having none of that. We're fighting for our independence.

So you can see that it's going to get harder and harder to become a member of our Party. And this vanguard that we've created, this instrument that we built in order to build independence in our land the way a man builds a house, will have to be refined, fine-tuned, and perfected more and more each day, and our people will have to make it more and more beautiful each day.

It's essential that all comrades, but especially the younger ones, study the Party's Program, understand it well, in order to prepare themselves for truly being of the Party. And what's more, to sign up to the Party early on, because we're increasingly going to have to demand total commitment to the Party from all our supervisors. Not commitment to their own heads, not commitment to Amílcar Cabral, or to João or N'Bana or Bacar or anyone else who might happen to be their boss, but to the Party, to the ideas of the Party, to the living force that is the Party. They will have to prove that they have in their heads all the ideas the Party has laid out, as will everyone else. Anyone who doesn't do this is wrong. But later on, before anyone can become a Party member, they will have to be a Party candidate first. They will have to prove that they really do deserve to join our Party. It has to be done this way, because we really do want to serve the people of our land. Let's not fool ourselves.

It's easy to put everyone into a party: a child is born and you immediately sign them up to the Party. But what's the point of that? What is the Party then? In a football club you have to pay membership fees, go to the field, clap, and cheer. Can't we just allow everyone to join the Party, children, men, women? No. It might be good in a liberation struggle, necessary even: with everyone included, we march forward. But in the process of doing all this, we learn, as the days go by, who really is for and of the Party. We have to be able to walk into a room like this one and say: he's of the Party, so is she, and that other one over there, but he isn't, not yet.

That's the way it's got to be; that's the only way we can serve our people. If we mix everyone up, we'll go wrong. Anyone who is a true component of the Party demonstrates their willingness to improve each and every day, because whoever stands still dies. A lot of comrades still haven't realized this, some comrades take advantage of the Party. For them, being in the Party or being a Party leader means living the good life, it means benefiting from the Party, and they want to take advantage of the Party as soon as possible because they do not believe in the Party, they do not believe in the future. They want to benefit from it right now, with nice clothes and money in their pockets, they want to rule, abuse their power, turn comrades into servants, and commit other abuses besides. Such people are almost asking to leave the Party and there are a good many who, if they don't leave today, will certainly be made to leave tomorrow, no matter how much work they've done, no matter how much help they've given. They'll either tear the Party apart or be made to leave.

The best response is to quickly mend your ways and fall back in line. We've made every effort to allow comrades to fall back in line so that they won't have to leave the Party tomorrow.

We've lost some people along the way because they found it impossible to mend their ways and, given our sorry circumstances, if someone does not seek to make amends, they're deemed to have turned against us, they become traitors. We have to combat this, step by step, with due care, to give everyone the greatest possible opportunity to be for and of the Party. But nor can we let people deceive us, pretend they're for and of the Party when they're not.

Any comrade who has in his head the notion that his "race" should rule our land had better be prepared, for we will wage war against him. Some comrades still seem incapable of entirely abandoning the idea of "race" they have in their heads. They have their own ambitions and want to be in charge of everything. People like that are not for and of the Party. In our Party, the people in charge are those who have proved their worth, those who are most capable of taking charge, having already provided concrete proof that they know how to take charge, and who have only one aim: to serve the people.

Nowadays, anyone in our land who is ready to put an end to Portuguese colonialism, follow the Party's Guidelines, respect the Party leadership, and carry out their orders, is for and of the Party. These people are of the Party today but only those who have demonstrated exemplary moral conduct will be of the Party tomorrow, only men and women of dignity who work hard and really do have work to do, because we've no room for the idle in our Party; only those who treat the Party's Program like their lifeblood, like the fire in their souls, and who strive to overcome everything and everyone in their way in order to fulfill that program. What is the Party's Program? It's the one you all already know and are getting to know more and more. Only these people will be for and of our Party tomorrow and some will become the de facto custodians of the Party, capable of transforming the Party, each and every day, into a better organization, one evermore in service to the people.

What We Mean by 'The People'

A lot of comrades say: "Oh, my people!" A lot of comrades, when they make mistakes or are confused by Party things, immediately start talking about the people. This will gradually stop, but for now we have to be clear about who the people are.

Defining "the people" depends on the historical moment in which we live on earth.

The population is everyone, but the people must be considered in relation to history itself. We therefore have to clearly define who the people are, or were, at any given moment in the lifetime of a population. Today, as far as we're concerned, in Guinea and in Cabo Verde, everyone who wants to drive the Portuguese colonialists out of our land are the people. Anyone else is not of our land, even if they were born in it. They are not the people, they are the population. That's how we define the people of our land today: anyone born in Guinea or Cabo Verde who wants what is essentially a historical necessity: to put an end to foreign domination. Those who are ready to work hard for this, to take a firm stand, who are for and of the Party. Therefore, the majority of our people are of our Party and the Party's leadership best represents our people. No one should think that, just because they were born on Pico da Antónia or in deepest Oio, they're more "of the people" than our Party's leaders. The foremost group among the people in our land, the truest and most genuine, are the Party's leaders, for they managed to create an entire movement in order to defend the interests of the people.

Let me try and clarify the matter a bit further:

Within the population of our land, all those who currently want the Portuguese colonialists to leave so that we can gain our liberty and independence, are our people. Some among them are putting in serious work, fighting with weapons in hand or doing political work or working in education or in any other field, under the Party leadership; they are our Party. If you like, we could say that our Party is our people's vanguard and, at present, its primary element is the Party leadership. It follows, then, that anyone who loves our people must love the Party leadership. Anyone who hasn't understood this yet hasn't understood a thing.

This is at the present stage, the current moment. But in time, when we gain our independence, for example, anyone who wants our land to be independent but doesn't want women to be free, anyone who wants to carry on exploiting the women of our land, may well be considered "of the people" today but they will not be tomorrow. If we want every child of our land to be respected and some among us do not, then that group must be considered to be of the population, not the people.

Our aim is to bring progress and happiness to our people, but we cannot do it against the will of our people. Now, if someone from our land does not want progress and happiness, they are either not of the people, in which case we may do everything in our power against them, maybe even put them in jail, or they are, they are one of many and so they represent the people, at which point we stop; there's nothing we can do, because you can't bring progress and happiness to people against their will.

We have to understand, then, that at each stage in the history of a nation, land, population, or society, "the people" must be defined according to the main current in that society's history, according to the primary interest of the majority in that society.

The term democracy was created in Greece, in Athens (*Demo* + *cracia* = government of the people). But who created it? In Athens there were nobles, lords (owners of the land), and then slaves, who worked for the others. Democracy then was only for those at the top: they were "the people," the others were slaves. It's still the same thing today in many places. Whoever has the upper hand, the power, creates democracy to suit themselves. But in our land, we want power to be in the hands of the majority. We want power to be in the hands of our people. Those who keep on going down this path, who each and every day want ever more progress and happiness in our land, progress not just for the Fulas, not just for the Mandingas, not just for the sons and daughters of Caboverdeans, not just for the Balantas, but progress for everyone, in Guinea and in Cabo Verde, they constitute our people.

Parties and Movements

I'll say a little bit more about this instrument our people have created in order to further the actions begun by some of their sons and daughters in the struggle for liberation and progress in our land. I wish to emphasize the fact that, right from the start, we always had the sense, indeed the conviction, that we didn't need to create several movements in order to liberate our land. On the contrary, what we needed to do was make a big effort to have one single organization lead the struggle in Guinea and Cabo Verde. That was the line we drew after analyzing our specific circumstances, our reality, and the line we've firmly defended, for several years now, despite the fact that at certain points we've had to take a step back to reflect upon whether or not we were right.

Yesterday, we talked about conflicts within our society and we saw that on what we should properly call the social level, that is to say the various layers of society, or between different classes, if you prefer, conflicts are not particularly big, especially not in Guinea, though they are a little more marked in Cabo Verde where some people own land and property, and where there are some owners of small businesses and industries. But I pointed out to comrades that all of this is really quite limited, not enough to form what might properly be called a class, from a quantitative, numerical perspective. But we sensed that, influenced by past times and as a consequence of the enemy seeking to create division in our midst, conflicts do exist between different ethnic groups, what we call "races" in Guinea. And, of course, in Cabo Verde, there are conflicts essentially between landless peasants on the one hand and those of secure means on the other, landowners included.

The stupidest thing we could do in our land would be to create parties or movements in Guinea based on ethnicity, for this would not only provide a very good way for the enemy to divide us in our struggle, but also ensure that the enemy came out of the struggle victorious, with our independence destroyed, for comrades will have seen what has happened in other African countries. In Cabo Verde, it would be ridiculous to consider creating one Party for people who have something and a separate Party for people who have nothing, and then try and fight Portuguese colonialism.

In fighting against colonialism, it is fundamentally important, decisive even, that we join everyone who wants independence together, everyone who wants to fight against colonialism. That's why, in 1959, when a few small groups of nationalists emerged in Bissau who weren't under our control, some comrades from our Party, especially comrades Aristides Pereira, Fortes, and Luís, did their utmost to try and make sure these small groups were integrated into our Party so that our strength was not dispersed.

As you all know, the Party was created in 1956, and what I'm talking about didn't happen until 1959. Later on, some people from our land started talking about a front, the Party itself even talked about forming a front, and some comrades might ask why we did not in fact create a front in our land. We did not precisely because a front means uniting several organizations. We did not know of any other organizations in our land. When our Party made contact with the outside world, from 1960 onward, we realized there were people outside our land, whether that be Guinea or Cabo Verde, who had created so-called movements based outside our land. Our Party had to make concessions, we took a step back from this idea of only having one Party and not a united front, to see if we could bring these people together in our struggle for the independence of Guinea and Cabo Verde. That's why, on the one hand, we formed the so-called Front with the Movement for the Liberation of Guinea and Cabo Verde, which was based in Conakry but had been set up by comrades as a group already linked to the PAIGC, and with the Movement for the Liberation of Guinea and Cabo Verde, which was based in Ziguinchor.

I can tell comrades the story of what happened in Conakry later, but the fact is, amid a lot of noise, with our Guinean and Caboverdean brothers in Senegal causing trouble, we decided to launch an appeal for unity between all the liberation movements for Guinea and Cabo Verde. The PAIGC called on anyone who said they were a movement to unite. We held a conference in Dakar with what was then called the Movement for the Liberation of Guinea and Cabo Verde, a group based in Dakar that included Guineans and Caboverdeans, including a few fellas you will know of; there's no need to afford them special importance by citing their names. This conference was also attended by the Ziguinchor movement and the Movement for the Liberation of Guinea and Cabo Verde, from Conakry, as well as the PAIGC, represented by a few members. All of this was essentially a concession on our part, and a tactic for seeing what these people really wanted, what their intentions were, to what extent they were seriously committed to the struggle, and whether they really wanted to fight or just secure cushy roles for themselves. We practically ran the whole conference ourselves. We brought well-prepared documents while they, having been asked to prepare something for the conference, didn't even have a program drawn up yet. The conference actually took place with assistance from the Senegalese authorities, Comrade Marcelino dos Santos, representing the CONCP, and other organizations.

Our representatives robustly defended the Party's point of view, which was supported by the Conakry and Ziguinchor-based liberation movements for Guinea and Cabo Verde. Of course, the Dakar group had never been aiming for unity, they were trying to break up the PAIGC. That was their plan and, when they realized it would be impossible, they accepted all the resolutions that were presented at the conference. But soon afterwards they started sabotaging things. Of course, they were then unmasked as people who didn't want unity because they didn't want to fight, people who pretended to talk about unity but were only really looking for ways to maneuver themselves into a nice position, earn themselves a cushy role, and destroy our Party.

Comrades will therefore see how the Party, although established with the principle for life of being a single organization, under a single flag, and without the confusion of being a liberation movement, was able to make concessions, was able to step back and give everyone the chance to clearly express whether or not they wanted to fight for independence. When we came to the conclusion that these people were ultimately only lying, that they were being dishonest and really only looking to secure positions for themselves and cause confusion, thus serving the Portuguese colonialists, the Party decided on the following: we no longer want unity with anyone, anyone who wants unity with the PAIGC can come to the land and see us. That became our position and we resisted all pressure to do otherwise, convinced that we were on the right path, the most secure.

Rejecting Opportunism

Another issue we wish to clarify as regards our Party, our organization, is the following: right from day one (and we've already talked to comrades about this in relation to our principles) we have rejected opportunism. We could, for example, try to bring into the Party certain men who have a lot of influence in Guinea, invite them to join the Party in order to make use of their influence, certain big men in Bissau and a few *régulos*—I recall that several *régulos* did in fact become members of the Party, but without us ever telling them they'd be in charge.

There were *régulos* from the Manjacos territory, for example, or from the Mancanhas territory, who called for others to wave the Party flag, and there were chiefs in the Mansoa area and in other areas who were imprisoned because of the Party flag, but we never told them that, just because they were chiefs among our population, they would also be chiefs in the Party. We rejected this idea once and for all, for we didn't want to mislead anyone. In a new organization, created to liberate our land, our leaders are and will be those best equipped for the task, not people appointed just because they were chiefs yesterday. For example, it was felt, and you can sense it today in various parts of Africa, that putting traditional chiefs in leadership roles in national liberation organizations was inviting trouble for tomorrow, encouraging opportunism, and delaying our embrace of the future.

7. REVOLUTIONARY DEMOCRACY

Within the framework of the principle of revolutionary democracy, which we have already referred to several times, every supervisor must be courageous in assuming their responsibilities, demand respect from others for their actions, and respect the actions of others.

On the other hand, we mustn't hide anything from our people, we must not deceive them, for this only causes trouble for the Party further down the line. We have to be firm in combating this with some comrades. We cannot, for example, have members of the population going to the border to fetch goods for the people's warehouses, only to then be made to carry war materials when they get there. If we do things like this, we're behaving worse than the colonialists, abusing our authority, abusing the good faith and goodwill of our people. It's much better to tell members of the population quite clearly that they need to get ready to go and get some war materials, because the war is being fought for our land, and if they don't want to go, they'll be arrested and made to do it by force. If necessary, arrest them, but they must be told what's happening. It's better than lying, because deceiving them diminishes us in the eyes of our people, who may live and suffer in poverty but just like any other people, they have a conscience, they know what's true and what's a lie, what's fair and what's unfair, what's right and what's wrong, and they have enough of a conscience to lose respect for anyone who has lied to them.

We have to put a stop to lying, we have to be prepared not to mislead anyone about the difficulties of the struggle, about the mistakes we've made, about the defeats we may one day suffer, and we must not assume that victory will come easily. Nor must we assume that things are the way they "seem" or say "I just presumed . . . . " This is a big fault with some comrades. "Comrade, how did this happen?"—"It seems that . . . " That's not good enough for people who are supposed to be carrying out a revolution, who want to bring progress and happiness to their people through a liberation struggle. We have to be conscious of this.

Some comrades are incapable of providing a clear explanation of what's going on in their area; others are capable, thankfully. I'm focusing on negative aspects here, but everyone knows there are many positive aspects. That's why we're sitting here in the first place and shame on us if there were only negative aspects. But it's my duty to point out what's not right so that we can improve, so that we can move forward. We trust in appearances, our own imagination; we all tend to do this, to trust in our imagination.

Revolutionary democracy demands that we fight all opportunism, as I've already told you, but also that we fight the habit comrades have of forgiving mistakes too quickly. I'm a supervisor, you make a mistake, and I forgive you for the following reason: you now know I've got something on you. It cannot be like this, no one has the right to forgive mistakes without first discussing them in front of everyone, because the Party is ours, not one individual's, it's all of ours. We find it too easy to excuse comrades, we're very quick to forgive and we have to combat this. The time has come for the excuses to stop. There's a job that needs doing and needs doing well, no more excuses.

We're capable of making up all sorts of excuses. For example, there are supervisors whose work entirely consists of making excuses for why their people aren't doing anything, of trying to explain to the Party leadership why nothing is getting done: "difficulties with the terrain"; "adverse conditions"; "the enemy is advancing"; "there is a lot of bombing," etc., instead of showing strength, working hard to overcome these difficulties, because a struggle consists of constantly triumphing over difficulties. If there were no difficulties, it wouldn't be a struggle, it would be a walk in the park, a picnic.

We must combat the tendency for camaraderie and for friendships that do not serve the Party, that serve only those involved and not the interests of our Party and our people. We know this exists within our Party. There are even some comrades who get upset when a comrade is relocated, as if they can no longer live without him. We must be firm in combating this, in our heads and in the heads of others. Here there should be no *mandjuandade*[1] that does not serve the Party, no friendship or comradeship that does not serve the people of our land. Sitting around drinking cane or palm wine, hiding from other comrades what someone is up to with the *badjudas* of our land, hiding mistakes even, related to the armed struggle, or keeping quiet because a supervisor isn't fighting the way they should; all of this is not friendship and comradeship, it's a betrayal of our Party and our people; it serves the Tugas, it's forming friendships that favor the Tugas. This exists among us and we have to be firm in combating it, we have to show courage. You all know it exists and some of you here are, unfortunately, guilty of it.

Our criteria for friendship, for *mandjuandade* or comradeship should be the following: if you are of worth to the Party and respect its Guidelines properly, then you're my comrade, my friend; if you don't, it's best you go and join the opportunists or serve the Tugas. But our obsession with forging friendships is so great that certain comrades are happy to hang out at a man's house even though they know he's a Tugas agent, of going to his home even, eating and drinking at his house. How can this be? Yet comrades will say: "I've known this person for a long time," or "He's related to my mother." This is a lack of political consciousness, a lack of consciousness for the sacrifice they themselves have been making, for the struggle, for our people, for our land. Yet even Party leaders do this! Fortunately, it seems to be coming to an end.

Another thing that happens, for example, is that everyone in the Party knows a certain comrade has committed a serious wrong, whether inside or outside our land, and he gets summoned. We're waiting for him, he arrives, and then comrades leap up to greet him with hugs and kisses as if he were the best comrade in the world. What kind of a lack of conscience is this? What kind of absence of all sense of responsibility? If someone has proved himself to be of no use then we have to show him that we think he's of no worth, there should be no friendliness or consideration for him. We have to set all that to one side.

The time has come to be friends only with those who prove their worth, because people who prove themselves to be useless are not

---

1   "Tribalism"—referring to the organization of society based on tribal relations

worthy of our friendship, our comradeship. Anyone who betrays the Party, who seeks to divide us, who makes plans to sabotage us, who serves the enemy, who socializes with enemies of our Party, cannot sit down with us, cannot eat from the same bowl as us, cannot drink from the same glass or mug, cannot sleep in the same bed as us. We need to be able to distinguish between the worthy and the worthless in our heads otherwise there's no point in carrying on with the struggle, because sooner or later we'll drown in a sea of entanglements of our own making.

The Irreplaceables

We have to be able to avoid the way certain comrades get a complex whereby they think that if they were to leave their posts everything would collapse, game over. No one is indispensable in this struggle; we are all necessary, but no one is indispensable. If someone has to go, let them go, and if the struggle ends because of it then it clearly wasn't being carried out properly. These days the only thing we take pride in, myself included, is the certain knowledge that given the work we've already done, were I to leave, were I to stop, die, or disappear, then there are people in the Party capable of moving the struggle forward. If there weren't, after all this time, that would be a disgrace! I wouldn't have achieved a thing, because a man who makes something that only he himself is capable of continuing, hasn't made anything at all. A work is only worthwhile to the extent that it's the work of several people, many of whom are capable of taking the lead and moving it forward, even if one hand leaves.

But there are comrades who have this complex in their head that if they were to leave wherever it is they're placed then everything would fall apart. We have to combat and eliminate pretensions like this. Not to mention cases of comrades who treat being transferred like a death sentence, all because they've set up their working conditions in one place and now they've been called somewhere else. What a failure of consciousness! As if our land is no more than the one little corner you find yourself in! This shows that consciousness is still lacking in regards to the real reasons, objectives, and characteristics of our struggle.

We must be capable of defending the truth, of telling the truth in front of everyone, without any fear, even if difficulties arise because of that truth being told. Specifically, we must be able to speak the truth to people's faces.

Militants must not be afraid of any supervisor in our Party. Anyone who is afraid either hasn't understood anything yet or is a coward by nature. Our Party has given everyone the same power to ensure they need not fear anyone, for we have repeatedly said that we are fighting to put an end to the fear that exists among our people, in Guinea and Cabo Verde. We should not be afraid of anyone; even the humblest militant should not be afraid of anyone, and that includes the Secretary General. Respect him, yes, because that is also self-respect, but not fear him.

Supervisors should not be nervous of militants. There are certain supervisors who militants and soldiers are afraid of. They are barbarous *régulos* from ancient times, not PAIGC leaders or supervisors. But they themselves are sometimes nervous of militants. If they overhear a bit of chitchat, they immediately want to know what it's all about, for they're afraid of anything that might cause them problems with the Party leadership. We have to put a stop to all this.

Revolutionary democracy demands that supervisors and leaders live among the people, appear before the people, have the backs of the people. They must be in no doubt that when they are working for the Party, they are working for the people of our land. And we have to fight, no matter what the cost, so that our people sense that they themselves hold the power in our land. They haven't got much of a sense of this so far. In the liberated areas, some comrades have usurped that power—we have to put it in the hands of our people. We're still at war; it's a bit difficult, but as we advance, we have to hand power over to our people, give them the sure sense that power really is theirs.

Nobody in the Party should be afraid of losing power. Lots of countries have ended up in a terrible mess because the people in charge were afraid of losing their place in the chain of command. We must not be afraid of anything, we must clearly speak the truth to our people, to our militants, to our comrades, and if they're unhappy with us and are capable of it, then they can get rid of us, drive us out. But we should none of us be afraid of anything, and we should not hide the truth in order to protect our position. That would be to betray the interests of our people, our land and all those who have trusted in us.

We must not mislead people in what we say or make false promises, we must speak frankly about the difficulties we face. For example, at the Boé meeting, people said to me: "Send us this and that, we want this, that, and the other etc. for the shop." I said to the local population: "No, we cannot do that; we're already making a huge sacrifice to send you what we do send you; if you're not happy, fine, do whatever you want, leave the Party even, but we cannot send you what you're asking for. You have to remember you're not the only ones who need it, other people in our land need help too." And I took the opportunity to spend time with our people, to teach them, to raise their consciousness, without telling them any lies, without misleading them with false promises. They all understood.

As I said, we must move forward evermore by the day in terms of putting power in the hands of our people, in order to profoundly transform their lives, to even put our every available means of defense in their hands, so that it is the people themselves who defend our revolution. This is what revolutionary democracy will really look like, tomorrow, in our land. Anyone who rules a people while being afraid of them is going about things the wrong way. We must never be afraid of the people.

Within the framework of revolutionary democracy, as I've already said, we must, each and every day, bring forward the best sons and daughters of our land and leave the worst behind, those who are of no worth. Because our job is to prepare the hoe, the plow, and the hammer with which we will build our people's future, one of freedom, progress, and happiness. We're going to keep on improving our Party each and every day, because the better it is, the more certain we are of achieving what we want for our people. That is why, as we've already said, we must give the Party over, more and more by the day, to those who are capable of making it get better and better.

8. STAY TRUE TO PARTY PRINCIPLES

Another Party principle that we live by is that you must stay true to your principles.

Many people have principles but, when the moment to apply them comes, they forget them or aren't true to them. We must stay true to our principles, apply them every day, make no concessions to them, whether internally, in our inner lives, or externally, in our relationships with the outside world.

Our leaders and supervisors must always have the courage to fight the temptation of opportunism, of taking the easy route. Our struggle is never the easy route, but a lot of people in our midst are drawn towards easy things and the result is that at every step they forget yet another Party principle, and then they lie. And once you start lying, you end up lying so much that you inevitably get caught out.

We have to respect our principles. We have established our strategy, the general outline of our struggle, in accordance with these principles and we will yield to nothing, we will not take a backwards step for anyone, we will not accept this. But in matters of lesser importance, matters that do not damage our principles, we have to be able to make concessions, know how to yield, recognize the need to be tactical, at the political and military level, but especially the political level.

The skill of a leader or the leadership lies in knowing when to yield and when not to yield. In other words, when faced with a given problem, we have to ask ourselves the following question: What's of primary importance here and what's of secondary importance? Is this really a priority issue or is it secondary? Is this an issue of today or forever, is it permanent or temporary? We have to be able to distinguish between what's essential and what's preferable, we have to know how to make concessions, how to yield, in order to deepen the Party's roots and open a path for the Party to move forward.

In our relations with militants and soldiers, we have to yield on certain things, we have to concede on certain points, but without compromising our principles. For example, in the Armed Forces we mustn't yield on anything concerning discipline, but we can give a little leeway to comrades on things that do not spoil our work, that do not jeopardize our principles and our basic rules of working.

These are, then, very briefly, some of the basic principles upon which our Party's work is based, upon which we have based our own conduct and upon which we continue to base our struggle against Portuguese colonialism today and our struggle against poverty, suffering, and misfortune tomorrow, against every injustice in our land and for the progress and happiness of our people, in Guinea and Cabo Verde.

III. ANALYSIS OF DIFFERENT TYPES OF RESISTANCE

Our aim is to smash the colonial state in order to create a new state, a different state, one based on justice, work, and equal opportunity for every child of our land, here in Guinea and in Cabo Verde.

1. POLITICAL RESISTANCE

Meaning and Objective

Our resistance, comrades, might be compared to, for example, the following: a family or village in our land needs to grow rice. It has two helpings of rice. It knows that if it saves one helping to sow, there won't be enough rice to go around and give everyone something to eat. But it saves that helping and sows it, and if the field is worked well, that one helping might yield ten, twenty, even thirty helpings, depending on the terrain. This is similar to the resistance of a people, comrades.

We all had our lives, any one of you could be at home right now, with your family, living under colonialism, sure, but at home with your family. Some of you were maybe even lawyers working for the Tugas, just as there are people who still are lawyers working for the Tugas, or maybe you were a doctor working for the Tugas, just as there are people still working as doctors for the Tugas, or as engineers, or farmers, mechanics, carpenters, tailors, sepoys, soldiers etc. But we decided to make our heads into seeds that are sown in the ground to produce new plants. Some calamity may occur, of course. It might not rain, for example, and all the seeds will dry out. The seeds are then lost, we've achieved nothing, and on top of everything else, we're all hungry. Or maybe we don't properly protect the field we've tilled, and pests, birds, or monkeys get in and spoil our crops. The resistance of a people requires courage if we are to turn ourselves into seeds and grow to become a new plantation that will bring joy to our people through freedom. That's the risk, the so-called risk of resistance. Some will get left behind, but more will grow each day, others will push on ahead. And a resistance will only ever triumph if it grows day by day.

A people's struggle, a people's resistance, takes many forms. As I've said before, our resistance began a long time ago. Our resistance began in Guinea the day the Tugas got it into their heads that they would dominate us, exploit us. In Cabo Verde, our resistance began the day it became clear, from the state of our society, utterly dependent on the Portuguese colonizers, that our people were being exploited, humiliated, and exported like animals dying of hunger.

It was resistance at the individual level, people doing what they could. Resistance through emigration: our Mandjaco people who left for France, for Senegal, our Balanta people who left the Mansoa area, who resisted first there and then moved to the Nalus area, resisted there and then moved to the Bofá area, to the Cóia area etc., in the Republic of Guinea. All of this is resistance, comrades. The resistance of one or two souls brave enough to give a sepoy a slap and then be beaten to death for it; the resistance of people who were summoned by the chiefs of post, but fled. Individual resistance of every shape and form. But others come together to resist, based on race, based on age group, based on family, based on other things. All it takes in a land is for a few sons and daughters to gain consciousness and see the path they must take for that resistance to become clearly defined.

Resistance is a natural thing. Any force exerted on a given object produces resistance, that's to say a counterforce. And the counterforce to colonialist and imperialist force is a national liberation movement. Such a tension can only be resolved through political work or, in certain situations, it might take the form of armed struggle, as in our case. And then, bit by bit, certain types of resistance become defined within the overall scheme of resistance. It is essential that every militant and supervisor is fully aware of these different types of resistance. But it's even more important that we understand why we are resisting, what we are resisting for. We must clearly understand the aims of our resistance.

Resistance is the following: destroying something to construct something else. That's what resistance is. What do we want to destroy in our country? Portuguese colonial domination. Just that? No. At the same time we want to destroy any other kind of colonial domination, any other kind of foreign domination of our land. We want our own people, our sons and daughters, to control our destiny in Guinea and Cabo Verde. That's the number one thing we want.

Furthermore, and this has been a basic principle throughout the life of our Party, we want to destroy any possibility that those who liberate us today, abuse us tomorrow. Our aim is not to destroy the Portuguese colonialists and colonialist domination only to then have some group of our own to take their place. Our aim cannot be to take over the Palace of the Governor so that some new governor can do whatever he likes. The same goes for the chief of post's house, the administrator's house. *Our aim is to smash the colonial state in order to create a new state, a different state, one based on justice, work, and equal opportunity for every child of our land, here in Guinea and in Cabo Verde.*

We want, therefore, to destroy everything that obstructs our people's progress, every relationship in our society, in Guinea and Cabo Verde, that counters our people's progress, counters our people's freedom. Ultimately what we want is this: real and equal possibilities for every child of our land, for every man and woman to be able to advance as human beings, to fulfill their potential; to develop their physical and spiritual selves and reach the heights of their true potential. Anything that prevents this from happening in our country must be destroyed, comrades. Step by step, one step at a time, if need be, we must destroy it and build a new life. That is the main aim of our resistance.

We cannot accept any kind of abuse, any kind of group or clique privileges, anywhere in our land, if we really want to liberate our people. Because we are not only going to liberate our people from the Tuga colonialists, but from everything that blocks our people's path to progress. We must destroy all ignorance, poor health, and fears of every kind, bit by bit, step by step.

We understand that there is fear in our country today, fear within our struggle, and maybe there still will be tomorrow and for a good while after that. Fear of the *polon* tree, for example, or fear of horns. But one day, sooner or later, when all our people have learned to read and write well, when everyone has been to school and learned what fear really is, what life is, what nature is, when everyone understands what the *polon* tree is, what lightning flashes and bolts are, what the moon is, the stars, and everything else, then rest assured, comrades, no one in our country will fear horns anymore, or pop-eyed witches.

When we have achieved this, we will have truly liberated the people of our country. Because our people are under huge pressure, comrades, not from the colonialists and not from lack of work, but from fear. A fearful people is an enslaved people. Fearful of going hungry, fearful of not getting enough work, fearful of illness, fearful of beatings, fearful of being deported to São Tomé, fearful of being imprisoned unjustly. But even more than that, fearful of witches, fearful of fortune tellers, fearful of what marabouts say, fearful of the *irã*, fearful of the dark forest, fearful of lightning flashes and bolts. Only a wretched people has so much fear, comrades.

A people so full of fear, yet capable of taking up arms against the colonialists, hitting them hard in our land. See the contradiction there, comrades? This clearly shows we are capable of anything, and that's precisely our Party's aim: to reach our full potential. This is what we seek through our resistance. To eradicate everything that's preventing us from fulfilling our true potential.

We do not want our sons and daughters to be fearful of their parents, not tomorrow, though we can perhaps tolerate a little bit of it today. But no, they should be respectful, not fearful. We no longer want to see our sons and daughters tied up to be beaten. This belittles our people, comrades, it blocks our people's path. We no longer want to see anyone in our country tied up and beaten. Crooks and good-for-nothings will be judged, and if necessary, they will be shot, but they will not be treated like dogs. We no longer want to see any human beings in our country treated like dogs.

And it is our job to destroy, through our resistance, anything that makes puppies of our people—our men and our women—so that we may advance, grow, rise up like flowers from our soil, we must do everything we can to make our people feel like valued human beings. This is our task, comrades. If you haven't understood this yet, you haven't understood anything.

This is what we're sacrificing ourselves for, this is what we're fighting for. We must be aware of what we want to destroy in our country, and what we want to construct. This is the first set of circumstances we require for our resistance to truly advance. If this is to happen, it's imperative that we're all conscious of certain issues. For example: Who are we and who is our enemy? We've been explaining this for a long time now. But we have to understand where we've come from, our struggle's point of departure, our resistance. I've already explained this to you, a few days ago, right here. What we were before this struggle, before this organized struggle. The political, economic, cultural, and social circumstances of our country. And we must clearly define the ways in which we have carried out and will carry out our resistance.

Our resistance evolves in a variety of forms, comrades. First comes political resistance, first and foremost: political resistance. That is why we began our resistance by creating our Party, a political tool. But there are other types of resistance too: economic resistance, cultural resistance, and armed resistance; each one is an essential component of our struggle, comrades, of our resistance. These four types of resistance represent the minimum of what can be done and we have to develop each one more by the day. This is what our struggle has been about all along, comrades, whether we were aware of it or not. This is what our struggle has consisted of so far.

For this very reason, our Party's Program has, right from the start, clearly defined what we see as our political aims. It's easy to say "fight, take up arms, and go on strike," but it's not enough to just fight with a gun in your hand—you need to fight with political consciousness in your head too. We need to be aware that it is man's consciousness that guides the gun and not the gun that guides his consciousness. The gun's worth lies in the fact that there is a man behind it, holding it. And, of course, the more politically conscious the man is, the more the gun is worth, and if the man's consciousness serves a just and well-defined cause, then the gun is worth all the more.

We must ensure our political resistance is clearly defined because the enemy puts political pressure on our political resistance in order to try to destroy it. We must clearly define our political resistance, inside and outside our country, and know exactly what we need to do. And it has been clearly defined for a long time now. If anyone doesn't know it, then they simply haven't wanted to know.

The first requirement of political resistance, comrades, is to unite the people. We have already discussed this in terms of Party principles, what our political resistance is made up of has, by and large, already been defined. Unite, gradually create a national consciousness, because at our point of departure there was no national consciousness; we were, due to our own history and the work of the Tugas, divided into groups.

The "civilized" and the indigenous, city people and bush people, Balantas, Pepels, Manjacos, and Mandingas etc. So our first job is to create a national consciousness in a certain number of our people, in Guinea and in Cabo Verde. This is why our Party program states this so clearly: national unity in Guinea, national unity in Cabo Verde.

We must seek, through our political resistance, in service of our overall resistance, to unite all our people, as many as we can. But as I've told you before, this means uniting without any opportunism, rejecting opportunism of every kind, because our resistance is not designed to serve a particular clique or to produce chiefs; it's not Cabral's resistance, I don't need others to serve me. If I'd wanted to, in 1960 I could have become the leader of all the Dakar "movements," I could have united them all under me. Comrade Luís Cabral too; when he left here and went to Senegal, they met with him and made him the following proposition: leave the PAIGC, come work for us, and become our leader. He told them never to say such a thing again because he's PAIGC through and through. From that day forth, they became his enemies. Even people who had been guests in his house became enemies. Because we will not accept opportunism of any kind, we reject all opportunism, comrades.

National unity, yes, national consciousness, yes, but not with traitors, not with opportunists, not with people without morals. We cannot create national unity with thieves, liars, and crooks. We're creating national unity with one true objective: to combat the enemy, to fight the enemy, but at the same time to fight against every negative element in our midst. This is a fundamental aspect of our political resistance, one that comrades must fully understand in order to orientate themselves in their work, whether it be as militants or supervisors.

We have to be vigilant and not allow anyone to divide our people. We have to clearly define, as I've already said, who our people are at this stage in our history. So let me repeat it: our people are all the sons and daughters of our land, in Guinea and Cabo Verde, who want rid of the Portuguese colonialists, that's all. Anyone who wants to get rid of them is one of us, and we don't want anyone dividing our people. Be vigilant, because those who divide us are our enemies, worse even than the Tugas, who will undoubtedly soon be gone.

In our political resistance, we must continually raise the consciousness of every militant engaged in the struggle or with the Party. We must urge everyone to better themselves in terms of their work and knowledge. This is the only way to make our most valuable resource, our men and our women, even more invaluable.

We have to fight to ensure the principles we've established, and which we speak of here, are applied, so that everyone, every man and woman, has the opportunity to advance. Failure to do so is a betrayal, a sabotage of our political resistance. And we must organize and organize. This is why our Party started to organize itself, right from the beginning, clandestinely at first, in groups of three, in cells, in towns, and then in the bush, in small groups, out in the open where it was possible to do so and hidden wherever we had to hide. Then came organized villages and, step by step, we advanced: Party Committees, Area Committees, Regional Committees, Interregional Committees.

Step by step we transformed our Party leadership, continually improving the way we organized ourselves, according to the reality of our struggle, in order to improve our political resistance. And every day, every hour, we have endeavored to clarify why we are fighting, what we want, so that everyone advances knowing exactly what they're doing and why they're doing it. This foundation is essential to our being able to politically resist our enemy's maneuvers, their propaganda, and our being able to advance our political resistance, for our political resistance is the most essential form of resistance, comrades, within the overall scheme of our resistance.

We have spoken often about the need to enlighten the masses of our land, to do so on a daily basis, to tell the truth above all else, to never lie to them, to never trick anyone; we have no need to trick people. If we start tricking and lying, we are ruining our political resistance. If there are difficulties, say so, clearly; if we triumph, say so, clearly; if we lose, say so, clearly. Because no struggle brings only victories. If there were only victories, it would be no struggle at all. There are victories and defeats, there are difficulties, there is sometimes despair too, but we always move forward. We must seek, by enlightening the masses of our land, by clearly demonstrating the enemy's intentions, to stop the enemy from misleading them. This is one of our essential tasks, comrades, and one that, unfortunately, some comrades seem to have forgotten about.

Given the particular circumstances of our struggle, given our need to build national unity in Guinea, we must make more of an effort to win over those brothers and sisters who certain chiefs have turned away from the struggle, especially among the Fula and the Mandjaco. Our Party established an entire policy because of this, and to deal with this, distinguishing between the population and their chiefs. Treat the population well, do your utmost to cause them no harm. This is precisely why, when we started the fight in Gabú in early 1965, we gave orders for our command not to fire a single shot for a whole month against anyone from our land who, having been tricked by the Tugas, took up arms against us. We talked about this, we discussed it, and a few of our comrades even died without firing a single shot. Comrade Lúcio can tell us all about this, he saw it. But we did this to win people over, to reinforce our political resistance, to increase our unity in terms of our engagement.

In Cabo Verde, while we understand that our struggle is primarily being fought on behalf of those who are suffering, those who have no land to work, who have no jobs, who are contracted to go and die in São Tomé; those mothers who lug sacks around at the docks in São Vicente, who die of hunger alongside their sons and daughters in times of crisis; while we understand all this, our orders are to recruit as many people as possible to our cause. Even those on the Tugas' side. To those sons and daughters of Cabo Verde who are in good employment, living well, we state our case clearly: the country is yours, join us so that we may advance. Because the first step in a political resistance is joining as many people as possible together for the fight.

In Guinea, it's the same thing. Our struggle in Guinea is not, as far as I'm concerned, being fought to improve my life in material terms. If I were ever to have in our country, in Guinea or in Cabo Verde, the lifestyle I used to have . . . Or if the leaders of our country tomorrow, in Guinea or in Cabo Verde, were to live as well as I used to live in Portugal, then that would mean our country was very rich. But we must be vigilant and not let our leaders live like this, because it is too good a life for a poor country that still has so much work to do. Our struggle in Guinea is, to begin with, being fought on behalf of our people in the bush, people who have lived for centuries and centuries within the same village, never straying more than five kilometers from their homes; people who don't know what schools are or that medicines exist to treat the illnesses that swell their bodies.

Our resistance in Guinea sets out to end every kind of abuse: it is against anyone who's abusive, in the bush just as much as the towns. It is in order for the sons and daughters of our land to be able to gain a proper understanding of their professions and so that no foreigner gets to rule over our land. And knowing this, or in spite of this, we seek to join everyone together in our cause, people of every social class, even Jaime Pinto Bull, as I said to you only today. To Jaime Pinto Bull I say: leave the Tugas and come and join us. In Cabo Verde I say the same thing, loud and clear, to Júlio Monteiro, to Aguinaldo Veiga, to Antero Barros and so many others: leave the Tugas, stick with us, for the country is yours too. We are not the only ones who have the right and the duty to fight for our country, there's plenty of room for all of us. This is the path of political resistance for those of us who really want to fight and give it our all, for those who want to serve their people and not just their own stomachs.

In terms of our political resistance within our land, we must do everything we can to channel all our forces into our political resistance. Our Party has done a lot in this regard, maybe we should or could have done more, but we've done a lot. And the triumphs of our struggle, the successes of our struggle, the continuity of our struggle, the prospects of our struggle today, show that our Party has won some great victories in this sense. Nevertheless, there are still traitors within our land, there are still Tugistas, Tuga lapdogs. There are still people in our midst who might pass over to the Tugas tomorrow, because their ambitions, their pretensions, their vanities, their vices mean they cannot put up with the demands and rigors of our Party's work.

Political Resistance in External Terms

In terms of external political resistance, we also have to make a big effort there. Our principal objective externally, given our circumstances, is to gain everyone's political support, in order to reinforce our political resistance.

Our Party has worked hard to win, fought to win outside political support within Africa and in the wider world. Since 1960, we, the people of Guinea and Cabo Verde, have been fortunate in that I was elected, chosen from among all our comrades in the Portuguese colonies who are with us in this struggle, to go out and denounce

Portuguese colonialism to the rest of the world. And in February 1960, we gave our first international press conference in London, revealing Portuguese colonialism for what it is, and we wrote our first pamphlet, the first pamphlet against Portuguese colonialism written by a son or daughter of the Portuguese colonies. It was published in English in England, under the name of Abel Djassi. There and then our political resistance in the international realm, in the external realm, began to take shape, within the framework of the Portuguese colonies generally, but moving towards our own framework, that of Guinea and Cabo Verde, and therefore the framework of our Party.

Externally, the principal objective of our political resistance is to gain allies, to gain political support and thus to isolate the enemy politically. To this end, from as early as 1960, while preparing our people for the armed struggle, we began to go to conferences and international meetings, raising our issue, fighting to be heard, multiplying our efforts, courting all the necessary support, and seeking to isolate the enemy internationally.

Seeking to isolate the enemy in regards to its own people is another issue. This is why, right from the beginning, within the framework of our political resistance, we have made it clear that we are not fighting against the Portuguese people. Everyone in our Party knows this. We are not fighting against the Portuguese people—we are fighting against Portuguese colonialism, against Portuguese colonialists. We are fighting to get the Portuguese colonialists out of our land. But we've been even more clear about it than that: we, the people of Guinea and Cabo Verde, the PAIGC, are not fighting against Salazarism or fascism in Portugal. That's the Portuguese people's job, not ours. This is an important point to make in order to isolate the Tugas from their own people.

Within Guinea, we have managed to isolate them a little. We saw that, whereas in early 1959, as well as during the August 1959 strike, the Pidjiguiti massacre, some Portuguese civilians took up arms against us, civilians have not been willing to take up arms in the war. A number of civilians have even sided with us. This is a triumph for our Party, for it shows that they fully understand we are not against them. This is what isolating the enemy from its own people is, isolating them from the masses.

And in Portugal today, an increasing number of people, more and more by the day, look favorably upon the PAIGC. There is great respect for our Party in Portugal, more than you might imagine, comrades. Some of the Tugas in Portugal maybe have more respect for our Party than some of you do sitting here. Forgive me, but it's true. And public opinion against the colonial war being waged in our country grows by the day, because our Party has managed to nurture this aspect of political resistance, isolating the enemy, distinguishing between the enemy and the masses, isolating the enemy in relation to its people.

It could be better, of course, but there's not enough time for everything to be brilliant. We have stated our case in relation to the Portuguese people and defined how prisoners are to be treated, how deserters are to be treated, in order to win over more and more of the Portuguese people, to isolate the people from our enemy, the Portuguese colonialists. And now we understand that the best form of propaganda our Party has ever had, the best propaganda concerning our struggle, our resistance, has come from Portuguese deserters, from Portuguese prisoners even. This is one of the greatest triumphs of our struggle. There have even been Portuguese deserters who, after we sent them away, wrote to us asking us to accept them as naturalized sons of the land, because they want to spend their lives working for the PAIGC. This shows how successful we've been in our work. Since the very start of the struggle, in documents some comrades will perhaps know, we have addressed settlers in our country, saying to them clearly: "You are the wheels on the old colonialist car that wants to carry on exploiting our people." But even settlers have a place in our country, if they want it. We want to make a country where anyone from anywhere in the world can come and live, provided that they respect our people's right to rule themselves, to come and live and work, for that's the way it should be. This was the first reason why many civilian Tuga settlers demobilized, rejecting the colonialist path.

We reached a point around 1964 whereby, had the authorities allowed it, the Tuga settlers would have all left. But although our struggle is an armed one, we refuse, out of respect for our own form of political consciousness, to abuse Portuguese soldiers in any way. If any of our comrades have committed crimes like those the Tugas commit against us, then they have been disobeying Party orders.

At the start of our struggle there were comrades who suggested that, within the scheme of our overall struggle, we should commit certain atrocities. But we refused to do so. Certain things that have happened in other African countries have no place in our struggle. No matter what justification an African might give for killing women, for killing white children of our land, just because they are white, we reject these actions once and for all. Why? Because what we want is political resistance in service to our people, we do not want our people to become bloodthirsty, we do not want our people to shed blood just for the sake of shedding blood. If blood is to be shed, it is to be shed politically, to serve the future of our country.

Every time we kill someone, it is because that someone has a gun pointed at us, turned against the rights of our people. We have issued orders saying that anyone who took up arms against us but lays down their weapons will no longer be considered our enemy: they will be seen as a human being and must be treated well. Our comrades have, thankfully, understood this properly and respected it. And if someone does not respect it, they are sabotaging our Party's work, our political resistance.

The work we do with the people of other Portuguese colonies is very important within the scheme of our own political resistance. We've said it before, but of all the resistance movements in the Portuguese colonies, our Party has concerned itself most with this. Right from the start, we have always raised the issue: we are one, fighting together, because there is but one enemy. There have been ups and downs in terms of our forming an alliance with other movements, there have been betrayals from other movements, but the PAIGC, comrades, has always been loyal and shown unconditional solidarity to resistance movements in other Portuguese colonies. Certain comrades within our Party have even raised this as an issue: How is it that we're the only ones who honor our CONCP [Conferência das Organizações Nacionalistas-das Colónias Portuguesas (Conference of Nationalist Organizations of the Portuguese Colonies)] commitments? Our answer is that we honor them because it's in our interest to do so—it's not just in other people's interests, but ours too. We had to sacrifice members of the Party command to go and work for the CONCP, when other movements gave none. But in the same spirit, we will always defend, against anyone and anything, the need for all students of the Portuguese colonies to join together in a single organization, UGEAN [the General Union of Students from Black Africa under Portuguese colonial domination]. Fortunately, our more disciplined comrades understood this well.

There is only one thing we refuse to do and that is to join forces with false resistance movements in other Portuguese colonies. We will not join up with movements that do not advance and that give themselves over to the imperialists, for we do not want to replace one kind of domination of our land with another. We join with those movements our analysis has shown are pure, those that intend to fight the proper way, and we have no regrets in this area so far. This, comrades, is a fundamental aspect of our political resistance: our unity, our comradeship, our collaboration, our close bonds to the liberation movements of Angola, Mozambique, and São Tomé.

We ourselves, the PAIGC, are working hard to help unite different movements in Mozambique, towards the creation of FRELIMO. And we ourselves, the PAIGC, helped form the MPLA [Movimento Popular de Libertação de Angola (People's Movement for the Liberation of Angola)] in Angola. This is not vanity speaking, it is common knowledge; the sons and daughters of Angola know this well. To serve the interests of our own people, comrades, we have taken risks in Angola, attending clandestine meetings at a time when several Angolans had been imprisoned by the PIDE. But we had to go to Angola and hold meetings. We set up an agronomy contract in Angola and used it to go to Angola and gather comrades together to discuss the path we must all follow in the struggle to free our lands. All this under the PIDE's watchful eye, comrades. And after having done other work in Angola besides. What for? To serve the people of Guinea and Cabo Verde, comrades. We have no pretensions about trying to serve the people of Angola: Angola's own sons and daughters are perfectly capable of serving their own people, although our consciousness as human beings means we would be happy to serve in Angola just as we would be happy to serve in Mozambique, the same as in Guinea or Cabo Verde. And only members of the Party who have attained true political consciousness are capable of serving in any country, fighting the common enemy. We have always staunchly defended the need for unity among resistance movements in the Portuguese colonies.

Thankfully, after all the difficulties, after all the problems, we are now all in agreement on this and this is very important. It is another great victory against Portuguese colonialism, comrades.

And together we are working to realize another of our Party's dreams, which is to gather together all the students from the Portuguese colonies in a single organization. This would be another great triumph within the overall scheme of our political resistance, because the enemies of our people, the enemies of today or tomorrow, are also active within the student realm, trying to win people over and hold back the lives of our people.

In terms of our political resistance outside our land, we are constantly seeking to develop and reinforce our relationships across Africa. To start with, we fought with great courage in Conakry, for example, in order to win the friendship, esteem, and solidarity of the Republic of Guinea. This was an essential aspect of our political resistance, comrades. Indeed, at that stage of our struggle, it was arguably our Party's biggest triumph, the most far-reaching, by which I mean it had the biggest consequences, way beyond what most of you can imagine. We have also made a big effort and showed great patience, determination and persistence, to win over the people of Senegal, despite Senegal's reluctance, despite Senegal's rejection, despite Senegal creating "movements" against our Party. But after several years' work, we reached an agreement with the Government of Senegal, another great victory in the overall scheme of our political resistance and one we must work to reinforce every day, indeed take to another level because our circumstances are very different today.

In African terms, working within the limits of what's possible, of course, and according to our limited time and resources, we have endeavored to reinforce friendships with other independent African states. Our Party has developed a deep friendship with a number of African heads of states. Let us recall the deep bonds of friendship that link us to Algeria, to the United Arab Republic, to Tanzania, to Congo-Brazzaville, to name but a few. We seek to develop friendships with the Ivory Coast and with Tunisia. As a Party we have decided to push further and reach out to all the independent states of Africa. This is important work in our political resistance.

Through our bravery and hard work, through our victories, through our resistance and our endeavor, we have managed to win over all the African people aligned under the OAU [Organization of African Unity] and establish ourselves, that's to say we as a Party and a people, as the leading liberation movement in Africa. This is a great victory in political terms, comrades, in terms of our political resistance. And we are constantly working to strengthen our friendship and collaboration with other liberation movements in Africa. We have a great sense of unity and trust with the movements in South Africa, who are fighting against colonialist racism; with movements in Rhodesia, in Southwest Africa,[1] and, before they became independent, in Zambia and Kenya. Through persistent work, we are developing friendships with them all, but always based on consciousness, never on opportunism, knowing how and who we choose to be friends with. Because if you don't know how to choose your friends properly, if you don't have some sort of criteria, if it's not based on principles of respect, then you end up choosing mischief-makers, not friends.

One of our Party's greatest triumphs within the context of our political resistance, the result of intense work over a number of years, has been to demonstrate the value of our struggle to progressive forces around the world, especially within the socialist community. We have shown them the value of our work and demonstrated our sense of responsibility as a party, while earning their trust, appreciation, and indeed admiration, so much so that, thanks to our political consciousness and the triumphs of our political resistance, they have become firm friends who help us in our struggle.

Our Party has even had some success in terms of political resistance relating to countries allied with Portugal. We've never gone around claiming that our struggle is against all the capitalist countries in the world. We've never done this, we say we're fighting Portuguese colonialism, that's our task.

We make the issue very clear, be it to the Americans or the Germans, the English, the French, we say we're not fighting you, we're fighting Portuguese colonialism. And if we haven't got more out of them yet, or haven't got anything at all, then the fault lies with them rather than our Party, because they have commitments with the Portuguese colonialists, because they have imperial interests, and those interests are bigger than any kind of humanitarian interest they might have for our struggle.

---

1   Namibia

Even so, we have achieved a number of victories. We have some-times seen Western countries abstain and vote neither for nor against Portugal. This, in itself, is a huge victory for us, comrades. A huge victory. We have managed, for example, to visit certain countries and hold press conferences, raise our issues and, above all else, win the support of anti-colonialists in those countries. This is important, comrades. Be it in America, in England, in Italy, in France, etc., pro-gressive forces have huge admiration for the PAIGC, comrades. Only those unacquainted with our relationships and all the correspondence we receive fail to appreciate this.

But we recently achieved an even bigger victory. A Western country that has dealt with Portugal in commercial terms has declared itself to be entirely on our side: Sweden. And now it is helping us, substan-tially. This year we will start to receive this help, not in the form of money but in goods, in medicines and school materials, to help our people economically and culturally. Comrades, this is a real triumph for us and opens up a great breach in Portugal's international alliance. Colonialist Portugal is fully aware of this and furious.

The Soviet Union has helped us, but the Tugas didn't get furious about that; they complained, but not much, they knew this was only to be expected. It was the same thing with China, with Cuba. Portu-gal has diplomatic relations with Cuba, but didn't cut off those rela-tions. The Tugas know we get arms and other things from Cuba; they know there are Cuban doctors who assist us; they know all of this full well, it's not like they've suddenly arrested a Cuban and found it all out. But they didn't make much fuss about it, they didn't get as furious as they did about Sweden.

Sweden said it would help us and the Tugas became immediately furious, they recalled their ambassador, cut off commercial ties, sent people out onto the streets to protest, prevented dockers from unload-ing Swedish ships. Because they know the significance of this. They know this was a breach in terms of their Western alliance, they knew it could serve as a lead for other progressive forces to follow, in America, England, and France, for example, where people might rise up and petition their governments to help freedom movements in Africa. The Tugas are afraid of this precedent, comrades. This should give you an idea of just how successful the Party has been this year, a great victory achieved through our political resistance in the international sphere.

In summary, comrades, our political resistance must revolve around three fundamental points: to achieve national unity in our land and to put that unity entirely at the service of our struggle, at the service of our people, under the flag cf our Party; to further isolate the enemy from its allies, from its partner countries, from anyone that might support it; and to win more allies over to our cause, gaining ever more support without ever compromising on our principles. This is how we must orientate our struggle, doing our work properly and never forgetting that our fight is fundamentally a political fight, which is why we must ensure our political resistance triumphs.

2. ECONOMIC RESISTANCE

In our afternoon session yesterday, we looked at how our resistance is a response to Portugal's colonial dominance of Guinea and Cabo Verde; we showed comrades what this means, what the principal aspects of our resistance are and how, throughout our struggle, the Party has followed a trajectory that responds to the needs of the resistance according to the concrete situation in our land.

We spoke yesterday about political resistance and saw how, operating in conjunction with political resistance, there is also economic resistance, cultural resistance, and armed resistance. All these types of resistance exist in our country and have ever since we began our struggle, each one developing by the day without most comrades being aware of it.

Today, we will speak a bit about another important aspect of our resistance: economic resistance.

As every comrade knows, our struggle is a political struggle because we are seeking to win our right to be a free and sovereign people; in other words to govern ourselves by gaining national independence for our country. But at the root of this truth lies another truth, which is the following: colonialism is, first and foremost, economic domination. Colonialism, or imperialist domination, seeks, in the first instance, to dominate others economically. To this end it adds a political domain and spreads its imperialist or colonialist state forces throughout the land it wants to dominate economically. This being the case, we must recognize that the principle aim of our resistance and our struggle is, at root, to free ourselves economically, although to do this we must first achieve political freedom.

In other words, a country is only truly liberated if it manages to rid itself of every aspect of foreign dominance over its economy, if it truly manages to free itself from foreign exploitation. This is what freedom is for a country dominated by colonialists. Every country has its natural resources and its population, which is its greatest resource, for the population provides the labor-power to develop its natural resources, existing or potential, and its means of production. But under colonialist or imperialist domination, none of these things are free: they're not developed freely, they're subjected to imperialist domination. Winning true independence is being able to freely develop a combination of factors known as the productive forces of a country. You can see, therefore, that, when it comes down to it, our resistance is aimed at resolving an economic issue, although it has to achieve political aims first, the political aspect always being very important. But in any case, this is why our economic resistance is so important.

As I've said before, every struggle, but specifically our liberation struggle, has two components that must come together: destruction and construction. We see this clearly in our political resistance: we have to destroy the Portuguese state, we have to destroy the political concepts the colonialist Tugas have put in our heads, and we have to destroy, in the long term, and overcome, in the short term, any erroneous political assumptions that might exist in people's heads, within our population, within our different classes and ethnic groups, assumptions that might hinder our people's march down the path towards progress.

We have to construct a new state for our country, one based on the freedom of our people, on democracy, on working towards progress. We have to construct a national consciousness among our people, we have to constantly develop our population's political consciousness, and we have to construct all the necessary political means, organisms, and organizations required to defend the national liberty that we've won.

Destroy the Colonial Economy

Economic resistance is likewise a matter of destruction and construction. The objective of our economic resistance is to destroy the Portuguese colonialists' exploitation of our people. This means that our struggle had to be aimed, right from the start, at putting a complete stop to the exploitation of our land by the Portuguese colonial regime. We know that exploitation in Guinea works principally through our people being essentially forced to buy agricultural products at prices determined by businessmen of the colonialist state, and through our people being obliged to grow peanuts and sell them at prices likewise determined by the Tugas. The level of exploitation is such that, were anyone to properly do the sums, they would conclude that peanut cultivation in Guinea is in fact forced labor, because the money a family farming peanuts gets for however many peanuts they harvest, regardless of their area of land, is not enough to pay a wage, even a tiny one, to all the people in the family who work at it all year round. In other words, we must draw the conclusion that our people work for Gouveia, Ultramarino, and all the other companies that buy peanuts, for free, because the money they get for these peanuts may be enough for them to pay the family tax, buy a cut of fabric for the mother, and a few other bits and bobs, but if we make proper calculations, if we take wages into account and other expenses that should be factored in, we see that the price paid for the peanuts doesn't cover it, that this is agricultural exploitation. And this is what we want to destroy, what we knew we had to destroy: we had to destroy the relationship of economic exploitation the colonialists had with our people. And we had to destroy other forms of economic exploitation besides, even if they were dressed up as legitimate administrative running costs, such as the various types of unfair taxes our people had to pay to the colonial Portuguese state.

In Cabo Verde, our principal aim is to destroy a system of exploitation based on large properties that afford no land to our people. Our people are forced into being tenants, whether they farm or not, they have to pay rent, live in poverty, suffer from hunger, and even risk being sold or contracted as forced labor in other colonies. We must destroy this.

In Guinea, we have managed to destroy a lot already. Just a few days ago, for example, Radio Bissau announced that a Greek ship had docked bringing three tonnes of rice. We can see from this that we have managed to inflict a degree of destruction on the Portuguese regime because, as we know, our people were practically forced to sell the rice they grew to Ultramarino to be milled and then sold back to us. But the Tugas now have to import rice. Last year they imported over ten thousand tonnes of rice from Brazil alone; this year they've already taken delivery of three thousand tonnes. And anyone who's been following the official statistics will have seen that peanut exports have fallen a lot. There are practically no exports from our land at present. Portuguese ships bring in war materials and provisions for the troops or goods for the towns, and leave almost empty. They mostly just take away scrap metal from trucks and other things our soldiers have destroyed.

We have, therefore, already destroyed much of the Portuguese economic system in our land, but we must destroy it all, completely. But then what do we construct? We must start constructing our own economy now. Indeed, we have been constructing it for a few years now because it's all very well and good to say let's fight, in political terms, in military terms, but people cannot fight properly with an empty stomach and poor health. This is another form of resistance. It's impossible to resist without food, it's impossible to resist without good health. We therefore have to develop our economy, find the best way to move our economy forward, even during our struggle, because we have to guarantee the minimum conditions necessary for our people to make a living, for our soldiers to have the means to live. Furthermore, we have to make a real effort to gradually improve living conditions for our people, so that they sense the sacrifices they're making, for our country's independence, for our Party's flag, are worthwhile.

As a party we've done what we can, but we—Party militants, supervisors, soldiers, leaders—haven't been able to improve the living conditions of our people or show them that poverty can and will end. Above all else, we need to raise consciousness so that everyone understands that, while there is poverty in our country today, it will end tomorrow, but that it depends on us, on our work and us advancing the struggle. Because anyone who has practically nothing today but trusts that they'll have plenty tomorrow if they work hard, is no longer poor; they're rich, because they trust in the path and see that it's open to them. We must do our utmost in this regard, because we know that anyone living in poverty is easy prey for the enemy, is easily captured to work against the interests of our people. For example, we only have to consider the following: Who in our land serves the Tugas the most? It's plain to see that most people who serve the Tugas are people without means. In Bissau, the PIDE recruits most of its agents from among the unemployed and the idle.

Faced with our need to put up economic resistance, we must clarify the following: What is the enemy doing to destroy our economic resistance? Because they aren't just fighting us with arms, they're fighting us economically too. On the one hand, in the areas they still control, they're making a big push for economic development, saying life is going to improve, giving jobs to people to show that life really is improving, trying to establish rice fields, provide goods etc. For example, everyone knows that more goods and nice things are arriving in Cabo Verde than ever before. This is in order to put a stop to the kind of shortages that foster revolts. Even in Guinea, numerous things the Tugas used to buy off us, like rice, they're now buying elsewhere for much higher prices. This is in order to exhaust our economic resistance. They are making a big show of creating large rice fields in the Tite area—the island of Bissau has been almost entirely transformed into rice fields—and so they are trying to find ways to provide an economic lift to the areas they still control in order to show people that life is improving, that people don't need to join our struggle.

On the other hand, the Tugas are going to great lengths to try to completely destroy the economic base of our struggle. Bombings, napalm, helicopter attacks that terrorize local populations so that people take flight and leave our country for Senegal or the Republic of Guinea. This is good for the Tugas because local populations are not then working the land in the liberated areas and providing us with the economic means needed to support our struggle. And if that doesn't suffice, if local populations hide or refuse to bow to Tuga demands, the Tugas burn our crops and our villages, destroying everything, killing our cows, killing any creature that moves. And criminals that they are, they kill our local populations too, children, women, the elderly, never mind adult men. This is not just because of the war, no, it's in order to destroy our economic resistance, to end it, because they know as well as we do that if we don't have an economy, if our land does not have the economic means to support our struggle, if we don't have food, if we don't have the capacity to provide our people and soldiers with food, then there can be no war, comrades, there can be no struggle.

The enemy, therefore, is destroying everything it can, even in terms of things like medicines and fabrics, things we get for our people, for our people's warehouses, for our hospitals, etc. The enemy is making every effort to put a stop to these things. That we've managed to establish warehouses in certain areas, where our people can go and get fabrics, shoes, and other things they need is one of our enemy's biggest defeats in economic terms. The Tugas want to find our warehouses and burn them down as soon as possible, because they know these warehouses give us economic strength and that this translates into political strength in the context of our struggle.

To combat our economic resistance, the Tugas are prepared to torch the entire country if necessary, employing what's known as the scorched earth policy, in other words, to reduce everything to ashes rather than have us win our fight. We must therefore be vigilant and know exactly what we must do when faced with such criminal intent on the part of the Tugas, intent that we have ample proof of being carried out in certain areas of our land. We must be firm in our economic fight.

This is why, right from the start, our Party has thought about and tried to implement a program of economic resistance. We must adapt it, of course, tailor it to suit our conditions as best we can, and we must mobilize all our forces, channel our energies into our economic resistance, especially the energy of local populations, of militants in the villages and the liberated areas. At the same time, we must gradually increase our destruction of the enemy's colonial economy and make secure plans to boost our own production, agricultural products, artisanal products, and other things besides. We must try to destroy the enemy's economic means, their cars, their factories, their reserves, their warehouses, their boats, their roads, to completely shut down their economic exploitation of our land.

You will have seen, comrades, that we started out by sabotaging roads, bridges, and everything else. This was our first act of economic resistance, and an act of political and military resistance besides, carried out against the colonialist enemy. And if the enemy has established itself in a particular area and in such a way that the only way to force them out is by setting fire to everything, then we too will do so, we have the right to do so because it is our land. It's better to completely torch everything and force the Tugas out, and then rebuild the area, than leave the area untouched and let the Tugas remain there indefinitely, dominating our people. This is something we need to be conscious of, while pursuing a strategy that seeks to minimize the need to destroy things, things that may currently be under colonial control but that were originally made by us.

This has, in fact, always been our Party's policy. It's important to understand our great need to destroy the Tugas' supply chains. This is why our Party has been so insistent on the need to attack boats on rivers and trucks on roads, because boats and trucks not only bring war supplies but serve the enemy's economy. When we attack boats and trucks, we attack the enemy from a military perspective and, just as importantly, from an economic perspective too. We have to do everything in our power to boost the economy of our land, as part of our struggle, just as we've been trying to do, but more so, more and more every day, boost our economy even in a time of war, improve living conditions throughout the land. And we have to do our utmost so that we depend less and less each day on things that come from outside our land, in other words we have to try and become self-sufficient.

The Party issued important Guidelines regarding agricultural development, improving our production, increasing our agricultural output, making other things such as artisanal items, even to make more soap within our land, to try and develop our population's every cottage industry. This is all in our Party Guidelines. Why? To see if we can become self-sufficient. Our land has its own particular conditions, of course, some of which, unfortunately, severely limit the scope of what we can do in this field. We were already substantially behind the rest of the world, economically speaking, and being so far behind made successfully carrying out certain basic principles of economic resistance all but impossible, but that's no reason not to do the best we can. We cannot expect ourselves to be self-sufficient in terms of fabrics, for example, which our people are used to buying, as they are shoes, collars, needles, sewing machines etc., etc., things that count among the basic needs of our people, albeit needs created under colonialism. We cannot expect this because there are no factories that make these things in our land.

Numerous agricultural crops have never been introduced and they cannot be quickly established in a time of war. But we ought

THINK TO BETTER ACT, Vol. 1

to be able to get some of them going all the same. We cannot expect ourselves to be self-sufficient in medicines, even simple medicines, but there are other things we can in fact do. Increase rice production, increase manioc production, grow more potatoes and other types of produce, and safeguard production in all the areas of land we control, for example. Vastly increase production. This we can do and, given the circumstances of our struggle, it needs to be the bedrock of our economic resistance.

We must also, and I've already spoken about this, seek to develop our artisanal industries: earthenware, mats, cloths, weaves, etc. Our Party did some work in this area, but it didn't have the desired effect. Because in the midst of war, the situation in our land being what it is, certain supervisors forgot about our Guidelines in this respect—to develop production, to increase production, to multiply and diversify production, to vary our country's agricultural produce. We have achieved one or two successes, of course, there are areas where rice production has increased a lot, areas where more manioc is now being produced, where more potatoes are being grown, but we must nonetheless recognize that we are a long way off what we are capable of. While it is true that in some areas, Quinara, for example, local populations that did not previously farm are now farming, it is also true that other areas, where the local population used to farm a lot, are now farming less, because of the war. And the departure of so many people to Senegal has been, and continues to be, a great setback to our economic resistance. It is a setback because all these people who leave our land are potential farmhands who might be working in our liberated areas, but they go and work in Senegal instead, boosting the Senegalese economy and diminishing our own economy and our economic resistance against the Portuguese colonialists.

We must be clear and say that certain Party leaders and supervisors, at all levels, have not treated our economic resistance importantly enough. We have always said that it's not only the people who should work the land, that it's not enough to simply ask local populations to produce more, but that soldiers should also work the land and produce too. In the rainy season we have to mobilize all our available forces, make the entire population work harder, make soldiers plant, make the militias plant. In some areas this has been possible, but we have to recognize that in other areas, even where the soldiers have had little to do, because the area is liberated, they don't plant and they simply wait for the local population to provide them with food. And in some areas we have now reached a point where, because of a lack of rain the previous year, for example, the local population cannot provide them with food, the soldiers have grown nothing for themselves and they have to ask the Party leadership to send them food.

We must be clear and say to comrades that if, in order to fight the Portuguese colonialists, we have to provide food to our soldiers deep in the bush, then the Portuguese colonialists will be in our land for the next hundred years. And this will primarily be the fault of Party supervisors who have proved themselves incapable of getting soldiers to plant in planting season. Some soldiers won't even help the local population to plant when we've told them they must do.

Within the context of our economic resistance, we need to coordinate our work in order to safeguard our war economy and ensure we get supplies to the front, to our soldiers, and to our people, providing them with the necessary staples. Unfortunately, we face great difficulties in getting hold of staple products because we don't have enough money and, the situation in our land being what it is—whereby we have destroyed bridges, roads etc. and when we haven't got any cars anyway—even if it were possible to use the roads, we cannot establish an overseas trade that would allow us to sell things to the outside world and buy things in return. Providing the necessary staples to our population is, therefore, essentially a matter of relying on offerings and donations sent by our friends and allies. In the meantime, we must, and I've said this before, campaign daily to raise people's respect for those who work, make sure working is highly valued, convince the sons and daughters of our land that working the land is not something to be scorned, on the contrary, it's the noblest, healthiest, and most invaluable work anyone in the land can do right now. Unfortunately, in our African heads we still view work as an activity of little value, especially working the land—that anyone who works the land only does so to give themselves something to eat, that it's the work of the desperate. But we have to, within the context of our economic resistance, do a better political job of persuading our people, our population, all of us, that working the land, growing crops, is not just something you do in order to eat, but in order to provide the country with produce to export, to have plentiful things to sell and thus convert into other things—that growing things is the most important, most dignified, most invaluable work there is in our land, comrades, whether it be in Guinea or Cabo Verde.

Within the context of our economic resistance, we must be capable, today, but above all else tomorrow, of getting every social class in our country to produce a little bit more, of getting every ethnic group in Guinea, or every race, as we tend to say, to expand the range of products it produces. We cannot allow one ethnic group to just produce rice; they have to produce rice, corn, beans, manioc, etc., greens even, and other things like that, because we must improve our people's diet. The entire population of our land can and must produce everything; we have to develop a range of different crops everywhere in order to boost our productivity. And we must steadily urge, that's to say encourage, or coax, our most valued producers to produce even more. We have to develop friendships with our most enthusiastic and committed rice growers, show our appreciation for them, our commitment to them, turn these sons and daughters of our land into household names, hold them up as examples for others to follow.

We must gradually find a way to solve the problem of smallholder farming in our land, because at present our country, due to it being so far behind, doesn't really even have smallholders, not in Guinea. In Cabo Verde, the problem is different because there are a lot of smallholder farmers, albeit not as many as we'd like, because the majority are tenant or associate farmers. The fundamental problem is getting people to work together in these conditions. In Guinea, we'll have to set up cooperatives, bit by bit, at first fostering increased cooperation between families, and later selecting our best militants to manage the cooperatives as a whole, to develop a cooperative system, for this is, as we see it, the fastest way of developing our agricultural sector and, therefore, the future economy of our land.

And we should immediately start to experiment with properties previously controlled by the colonial state. This is why our Party issued orders for any farms or allotments abandoned by the enemy, or by those fleeing the war, to be taken over by the Party and run by designated management committees. But we have to admit that, in the vast majority of cases, comrades and supervisors have paid insufficient attention to these instructions, to our Party's Guidelines, and most of these farms and allotments have failed, thus far, to deliver the yields that ought to have been possible, nor have they been kept in the kind of conditions they ought to have. Some of them lie abandoned, full of straw, with crops withering away or spoiled, while others have been targeted with bombings by the Tugas, their bombs destroying our fruit trees and whatever else was there.

As part of our overall struggle, we must all be clearheaded about what our main area of activity is in terms of our economic resistance. Given our specific situation, as you all well know, our main activity is agriculture, we haven't anything else in our land. It's agriculture today, it will be agriculture tomorrow, and it may very well be agriculture for long after that. We therefore have to make every effort to advance our agricultural sector, raising political consciousness among our farmer comrades and among our countrymen farmhands, showing everyone that the agriculture route is the first and surest route to success and the advancement of our people. Furthermore, that taking the agricultural route today opens the way to our potentially developing industry tomorrow, to create a higher standard of living. But we have to make our agriculture as productive as possible first, for we are still some ways behind, conditioned by our African lives into thinking that agriculture is just subsistence farming, whereby everyone produces no more than what's needed to feed their own family. This is an agriculture with no surplus whatsoever, where nothing is saved for tomorrow, sometimes not even enough to plant for next season. And in economic terms, in the colonial context, agriculture was a means of exchange with the Tugas and no more, with them exploiting us, our people producing peanuts, harvesting coconuts, beeswax, and honey, to exchange with the Tugas or to sell them a bit of rice, and that was it. What little money this generated soon consumed itself and every year the sons and daughters of our land, the farmers and planters, started the season in the exact same miserable position they started the previous one, advancing not one iota. That's the nature of our agricultural sector.

In some places people used to say agriculture was the art of being poor but happy and carefree. In our case, agriculture will likely remain the art of being poor forever, unless we change the type of agriculture we do, unless we truly revolutionize our agricultural sector. We actually have pretty good agricultural conditions, both here in Guinea and in Cabo Verde, despite there being periods of drought in Cabo Verde, for this need not be disastrous to agriculture nowadays, not with all the scientific advances mankind has made and that anyone can make use of.

Only by making genuine advances in agriculture will our land become properly productive. We are sure that certain areas of our land can produce two, three, four, even ten times more than they produce now, if techniques are improved, if the soil is properly looked after, if seeds are carefully selected, if crops are properly cared for, if we put in a lot of good, hard work. In many areas of our land, were we to have fertilizer and manure, were agriculture to be combined with raising livestock, as it ought to be, then we might increase production dramatically, and in terms of agriculture, raising livestock, rearing livestock on a large scale, pedigree cattle—we can do it!—poultry, of every type—we can do it! If we truly have the will, we can do it, if we're truly committed, if everyone shows willingness and commitment and puts the work in. Our country cannot advance if we just raise a few chickens, if we just let a few chickens loose in the bush and then catch them when they're ready to eat or sell. That's not raising chickens, it's picking them the way you might pick *dênde*[1] or toll fruit off a tree out in the bush.

We have to truly improve all this before we can start thinking about how our country can advance in other areas. In industrial terms, for example. And we have to consider the specific issue of cattle raising, that's to say livestock, for it could provide us with tremendous riches, comrades, both in Guinea and in Cabo Verde. Guinea, within the overall African context, is among the countries with the highest density of livestock, but Cabo Verde, despite the occasional droughts and lack of rain, is capable even now of exporting leather, of exporting hides to Portugal and other places. So, as we can see, we must, starting from now, lead our lives down the agricultural route and, precisely so that our agriculture can properly advance, develop our cattle raising.

Unfortunately, due to this war, in the midst of our struggle, we have not given due attention to this aspect of our work, we have not controlled our livestock riches. A lot of our livestock in the North went to Senegal with the refugees, to the great satisfaction of our Senegalese brothers. Other people moved to the Kundara area. The Tugas then feasted on our cows in a frenzy, they've even exported our

---

1   Palm oil

cows. But we ourselves, supervisors and leaders, have not paid this sufficient attention, have not worked properly with local populations and shown them how important it is that we preserve our livestock riches. Today, hardly any of our chickens and goats are eaten by the chiefs of post and sepoys, thankfully, but what have we done so far to preserve our animals, to look after them properly, to get our people to take better care of them, to handle the matter better?

Our political, security, and health commissars and supervisors have not given a moment's thought to our livestock riches, with one or two exceptions, obviously. I could mention, for example, the case of one of our supervisors who, in an area where there are calving cows, where all the cows are calving cows, wrote to me asking me to send milk because two children had been born and they didn't have any milk to give them, when in actual fact, anywhere there are calving cows, there is milk. He might have found milk for the children in any house where cows were calving, so I sent word back telling him to go out and find some cows to milk because I certainly wasn't sending any. And he managed it. Comrades often don't think for themselves, don't consider the context, as in this case and many others, unfortunately. They want to have things easy, whereas if we work at it, we could have milk whenever we want it in our land. We might even make cheese in the liberated areas, we could make butter in the liberated areas, it's not that hard, anyone out there can be taught to make butter.

During the rainy season, for example, you cannot plant onions, but in the dry season, which is coming up in November, you can; any army unit, no matter where it is, can find a spot by their hut to set aside as a vegetable patch and plant onions, garlic. All you have to do is designate a couple of comrades to keep an eye on things, near a river so they can be watered properly. This could be in Corubal just as much as it could be in Candjambari or anywhere else, we can grow things throughout the land, near a spring in the south, in Cubisecco, or in Quinara, or in any other spot. But no one does this because they just wait for the Party to send whatever they need. They forget that this is just wasting time, precious time that could be spent on helping our people to advance, on helping our struggle to advance, instead of on satisfying basic needs.

We must admit that our Party has not achieved any major successes in this area, beyond the fact that there are more rice fields in a few places, rice production has increased a bit, manioc and a few other things are being farmed more than they were. There has been moderate success in terms of the political work of persuading local populations to grow things they're not accustomed to growing, but no more than moderate success because our supervisors have not afforded due importance to the matter of developing our economy as much as we possibly can. We're not asking for miracles, just doing what's possible.

We are an agricultural country, we must get everyone to grow things—local populations, troops, even schoolchildren, they must grow things too. We issued orders, for example, for every school to have a field for growing produce. It's still very unusual to find a school that uses its field for growing produce, but supervisors go there, see this and say nothing; leaders go there, see this and say nothing. And the result is that we even have to send rice to our boarding schools for the children to eat. We might very well ask ourselves: What are these children doing there? What is the point of teaching them to read if they cannot work a patch of land? We cannot let our people fall into bad habits. We want to learn to read, to learn about everything, but we have to work to become self-sufficient first because no one else in the world is going to provide us with food, and a people incapable of feeding itself cannot aspire to anything else in life.

We must, of course, avoid all luxuries, all fineries and fripperies, during our struggle, our war. And what little we have, in our people's warehouses, we have to manage to ration properly, to distribute fairly so that the greatest possible number of people can benefit from a resource the Party has created.

And we should already be making plans for our country's economy under independence. We cannot just leave it until tomorrow, we have to start today, all of us. The Party has to properly understand the specific possibilities of our land, in every branch of the economy, and make conscientious, science-based plans for the development of our country. If we aren't capable of doing this, of establishing what specific economic path we need to take for our country to advance, of establishing an economic policy specific to our land, then we are getting ourselves killed and running ourselves into the ground for nothing; our bodies will be wounded and our lives pointlessly ruined, because of our inability to generate the revenues required to advance, to move our people forward as we promised them we would after all the sacrifices we asked them to make for this war.

We must, therefore, today and tomorrow, in terms of our economic resistance, channel our efforts towards the following aim: to increase output of every kind of product throughout the land and to increase that output ever more by the day. We must be capable of getting the maximum out of our land, out of every patch of land the country has to give. We have to be economical, in other words increase our gains and reduce our expenses.

This is something comrades find hard to understand, even today, when our Party has practically no income, aside from selling a few kola nuts, or selling a few lizard or crocodile skins. The Party has practically no income, yet comrades are not in the least bit careful, they pay not the least attention to the fact that we have so little to spend. Whatever we give certain comrades flows through their hands like water in the Rio Corubal or Rio Geba. Come on, let's spend, it'll never run out! This happens even with things of great importance, like munitions. We've proved ourselves incapable of rationing our arms properly, our munitions. A good many weapons spoil through lack of care, munitions are wasted for lack of care and excessive usage.

But we do understand, all of this is a new experience, a new war, in our land, we're able to accept that, given the context, difficulties and inefficiencies are inevitable. But there are other instances, like with petrol, like with medicine, even with rice in areas that do not produce rice, for example, where, as many comrades know, things like this happen: a group of soldiers have to take rice with them because in the area where they're going, like the border zones, it's not possible to get rice from the local population. We have rice available at the moment so we give them two months' worth of rice. And what happens then is that they eat this rice within twenty days, all of it. How is this possible when we have no income? We have to put a stop to this, comrades.

Another important matter in the context of our economy is, of course, transport. It's a difficult issue to tackle at present because we are at war; we're in the midst of war and trying to destroy the enemy's economy; we're destroying roads and if we can destroy every last possible means for the enemy to move around our country, by road or by river, then all the better, for we haven't destroyed everything yet.

This is good for us on the one hand, but it's bad for us on the other, because if we wish to develop our economy in certain areas, we'll find we cannot, because we have no roads. We don't have time to tarmac roads, etc. But we should still start thinking about the issue today, as something to be tackled tomorrow. And we must think seriously about the benefits of ensuring a fluvial means of transport, that's to say river transport, because our land in Guinea is rich in channels, in waterways that we can move our produce along, and we should create new possibilities in this regard tomorrow. And at the same time, we have to think about the possibility of ensuring there are water links between our continental land and our Bijagós islands, between our continental land and our Cabo Verde islands. Because only when a land's communications network flows like blood around a human body can a country truly advance.

A transport system, its communications network, is as important to a country that wishes to advance as blood vessels, arteries, etc. are to a human body. We must give due thought to this, starting today, and indeed we've been thinking about it all year. But that doesn't mean we shouldn't do everything we can to safeguard our transport now. The Party has done its utmost to provide trucks to bring supplies to our people, to provide boats to bring supplies to our people. We're possibly the only liberation struggle in the world where supplies are delivered to certain areas by boat. Our Party has managed to safeguard this, despite the difficulties, despite the total lack of care comrades pay to our equipment. But in our interior, especially in Guinea, where we are already at war, we have to be able to safeguard our means of transport too. Can this not be done via the roads? We have lots of rivers, let's make sure there are enough canoes, let's build more canoes. The Tugas understand this so clearly that one of their main jobs is to go around smashing up our canoes. So we must be more resolute. For a start, we must not allow the Tugas to smash up our canoes, we must hide them. The canoes we use for transporting our materials, be it goods or people, must be hidden properly after use. Unfortunately, many comrades go down the river in their canoes and just leave them there, right where the Tugas can find them and smash them up. There are thousands of ways to hide a canoe. But if, through bad luck, the Tugas do manage to smash our canoes, then we must put more people to work building new ones, get people who know how to do wood-

work to build some more. We never lack boats in Boé. Why? Because
we gave Idrissa one job, to build canoes. But in other areas, the Tugas
have smashed our canoes and, although some comrades thankfully do
find ways of resolving this, of getting hold of more canoes, others send
me telegrams—Cabral, the Tugas smashed our canoe—and what am I
supposed to do, when he's the supervisor, he's there, he's in charge of
the local population, he's in charge of the soldiers? Why doesn't he get
someone to build canoes?

Many comrades think we should get motorboats, and in fact we
do have a few, but we cannot solve the problem this way because we
can't just buy boats to put everywhere. We have made a big effort to
get motorboats for some areas, boats with outboard motors, and we
still have a few outboard motors. But the fact is that in some areas, like
Quiláfine, for example, comrades completely wrecked the motor in a
matter of days. I myself went to Ghana to buy new motors, but they
were all wrecked within the month because comrades chose to play
with them rather than use them only when required. And comrades
pay no heed to the following simple rule: to use a motor you must mix
gasoline and oil. But no, they haven't any oil so they just put gasoline
in and off they go, wherever they want. This, comrades, is disastrous
from an economic point of view. Then they say they have no supplies
because they have no means of transporting them. This just cannot be.

Another form of transport we could make good use of in this
war is the bicycle, like the Vietnamese did. Our country has certain
characteristics that make it a little more difficult, perhaps, but our
land generally resembles Vietnam a lot. We've experimented with this.
We've got comrades to transport things by bike, but the bikes all broke
after a few days. Some comrades even stopped riding them halfway
through their journey and put the bikes on their heads, carried them
like that. Why? They said they weren't used to them. It can be difficult
to push a bike but it has been proven, by the experience of people elsewhere, that one bicycle, well-operated, well-prepared, with poles to
support the load, can carry 250 kilos. A man can't even carry 20 kilos.
We can deliver supplies to areas of our land, many areas, just by using
bikes. Of course, it's difficult, sometimes rivers have to be crossed,
flooded areas etc. It's difficult, but we can use bikes.

If we give a bicycle to a comrade to go, for example, from the
border to Cubacaré, the journey can be done by bike, but with a load

it's difficult, that's the problem. The bicycle could be a brilliant means of transport in our land, but we need our comrades in the vanguard to help, we need our more enlightened vanguard comrades to set the example, to stick at it, to show that it's possible. Then we can be like the Vietnamese people who were able to carry loads over long distances just by bicycle, until they defeated the enemy.

I remember, for example, a great thing our comrades did in the south of our land. We wanted to get some heavy artillery to Cubucaré and Tombali. It was very difficult to carry because these weapons weighed over 15 kilos. So our comrades built a raft and traveled up the Rio Balana to the border to collect the weapons and took them back that way. This just goes to show that when we want to be, when we really put our minds to it, we're capable of anything. We are capable of doing great things, things like this. How many times has the Rio Farim been blocked off, but comrades have managed to find a way through, to get past, because they had to, because a supervisor comrade said: come on, keep going, toughen up. Unfortunately, not all comrades are like this. We could do with more of them, given all our responsibilities, given all the things we need to do to advance our fight.

The issue of transport is an issue we have raised with comrades many times. No one can expect the Party leadership to send supply trucks into the interior of our country. There are some parts where we have entered with trucks, but they were very particular circumstances. Party supervisors have to be capable of resolving transport issues themselves. It's incredible, for example, incredible that Sector 2 on the Eastern Front sometimes lacks munitions but no other sector makes any effort to get munitions to them. There are munitions available, in vast quantities in some areas, and so the only reason there are munitions shortages in other places is that comrades can't be bothered to go and help others solve a problem. Even with rice, in some areas there's an abundance of rice, in other areas there's very little, but it's very unusual to see rice being taken from one place to the next because it doesn't even enter people's heads to try and find solutions to such issues. It is done sometimes, yes, but all that proves is that it could always be done if we so wanted. It's a matter of showing determination, dedication and interest, of turning thoughts into actions in order to better serve our Party.

Overcoming Our Weaknesses

To advance with our struggle we must, in terms of our economic resistance, avoid overburdening our people lest they start to think our Party wants to exploit them too. We have always issued comrades with Party Guidelines that say do not take people's belongings, people's chickens, people's cows. If things are given to us, fine, we accept them, but we must never demand things, we must never take anything by force. This rule has not always been well respected, not always. We must be aware that anyone who seeks to exploit our people like this is a criminal, that they benefit the Tugas, that they are enemies of our people and our Party. When these things occur, we need to know exactly who acted against our people so that they can be reprimanded and indeed shot, if necessary, even if they're a chief or a supervisor. Some comrades have made a big effort to prevent abuses being committed against our people. Some Party leaders have tried hard to prevent abuses, but not all: some. And some supervisors have tried hard to prevent them too. But we have to put a stop to abusive behavior of every kind in our country. We have to reduce the excessive burden on our people and show them that we do not mean, and never will mean, to cause them harm.

Furthermore, we need to encourage those in our land who produce the most, find ways to reward them with praise, with prizes, with awards. We want to see the following happen in our country tomorrow: for the names we most celebrate to be the names of people who produce the most. Whoever produces the most rice, the most palm oil, the most peanuts, etc. in the country, a person, a family, a cooperative, whoever it is, we must hail their name, give them prizes, proclaim them the best citizens in the land. And we have to come down hard on those who don't work to help our country get what it needs to get out of the land, as part of our economic resistance.

Of course, we'll have other problems to deal with in the future, important ones, like developing and stabilizing our internal market, commerce within our country, or like developing as much trade as possible with other countries, establishing, in other words, an entire system of international trade, or like looking into pricing issues within our country. Sometimes we're so engaged in the struggle that we think it's just a matter of killing the Tugas, of fighting them and taking over the country. But the biggest issues lie ahead of us, comrades. We have to be clear in our understanding of who's going to control our country's commerce. Our commerce remains in the hands of the Tugas for now, it's our land but the Tugas still control our imports and exports. This is something we will have to establish for ourselves in the future. Our Party will have to be clear in its planning of this, to avoid any confusion and to cut off, right from the start, any attempts at exploiting our people.

And we have to combat, starting now, any mistaken ideas about our economy. One major mistake we're still making today is the following: no one pays any taxes now that they've been liberated. This is a mistake. We have to be able, after we've liberated an area like Cubucaré, for example, to quickly establish what taxes people should pay. Taxes don't even have to be in money form, they might be in kind, as it's called, which means paying taxes in the form of produce, just so our people don't lose the habit of paying taxes, so that nobody thinks there will no longer be taxes to pay once we've taken control of the country. No country in the world can advance without taxes. This has been a mistake. But it has been a necessary mistake, in the context of a mentality that wasn't yet truly nationalistic. We, as a people, were yet to acquire consciousness as a nation. And in terms of land, if we had, at the same time as liberating Cubucaré, started collecting taxes there, then maybe the people would have sided with the Tugas. That's why we made this mistake, but we have to explain this to people, to clearly say, as we in fact have always said, that they may not be paying taxes today, but they will have to start paying them again tomorrow. Most of our people know this, they already understand this. But we must explain that the taxes they'll pay tomorrow will not be the same as the taxes they paid to the Tugas. Not in terms of the basis, that's to say the criteria, the rules governing who pays what taxes, nor in terms of expenditure, that's to say what the taxes are used for. Tax revenues in our land must be used to raise our people's standard of living, in economic, social and cultural terms.

We must always have a plan if we want our economic resistance to triumph, a plan designed to triumph over the Tugas today and our underdevelopment tomorrow, to triumph over our country being so far behind. We must gain a full understanding of our land's particular conditions, here in Guinea and in Cabo Verde, in order to make specific plans to advance our country's development. Otherwise, it's like entering a room in the dark and crashing into everything, knocking the furniture over, banging our heads against the wall, walking straight into it face-first, having no idea what we're doing. This is vitally important if we are to triumph tomorrow, comrades, vitally important in the context of our economic resistance. We must avoid, now and in the future, any obsession with making extravagant plans. We must do what is possible, at every stage of our evolution, this is something we really must understand.

We must avoid, or clamp down on, people standing around with their arms folded. Today and tomorrow in our country, everyone capable of working must work. People who don't work have no right to anything in our country, that's the way it has to be. People of worth, work; people who don't work are worthless. And the best people are those who work the most. That's the way it has to be in our country and it should be the same with our struggle too. At this stage of our life as a party, we have to move the hardest-working comrades to the front and let no one be in any doubt about the following: those who proved their worth by working hard yesterday move forward. But those who stop working today because they worked hard yesterday are of no worth to us, and never were of any worth. I often say that in terms of our Party's work, everyone is like a stalk on a banana tree, for you have to produce bananas every year. You can't think that because you were a stalk last year that you've done your bit, no. Everyone is capable of becoming another stalk. With the banana tree, every stalk that produces fruit has to be cut back to let a fresh stalk grow, to bear more fruit. It's the same with our lives and with the Party.

Nobody should think they can sleep in the shadow of the work they did yesterday. There are a number of comrades in our Party who think that because they put a lot of work in during mobilization, because they put a lot of work in during the early stages of the guerrilla struggle, because at a particular moment they put a lot of work in securing supplies, because they were good leaders of the guerrilla forces or the army etc. they can shrug their shoulders today, skulk and skive off work, put their lives on hold, hide themselves away at some base or even beyond our borders. We cannot have this, comrades. In our Party nobody wins unless we all give more every day; more work, more sacrifice, more willingness, and more determination.

Another serious issue in our Party, in our struggle, is the following: some comrades have been wounded but are now fit again, because thank God (we say thank God, but also thanks to our Party) out of every 500 wounded comrades, say, 480 recover and can, therefore, go back and fight. But there's now a tendency for the following to happen: I'm wounded, I'll turn my injury into something more serious so that I can stop fighting. I went to Ziguinchor, I was lucky enough to get as far as Conakry, I didn't die, I was slightly wounded, now I'll fight no more.

No, comrades, this is demobilization, it's deserting. In any country where people have gained political consciousness, in any struggle where soldiers fight with consciousness, taking a beating gives them more courage, more of a will to fight, because they are now not only defending a cause they believe in, they are now determined to make the enemy pay for what they did to them. In other countries, there are soldiers who have lost legs and beg for artificial legs so that they can go back and fight. In other countries, there are political commissars who have been, for example, wounded in the arm, the doctor tells them to rest for six months so that the arm can heal and they tell the doctor to cut the arm off, for that way they can recover in two weeks and return to the fight. Because a political commissar needs a head but he can do without his arms.

But in our country, there are commissars who are lucky enough to hurt no more than a finger, yet that's enough of an excuse for them to stop, they can't go on.

Comrades, thankfully the majority of our people are not like that, I know it's not everyone. Thankfully we have many comrades with bullets lodged in their bodies who are so firmly committed to our work that sometimes we're the ones who have to persuade them to withdraw from the front line. There are comrades who have been wounded three times, four times, who are firmly committed to our struggle, more enthusiastic by the day, more courageous. They are the custodians of our Party, comrades, they are the true sons and daughters of our people, the future custodians of our land, no question. They are the new leaders and I, for one, say this to them: comrades, you give me strength. Some of them are sitting here now. You give us all strength and vindicate all the sacrifices we're making to move forward. There are other wounded comrades who are not here today such as, for example, Comrade Kemo, who was wounded. He hadn't recovered yet but there was an attack and he went back to join it, isn't that right, comrades? We sent him to Europe for treatment and all he wanted was to get back as quickly as possible. And in fact, the day I went to visit him, in the country where he was being treated, I found him at the airport, ready to come straight back to the bush, no questions asked, no demands. Because there are others who get wounded or are taken sick and use it as an opportunity to demand things of the Party, like asking the Party to pay them. But those comrades who ask for nothing, who give us their effort, their energy, their all, are not only serving the armed struggle, the political struggle, they're contributing to our economic resistance too, in the face of an enemy that we must destroy economically.

Indeed, we must avoid any squandering, by which I mean spending where we can economize. We must avoid this, especially with food, for example, even at our schools, our rest houses and other places, there is sometimes a lot of food left over, a lot of rice, and people come and get these leftovers to use as pig feed. Why don't we make more of an effort to measure out the right amount of rice, enough for every comrade while also rationing the Party's rice supply? Comrades in Conakry, or Zinguinchor, who use cars, drive round and round as much as they like, when they could get all their things done in just a few trips. Besides, there are others driving around too, they could go in the same car at the same time with another person, but they refuse to do this, they even hide so that they can then go out on their own later. They don't understand that this is just wasting petrol and creating problems for the Party.

In our economic resistance we have to clamp down on any sneakiness, robbery, and bribery, any corrupt people who make the most of every opportunity to steal, be it money the Party has given to them to administer—for a rest house or boarding school—or other things like cows, taking them and sending them to be sold beyond our borders, for example. This is a form of robbery too. We must clamp down hard on this, comrades. We must proclaim our respect and consideration for those Party comrades who have never been tempted to do any of these things, quite the opposite in fact, those whose behavior has always been exemplary and who've sought to help others stay clean.

We Africans have a reputation, because of our underdevelopment, whereby it's assumed that everyone in a position of responsibility, for resources, money and other such things, is on the take. And the kind of things we've seen happen in other independent African countries ought to make us nervous. So too should things that have happened here, with our own comrades even, a few at least. This makes us nervous, comrades, very nervous. We must remind comrades, supervisors, and soldiers for the most part, that taking things from the enemy at a time of war, though justified, is still stealing. I'm not talking about taking things from our people in the villages, for there's no justifying that, I'm talking about taking things from the enemy at a time of war and keeping them for yourself. That is stealing and the first step to becoming a crook.

Our soldiers are honest people, reliable, decent, dignified, the best sons and daughters of our land. Therefore, when one of our soldiers takes a watch, a bracelet, a gold chain or whatever, takes it from the enemy, he must show it to his chief, his leader, he mustn't just keep it, because if he does then he's no longer a soldier fighting to liberate his country, he's a highwayman. Some comrades don't understand this, they don't understand how much, in the eyes of those of us who are serious about the Party's work, they fall in our estimation when they hang some great big gold medallion around their neck, taken from some village or some encounter with the enemy. Many comrades don't understand this, but they really fall down in our estimation. Even wristwatches—of course, if someone takes a wristwatch in a war they can keep it, but they must show it to their chief first, get permission from their chief to keep it. And if he already has a wristwatch and wants to keep a new one, he must first give his old one to a comrade who hasn't got a watch. But no, some comrades take things and keep quiet, and in this way, they show that they're still not conscious of their own worth, of the work they're doing, the sacrifice they're making. They value a watch more than they value themselves, when tomorrow they'll be able to acquire, and honestly, as many watches as they want. We have to stop this, comrades.

And in economic terms, as in any other terms, we have to clamp down on extremist tendencies, such as comrades who say: "Let's force our people to do a job." No, comrades. Make our people grow things by force: no. It might even work, but we still don't want it, we don't want any extremism, it shows a lack of understanding for the present and the future of our struggle. And especially in terms of our future, when planning for our life tomorrow, we must avoid all extremism, everything over-the-top, any ambitions to be excessively progressive. For example, there may be comrades who put things the following way: "We are somewhat behind in our country when it comes to agriculture, while everyone else wants to give up on agriculture; England became developed and now few people work in agriculture, the same way that as France advanced its number of farmers declined and its industry grew. We can see that the way countries advance today is through heavy industry, so we too, in Guinea and Cabo Verde, post-independence, should give up on agriculture and focus on heavy industry." But we must likewise be vigilant so as not to make the very opposite mistake, for there are those who think the following: "We should leave our country as it is, this is the way it's meant to be, we're Africans, we must have our *régulos*, people who work the land for them, people who sell things, etc., because then we'll be good Africans with our traditions, our customs, where the Balanta grow rice, the Fula grow peanuts, the Felupe grow rice, the Manjaco grow peanuts, and rice and other things, the Bijagós pick coconuts, the Caboverdeans produce corn, only to then die of hunger when there is no corn." No, this is the opposite end of extremism and we don't want this either. To put it in the language of today, what I described first is to lurch to the left and what I described second is to lurch to the right. This doesn't mean the center is necessarily best. A lot of people think the center is best but that's not true, what's best is knowing how to make the most of both sides in order to move forward. Finding the best path through an area of land doesn't mean going straight down the middle, you don't necessarily get anywhere by sticking to the center. But this is a complicated discussion to save for another day.

We must, then, in terms of our economic resistance, as with our other forms of resistance, overcome our weaknesses and constantly improve on our strengths. Cut out our weaknesses and nurture our strengths.

3. CULTURAL RESISTANCE

We must remember that it's not enough just to grow things, fill your belly, have good policies, and wage war. If a man or woman does all this without advancing as an intelligent human being, the primary being in nature, without sensing that their knowledge of the environment they live in, and the world in general, is growing by the day, without, in other words, advancing in a cultural sense, then everything that man or woman does—grow things, enact good politics, fight—amounts to nothing.

In our specific situation we have to pay particular attention to our cultural resistance. Our Party has paid considerable attention to this right from the start and launched a number of important initiatives, beginning with the Cassacá Congress, although we were advising people on the need to support our struggle through cultural resistance way before that. Indeed, it might be said that the very creation of our Party, which planned and advanced our national liberation struggle, was a cultural act in itself. Our very existence is a clear demonstration of cultural resistance, evidence that we want to be ourselves, Africans from Guinea and Cabo Verde, and not Tugas. Our culture is not the Tugas' culture, although our culture nowadays has some influences from Tuga culture. Therefore, every politically conscious soldier, supervisor, and militant should clearly understand that fighting the enemy is also a form of cultural resistance, indeed the armed struggle is possibly our primary act of cultural resistance.

A New Culture for Our People

We have to work hard to erase colonial culture from our heads, comrades. And whether we like it or not, in the city or in the bush, colonialism has filled our heads with a lot of things. Our work, therefore, should be to get rid of everything harmful and keep everything useful. Because not everything colonialism gave us is harmful. We must be able, therefore, to erase colonial culture from our heads while keeping those elements of human and scientific culture that the Tugas also brought to our land, inadvertently, that also ended up in our heads.

A specific example: I am African, maybe I think, like other Africans still do, that in order for certain things to happen in my life I need to satisfy the will of the *irã*. I go to talk to the *irã* and he tells me that whatever it is I want will only happen if I offer him a little girl, no more than three rainy seasons old, for him to kill and use in a sacrifice. This kind of thing still occurs in Africa, indeed if we look properly there are probably still people in our land who believe in this stuff. I remember a comrade called Alfucene who we sent to fight in Gabú—remember, Lúcio? One day he came to tell me that the *irã* in Gabú didn't want us fighting there unless his son was sacrificed first. I interpreted this in the following manner: Alfucene, who was originally from Gabú, was trying to find a way of becoming chief there, he wanted to be the chief of Gabú and so he wanted it to look like the *irã* was interested in his son, and therefore he should become chief. I said to him: Comrade, if this is how we're going to fight in Gabú then let's find this *irã* and kill him, because he's the Tugas' *irã*, the Tugas installed him, he's not of our land.

But it could be that I, as an African, still have this kind of thing in my head. There are children being killed right now, as I speak, in certain parts of Africa in order to satisfy the will of the *irã*. I never had this stuff in my head. I grew up in Africa, but I learned the following: "Children are the most wonderful and delicate things in the world. We must give our children the very best of what we've got. We must educate them to grow up free-spirited, to understand things, to be good and kind, to avoid all wickedness. We must, therefore, never cause them harm, much less kill them." I am therefore obliged to defend my country from people who get this kind of cultural thing in their heads.

But I, though I am African, have also had a lot of contact with the Tugas, so maybe I've got it into my head that I'm a child of civilized people, that I am civilized; I went to school, I never lived in the bush, the bush is dirty, I had a decent house even though my mother was poor. Maybe I think I've got nothing in common with people in the bush, that our brothers and sisters in the bush are backward and I'm superior to them. This is the colonial mentality, copying the mentality of the Tugas, the colonialists. We have to erase this, from my head and everyone else's.

I will, therefore, provide some concrete examples of what we should preserve from the contact we've had with other realities, and what we should erase from the contact we've had with our own reality. This will enable comrades to understand what our cultural resistance consists of. Because our cultural resistance consists of the following: removing colonial culture and the negative aspects of our own culture from our spirit and environment, while at the same time creating a new culture, one that is based on our traditions but that respects everything the world has achieved for the good of mankind.

A lot of people think that for Africa to resist culturally it has to do the same things it did five hundred years ago or a thousand years ago. Yes, Africa has its culture, we're firmly of that belief ourselves. Some aspects of that culture are eternal, they never end—they might be endlessly transformed along the way, but they never end. Our types of dance, for example, we have our own African rhythms. But nobody should think that the drum is solely an African thing, that certain types of dress are only to be found in Africa, straw skirts, palm leaf skirts, etc.; nobody should think that eating with your hands is solely an African thing, that sitting on the ground only happens in Africa. People all over the world go through periods like this, there are still people elsewhere in the world, in Brazil, for example, who are worse than us for some of these things, as there are in Indonesia, Polynesia, the Far East.

A lot of people think that to defend African culture, for Africa to culturally resist, we have to defend the negative things about our culture. No, we're not of that opinion. Because culture is also a product of a people's level of economic development. Our opinion is that eating with your hands, and even singing certain types of songs or dancing a particular way, depends on the lives people lead, what crops people grow, what riches they produce, what things they make. This is why Balanta songs are different from Mandinga songs, for example. When analyzed, Balanta songs, deep down, are songs about men on the plain. If we compare Balanta songs to European songs, we'll see how similar they are to Alentejo songs, slow and choral. Because there are certain types of economic lives and geographical environments that produce certain types of songs. People who live in the mountains have certain types of song, people who live with livestock have their own particular way of dancing, people who live in the woods, on their own, with no livestock, have a different kind of dance. People who live in the savannah, where there are giraffes and other things, have another kind of dance. That's the way it is, be it in Africa, Asia, or the Americas.

And so too does the type of relationship we have with nature vary according to our economy, our economic development. People who believe cows are gods, honor cows in their dances. The dance will represent God as a cow. But people who think God hides in the forest will perform a dance that shows their respect for the forest, their songs will have a certain kind of music and lyrics related to this. This scenario is repeated everywhere in the world, wherever there are particular economic conditions and a particular situation prevails related to nature. People who are still afraid of lightning bolts, thunderclaps, and flooding rivers will have the same kinds of songs and dances. There may be one or two differences, but they will be similar. Of course, if we compare our dances to European dances, to city dances, etc., we'll find not the least resemblance, but these are ultramodern dances; if we compare our dances to folkloric dances, let's say, the arts and customs of people from eastern Europe, and even more so, from Asia, we'll find dances that are very similar to our own, comrades.

Our point of view is, then, that we must show resistance to preserve what is genuinely helpful and constructive from our culture, but in the knowledge that as we advance, our clothes, our eating habits, our ways of dancing and singing, everything about us will inevitably, gradually change, especially inside our heads, especially in our relationship to nature, and even in our relationship to one another.

For example, we Africans are in a situation whereby we need protection because we still haven't dominated nature. So we need what is known as organic security. Organic security means the more people we have around us, the more secure we feel. If I'm out in the bush on my own, I'm afraid, but if I'm with several other people, I feel better. But there's a contradictory side to this rule of organic security, and that's when you don't trust the people around you. Our security needs are such that we always need someone beside us, but because security cannot be guaranteed, and because our need for security is so great, we start to distrust those we are with. And so, what happens in our environment, even with people we trust, is this: yesterday you trusted them, but when they come along today and offer you their hand, you don't trust them. You take their hand, but now you're suspicious. Some people might even wash their own hand afterwards, for fear of catching something. They might even be suspicious of eyes. And there are people who take advantage of this by popping out their eyes. I remember our comrade Luciano, strong, brave, a little confrontational sometimes, who was chief of our rest house when we were training comrades. There was this miserable creature in Conakry who was obsessed with his being Muslim and who sided with the opportunists of the moment. He was a nasty piece of work, truth be told, and Luciano was very afraid of him, he didn't want to have anything to do with him, unless it was to beat him up. One day the man came by our rest house, Luciano advanced on him, berating him etc. Then the man pulled out a horn, pointed it at Luciano and said to him, "Ah!" Luciano backed away immediately, afraid of the horn.

Comrades, we laugh about this now, but a number of comrades sitting here are still afraid of horns. Today, we laugh even though we're afraid, but rest assured that tomorrow the sons and daughters of our land, in Guinea and in Cabo Verde, where there is also a lot of fear (don't let the young fellas from São Vicente and Praia who come here with their own pretensions make you think there isn't also fear in the bush in Cabo Verde, or fear of marabouts—once, when I fell sick, my mother took me to see the marabout because she thought someone must have wished me ill—fear of how the cards fall, fear of hair—they make charms out of hair to free themselves from evil), but rest assured that tomorrow in Cabo Verde, just as much as in Guinea, the sons and daughters of our people will not be afraid of horns. A horn is just something that's rich in calcium and grows on the heads of certain animals, that's all it is, comrades. If we burn it, it has a particular smell, due to the proteins and other chemical properties it has. A horn does nothing. But today, it doesn't matter how loud I shout this, no one listens, you don't believe me. And I'd be a fool to try and argue with you over this, I know. So all I'll say is this: fight tough and work hard, because the sons and daughters of your sons and daughters are not going to believe in things like this, not if we fulfill our duty to our people, not if we do it properly. Because the Swedes, those two who you see sitting over there, the parents of the parents of their parents also believed in horns. And the way people were buried in ancient Sweden was the same as the way people are buried in our country today. They buried their kings in ancient times, in ancient Sweden, the same way we bury our kings, their kings took all their belongings with them to their graves, just like ours, that's when their wives weren't killed and put in the grave too. The Vikings, who are the ancestors of today's Swedes, never went to war without their charms. One day we were in Cuba, Osvaldo and I, sitting watching a Viking film on TV. I'd seen enough films about the Vikings by then, but Osvaldo was watching it. Suddenly the warriors appeared and Osvaldo said: Look, comrade, they've got loads of amulets! Well of course, nobody should think that we Africans are so smart we thought of amulets and no one else did, and because we've got amulets we can go to war. The Vikings loved their lucky charms; the Franks, comrades, the people of ancient France, when they fought Caesar of Rome, they covered themselves in lucky charms. The ancient English did, American Indians too. In China, Mao Zedong had his work cut out trying to end the use of charms and even today it hasn't entirely stopped, witchcraft hasn't stopped in China. There are ethnic groups in China that use spells. If we read Vietnamese books, we'll see that witchcraft exists in Vietnam too. One of the great Vietnamese chiefs said that they had to let people carry lucky charms in order to get them to fight. Some people shave their heads—we too shave ours before doing certain things, we make a ceremony of it, even when we know for certain that it's wrong, applying only the tiniest bit of rationality to avoid trouble.

No one should think that because these things exist here among us, because we are Africans, we are superior to other people, that we know about charms and no one else does. The *lopé* loincloth, people all over the world have used loincloths, some people still use them today, all over the place. The *bubu*, a cloth worn in the Ghanian style, they had much the same thing in ancient Rome. Look at films about the Romans, they called their cloths "togas," but it was a cloth like any other. Sandals and cloths, that's all they wore. But today people go about in cloths as if you only get them in Africa, as if we Africans are the only people who know what a cloth is. This is a consequence of our state of economic development, no more than that. It's good, it's ours, but we can't go around thinking it's anything more than that. The day will come when the sons and daughters of the sons and daughters of your sons and daughters will forget about all this. It's just a shame we won't live long enough to see it. They'll be like us today when we look back at the way the Vikings lived, thinking them fools, failing to comprehend that the Vikings lived their own lives in their own era. They didn't do anything without checking with their warlock first. The king never went anywhere without his warlock by his side. Before the Romans went to war, they cut open the stomach of a chicken to see if it was an opportune moment to fight. There were even people who were called "augurs" who the chiefs consulted to find out if they should go to war or not.

In ancient Greece, which was the center of the civilized world, witches who lived in the mountains, called "pythia," were consulted to learn of the destiny of wars, people's lives, etc., and people brought them offerings, because God was among them. It's like with our *irã* in Cobiana, comrades. But this was three thousand years ago in Greece. Even longer ago in Egypt, in ancient Egypt, where all the Pharaohs had their own witches and God was a bull, the Bull of Apis, so the cow was untouchable, because the cow was sacred, like it is today in India. In India, they don't eat beef; there are people who die of hunger sitting beside their cow, because the cow cannot be killed, for the cow is God. They take their cows to the river to wash them, and everyone goes into the water with the cow, to wash in God's water.

We have to understand all this properly in order to base our cultural resistance on what our cultural resistance should really be about. We have to erase from our country all the harmful influences of colonial culture, comrades. And the first cultural act we must perform in our land is the following: unite our people, develop a new sense of patriotism in each and every one of us, and make this patriotism, this love for our country, inseparable from our need to fight. This is the first part of the culture we must establish in our country.

And we must show the value in resisting the enemy, the foreigner in our land. Show that we are joining forces to stop our people, the sons and daughters of our land, from being downtrodden and humiliated by another people. We need to make sure that it is clearly understood that we have the same rights in our own land as anyone else has in their land. This will be a huge leap forward for our culture if we manage it, and we will manage it, very soon, because the war itself will do it for us.

Furthermore, comrades, we must foster a spirit of heroism in each and every one of us, but especially in our soldiers, the courage to rigorously follow our Party's Guidelines. If the enemy needs to be killed in a certain place, then go there and kill him dead. This has to be our culture, comrades. Only when a man is capable of doing this is he truly cultured. And when a group of men and women like those gathered here today, faced with a given fact, are capable of uniting together and acting like a single being, then they have become cultured.

Take this for an example: there is a lot of quarreling among our Mandinga population, arguing among themselves, some acting like they're better than others, confrontations, stealing—it's even said that when a Mandinga says one thing, he means the very opposite. So they seem like a divided people. But when it comes to a cultural activity, such as praying, they become one. Pick any other ethnic group and the way they're hopelessly reverential before the *irã*. For example, you might say to a Balanta or a Manjaco the following: Look, Bobô is a good lad, and they'll think you must be friends with Bobô to say a thing like that and they'll repeat this to others. Some will believe you, others won't. But if you say the *irã* of Cobiana said Bobô's a good lad, it doesn't matter whether they're in the Soviet Union or wherever, they'll believe you. All you have to say is the *irã* said it and everyone will believe you, Mandingas, Mancanhas, Pepel, Balantas, everyone. So you can see how, when it comes to cultural situations, people are capable of uniting, even a divided people like ours is.

That's why, when we say we're capable of uniting to resist our enemy, we are gaining in culture. It also proves that we do, in fact, have a culture and we must, as a party, as a political organization, be capable of nurturing this spirit of culture in our people, in Guinea and in Cabo Verde, nurture it more and more by the day, specifically the idea that you have to be a patriot to be a child of our people. Furthermore, at this stage in our struggle, that you have to love our Party to be a child of our people. That's the culture in our land nowadays. What's most essential in our culture today is not teaching people to read and write, that's necessary too, we've spoken about this, but right now it's not essential that you reach second grade. What is essential is that you properly understand what our Party wants, what we want, what we are seeking to do, what we are doing, what our struggle is, where we're going. That is what's important, comrades. Being prepared to give your life. Any man capable of giving his life for our Party, no questions asked, is a cultured man in our country right now.

And in considering our struggle, we might compare, for example, Guinea's different races to see which ones are more or less cultured. Sometimes those who know more about certain things may come across as being less cultured. But any Mané or N'Bana out there in the bush toiling away and sticking to their task is more cultured than an Alvarenga man or anyone else who might be more educated but continues to follow the Tugas. This is because their work in the bush conforms to mankind's relationship with society and with nature, while serving the interests of their own people, today, in order to achieve a higher standard of living tomorrow. That's culture, comrades. Properly understanding your country's concrete situation in order to transform it in progressive terms.

We must instill in each and every one of us a sense of how certain victory is, a spirit of trust in victory. This is a cultural act, comrades. It enables us to withstand hardship, to never give up, to not lose hope after a defeat, because every struggle has its defeats. There are defeats within our struggle too, this is part of the struggle, that is why it is a struggle. But we should be constantly building up people's confidence in victory, we should be doing everything we can to make the enemy lose hope, to make our enemy's agents lose hope, to show them that they have no chance, that they will definitely lose. That is culture, comrades.

And we must, based on our love of our country and our people, based on our love of our Party, develop our dances, our songs, our music, put on plays, even acrobatic displays, do impressions of other people etc. Impressions of the colonialist settlers: for example, Senhor Fulano. This is very important. We should develop all of this, to serve our struggle, to serve our cause, but with updated content, that's to say, with new words and facts.

This is the great value of, for example, Balanta, Beafada, and Mandinga songs, and others too, Crioulo ones, Macanha, Pepel, or the *mornas* and *coladeiras*,[1] music that has always been a basic part of our struggle, celebrating our Party, hailing the names of our courageous soldiers, singing about our battles, our attacks on Tuga planes, showing how far our people have come in this war. This is what our culture is, this is what we should be developing now.

In parallel, of course, we should move towards opening our people's minds, in terms of literature, science, etc. Because we know illiterate people cannot form a good country. We need people who can read and write. Everyone who can read and write should teach those who can't. This has been in our Party Guidelines for a long time now and a long time ago our Party started to open schools, to improve the training of our teachers, to establish a context in which we can advance down the path of scientific understanding in regards to life and the world.

Our new culture, whether inside or outside school, must serve our resistance, must serve to help fulfill our Party's Program. This is the way it has to be, comrades. Our culture must develop in national terms, in relation to our land, but without dismissing or disregarding other cultures. It must be developed with intelligence, making the most of what other cultures have to offer, taking what's useful to us, anything that can be adapted to suit our living conditions. Our culture should develop based on science, it should be scientific, that's to say it shouldn't believe in imaginary things. Our culture should make sure that, come tomorrow, none of us think a lightning flash is a sign of God's anger, that thunder is the sky's voice expressing the *irã*'s fury. In our culture, come tomorrow everyone must know that, although we dance when there is thunder, thunder is really just two clouds crashing into each other, one with a positive electrical charge and one with a negative electrical charge, and when they collide it causes a spark, which is the lightning, and a noise, which is the thunder. It's like when you put two electrical wires together, one positive and one negative, and it makes a spark. That's what lightning is, but in the sky, the electricity of the clouds. The noise is the collision of two clouds, which we call thunder.

---

1   Traditional Caboverdean music

Not only is this true, but bearing in mind the speed of sound through air, when you hear thunder you can even work out where the two clouds are colliding, because light moves faster than sound. You see the flash and then a bit later you hear the thunder clap. Let's say the difference between the moment when you see the lightning and the moment when you hear the noise is five seconds, you can work out where the two clouds met and how far away they are from us, because the speed of sound through air is 340 meters per second. So, if you count the number of seconds after the flash and get to five, and then multiply five by 340 you get 1,700. That means the two clouds collided 1,700 meters away from us, causing the lightning and thunder.

A lightning bolt is just an electrical spark that, due to particular conditions, falls to earth and sometimes does so with sufficient force to cause a bit of damage, just as an electric current can sometimes cause things to explode in a house. Or the bolt might hit the earth with minimal force, land somewhere and just disappear. It could even pass through a human body and disappear into the ground, because the earth is also charged with electricity and because it's the opposite kind, it attracts the spark. That's why they put lightning rods on houses, so that the lightning bolt goes straight through the house and into the earth, harming no one.

Comrades, we must base our culture on science. We have to remove everything unscientific from our culture, if not necessarily today, then tomorrow. If we work hard today, we can rest assured that this will be possible tomorrow.

Our culture has to be popular, that's to say a culture of the masses, everyone has the right to culture. It likewise has to respect the cultural values of our people, those that deserve to be respected. Our culture cannot be elitist, aimed at a group of people who know a lot, who understand things. No. Every son and daughter of our land, in Guinea and in Cabo Verde, has the right to advance culturally, to participate in our country's cultural acts, and to express and create culture.

We need to foster a spirit of understanding in terms of distinguishing between the town and the country. We should note that, while our towns develop foreign customs day by day—some good, others bad, although we're generally quicker to adopt the bad ones: alcoholism, prostitution, banditry, con artistry, muggings, certain types of theft, etc.—in the bush, life is purer, which isn't to say there aren't people who steal there. But there's a big difference between a thief in Bissau and a Balanta thief. The Balanta thief, generally speaking—and things have perhaps changed since the colonialists came, due to the colonialist influence—steals things here, there, and everywhere, but with no particular interest in keeping what he steals, what interests him is the stealing itself. That's why he'll often steal something and pass it on to someone else, never to see the stolen item again, because theft is a sport in Balanta custom, it's to show skill, intelligence. I wear glasses and I look after them carefully, but a person like that might think: I'll have to keep playing until I can grab them when he's not looking. The person is showing that they're more skillful than me, that they can get one over on me. This is what stealing means to the Balanta. It's stealing as an intellectual exercise, as an exercise in physical and intellectual skill, without any interest in owning what's stolen. That's why a young Balanta man, when the time comes to celebrate him reaching adulthood, might list all the things he's stolen over the years, in order to demonstrate his worth, his skill, and the elders praise him and are proud of him if he's their son, because he's shown himself to be a person of high caliber. Stealing in the towns is not like that. No, in the towns the thief steals to feed his people, or else to get rich. Not to mention another kind of stealing that's deemed legal in the business world, for example, legal theft.

We must be able to distinguish between our bush and our towns, to make sure that all our towns' impurities don't spread to the bush. Let me repeat, this doesn't mean there aren't bad things in the bush. There are many bad things there, even examples of human sacrifice, of children being beaten, etc. It's dreadful the way children are beaten in our country. We must clamp down on this. And we must dispel any notion that the bush is pure, that there's nothing bad there, that it's only the towns that are bad. No, there are good things and bad things in the towns and in the bush, it's just that, in comparative terms, the towns are less pure than the bush. And we must work hard to make sure our rural areas progress more by the day, in the cultural sphere as much as in every other sphere.

Striving for Perfection

We have to make all our people conscious, comrades; starting today, all our soldiers, our militants, our local populations, make them conscious of the following: when a human being is doing a job, they must do it well, as perfectly and as quickly as possible, and in the most straightforward of fashions. We must develop in our spirit, in the spirit of all our people, the idea of perfection. We still don't have much of a sense of perfection. Look at that curtain, for example, not a single comrade managed to notice it, get up, and straighten it. A nail we're knocking into a wall, an item of clothing we're making; if it's wonky, that's no problem for us. We don't have much of a sense of perfection. If we're doing an ambush, we'll do it as best we can. Any comrade who trained abroad, or already had the knowledge, knows how to do an ambush properly: such a weapon needs to be put in such a place, another weapon in such a place, so many men here, so many men there, so many men as back up, etc., attack the enemy at a particular point. But how many comrades actually do this, how many? When done well, the results are extraordinary. But comrades generally overlook these things.

As with ambushes, the same goes for meetings where people are to go and speak. Comrades must go and speak at a meeting, but they don't bother to make notes, they do nothing and just improvise. They might end up saying all kinds of things, when all they have to do is a little bit of preparation, to refresh their memory. Today, there is a meeting in such and such a village; sit down and think about what the issues are in that village, make notes. You're a political commissar, the Party trusts you, you are the Party at that moment, are you just going to go and talk for the sake of talking? A bit of research is required, that doesn't mean preparing a whole speech, there's no point in giving a big speech to our people in the bush. Or sometimes there is, but either way, you need to make notes on the various issues, think about what's going to be discussed. This is very important. There are supervisor meetings everyone wants to go to, without anyone having any idea what they're going to say when they get there.

Or meetings are held like this: several supervisors meet in the north or the south of the country and what do they decide? To do things that are already in the Party Guidelines. Comrades send me reports of meetings and when you look at what decisions were made, it's things that are already in our Guidelines, which they've not read. Not only that, they come up with a slightly lesser or worse version of the one we already have. When there's a supervisor meeting, it's to discuss the following: How are we progressing in fulfilling the Party's Guidelines? Make notes and then discuss. Or maybe a problem arises concerning the Interregional Committee; make notes beforehand and go and discuss them.

Perfection in our work, this is very important, but so too is perfection in the way we dress. How many times have I told comrades to straighten their collar, to tuck their shirt in. A people that is fighting for its independence, for its dignity, has to, starting today, walk around with clean feet. When we're walking in the mud, we can be patient about this, but once we're out of the mud, we wash our feet. Clean clothes. If you've only got one set, take them off, tie a cloth around you, wash them, then put them back on clean. Comb your hair. If you don't have a comb, if you can't buy one, then make one out of a bit of wood if necessary. It seems like some comrades are maybe quite proud of their untidy hair. Perhaps it seems like an unimportant thing, but it is important. The way we behave is very important in terms of dignity and opening up new paths in life.

The Tugas used to say we were very dirty, but then when we dressed well, they called us "negroes who think they're doctors with degrees." That's the Tugas' stance. But we have no such complex, we are simply against any kind of dirtiness, we are against filth. It amazes me, for example, that some comrades are just as capable of sleeping on the floor as in a bed; it's all the same to some comrades, though fortunately not all of them, and it doesn't matter to them whether the room is clean or full of rubbish. Some comrades, supervisors even, are incapable of cleaning, even in the midst of utter filth. They're prepared to give their life for their country, but they're not prepared to pick up a brush, to sweep the floor, the backyard, they're not prepared to tend a little garden, even when, despite their work duties, there is plenty of time for this.

There are some comrades who make their bases nice and tidy, and I would never, even if I'm not particularly in favor of a certain base, say a word against them because I see effort there, the will to keep tidy. But others don't want to know. Anyone, man or woman, who's willing to give their life to the cause should be clean; they should live in a clean environment and make sure everyone around them is clean. Because only then can they be clean of spirit, cleaner by the day.

We need to introduce the notion of timekeeping into our culture, comrades, into our actions. We didn't invent the clock but we can still embrace timekeeping. We are in fact going against the culture of our people in this, comrades, for they know perfectly well what timekeeping is, they understand it very well: they know, for example, that if they don't plow by a certain time, things will turn out bad, that seeds must be sown so many days after the first rains, otherwise things will turn out bad. So many days after the plant sprouts in the rice nursery by the house it must be transferred to the field, otherwise it won't take. After turning the rice field, after cutting the mangrove, a certain amount of time has to pass before you can start to plant, because otherwise it will be too salty, etc., etc.

But we, comrades, many of us have no concept of time whatsoever. There are people who have to get up at five in the morning, and they get up at nine; an ambush must be performed from four in the afternoon, but they don't get there then, they show up the next day and find the Tugas have already been and gone. A barrack must be attacked at six in the afternoon, but they arrive in the dead of night, or maybe it was arranged for midday but they get there late and leave it for the next day, but the same thing happens the next day. How many times have our commanders failed in attacks or ambushes due to lateness? Some delays are justifiable, because of our difficult conditions, but others are simply due to a lack of care, a lack of awareness, a lack of order, a lack of decisiveness.

Sometimes a comrade is given a mission to take a letter somewhere quickly. They stop off on the way for whatever reason, their own amusement, and so it takes three or four days when it should have gotten there in a day. This is not good enough. You cannot win a war like this, much less build a country. We must have a better concept of timekeeping. Our comrades, political commissars, security commissars, etc. have to be on time wherever they go. I don't want anyone coming to me and saying they couldn't make it on time because they haven't got a watch. We do not need clocks to be on time. We can decide to meet when the sun is at its highest. There is sun in our country. When the cockerel calls for the first time, it's time to get up. When the sun is at noon, it's time to go. You don't need a clock to respect the time, comrades. A clock is just to provide a little extra help. Our people lived without clocks for centuries, but those who lived under the right economic conditions to invent clocks, invented them. But it wasn't the clock that made the people of Europe advance, no. It was working for long hours and advancing so much that they could invent the clock, the modern clock, because everyone has the old clock, you just have to put a stick in the ground and, depending on where the shadow is, that's the time. It's a sun clock. A person's shadow can be a clock, because in the morning a shadow is on one side and in the afternoon it's on the other. At midday many people say shadows disappear, because it's right under their feet, the sun is right above us, it's noon.

We have a lot of work to do, comrades, we have to make the most of our time. We have to try and be practical in our work, we have to instill in our comrades the spirit of being practical. We need to stop overcomplicating things. Or dispel from our spirit our magical interpretation of reality, that's to say that we still often have a way of thinking whereby when we sit down and talk a thing through thoroughly, until we're all in agreement, we tend to think that the thing is already done, and we're happy as if we have in fact done the thing, and maybe we even ought to celebrate, because the discussion went so well. But the discussion ends, everyone goes away happy with life and satisfied because they're going to do such a great job, but they don't then get down to actually doing the job, because it's already done in their heads.

But if we look at this closely, we can see how this corresponds to our own way of life, to how we're convinced that marabouts or witches are capable of pointing a finger at us and making us fall over. Sooner or later, we'll have to realize that this is a lie, that they're capable of doing no such thing. But it's in our heads, we think it or believe in it. And there are many other things like this besides. We think like this before an ambush, for example: we end up very satisfied with our plan, but then take no practical measures to ensure its success, to make sure everything runs smoothly with no mishaps, because everything's fine in our heads, because in our magical interpretation of reality, we think the job's already been done.

We must eradicate this from our midst, we all have to do it, as some comrades already have been. Discuss things, but then put them into practice, correctly, properly, without any mishaps, because our problem is starting things but not finishing them. When we start on a job, we throw ourselves into it full of enthusiasm, for example, we're going to build an underground warehouse to keep materials in. We make an enthusiastic start, but after a while we stop and everyone forgets about it. Look at independent Africa, so many things are started and never finished. Because it's enough for us to get something in our heads and that's it, never think about it again. How many things have we planned during our struggle, in political terms, in military terms, in education, in health, and not done? We start, but all it takes is for one small difficulty to emerge and that's it, it advances no further. We have to clamp down on this hard, very hard.

I could give many examples of things we've started but never finished. People who've started things and never finished them, organizations that started things and never finished them, and always for one of two reasons: they either realized it wasn't worth doing or they were unable to finish it. If they realized it wasn't worth doing, they were doing something they shouldn't have been doing in the first place, the matter wasn't properly thought through. Before starting on something, we must study it to work out whether it's worth doing or not, not just start and then stop. This is a waste of energy, it's squandering. Or else they were unable to finish it, but if you can't finish something you've started then that's just pathetic, you'll never achieve anything in life. We must put a stop to this, comrades.

Perfection, making the most of our time and being practical in what we do, having the capacity to see a task through to the end, every task that needs doing. This is very important, comrades, it's fundamental to our culture, comrades, it's a new dynamic, for our culture and our land. Because even if an entire week is required for an ambush to be done well, at a particular point on a road, then we should do it, take the whole week, the whole month even. We should organize our troops in such a way so that a group is always on that road, circling, moving etc., but they must always be there. If we know the enemy has to pass there, we mustn't leave, we have to see the job through until the end. What we can't do, as I've already said, is come along to perform a great ambush, wait for an hour or two, three, or four—the enemy hasn't come, some people say they're still coming others say they're not, and so we end up leaving. The enemy passes by a little later on and delivers its supplies to the barrack. With rivers it's the same thing. The attack has to take place at the scheduled time, otherwise why set a time? An attack is scheduled for five o'clock, but five o'clock passes, six o'clock, and it's left for another day, and the attack never gets done. Why do comrades mess with their own heads like this? Why? We schedule something for five, having confirmed that five is the right time to do it, or we schedule something for ten having confirmed that ten is the best time to pull it off. Knowing the enemy as well as we do, we must know when the best time to attack them is. We have to exploit this knowledge to the maximum.

We must learn to use our resistance as propaganda: this too is a cultural act. Through all the means we have available. This is why one of the greatest triumphs of our Party is our Radio Libertação station, our newspapers, *Jornal, Imprensa, Informação*, both inside and outside our land. We all know the value and power of our Party broadcaster, which transmits messages to our people and which we ought to steadily try and improve, because it's a vital propaganda tool for us, a means of promoting our resistance.

And, within the framework of our other activities, we should fly the flag for literacy throughout the land. We are pleased because so many comrades have already improved their knowledge during the struggle. Many of our country's elders have learned to read and write, our youngsters even more so. These days it's rare to find a bi-group[2] without at least one person who can't read or write, but it used to be that most of them couldn't read or write, and there were a lot of bi-groups in which practically nobody knew how to read or write. So we have to keep increasing this level of learning.

But there are a lot of comrades who reached second grade, or first grade, or second year. University graduates sometimes spend several days with their fellow comrades, doing nothing, spending their spare time relaxing, sprawled out or telling tales, without thinking to say: Comrades, those of you who've had no learning, come here and I'll teach you. Or those of you who've had some, come and I'll teach you a bit more. But most comrades don't think like this, they prefer telling tales or wandering around in the bush or in Conakry or Zinguinchor or Dakar.

We've a lot of work to do if we're going to build a new life for our country, comrades. We must, for example, and the Party has already

---

2   A small, mobile military unit of two guerrilla groups under a joint military and political command within the PAIGC.

started doing this, instill the idea of cleanliness, or hygiene, as it's called, in our people. Our people are clean, they love washing, they like brushing their teeth, they do it all the time, but not everyone. There are those who don't like it much and those who might wash and then throw themselves in the mud again afterwards, for whatever reason. We have to work to show people that their lives, the length of their lives, depends a good deal on them having a clean home. If people live amid dirt and other things, it's bad for them because such an environment is good for bugs that can cause humans harm. Flies and other bugs that bring all kinds of illnesses thrive in dirt. We must explain the principles of hygiene to our people. This is a fundamental aspect of our cultural resistance.

We started to set up health brigades, but where did we get with them? Not very far given what was required. But the political commissar should be a hygiene advocate, the security commissar should be a hygiene advocate, the commander of the Armed Forces should be a hygiene advocate. Wherever we go, we must insist on cleanliness. Even in Boké, for example, inside a rest house, or outside, supervisors visit them, find everything dirty, and say nothing. Only one or two people worry about cleanliness. We cannot let things be so dirty, we must clean, we must sweep. We have to develop a spirit of cleanliness, comrades, of hygiene.

Every supervisor and militant in the land must be a hygiene advocate. Wherever they go, they must demand cleanliness, and they, as good supervisors, must be the first to pick up a sweeping brush if necessary, be the first to clean up, to show others there's no shame in it, that they're fighting for their country, that they're prepared to give their life to our struggle but they're not prepared to live among filth, just because nobody bothers cleaning up, because they think cleaning is beneath their status. How can this kind of attitude put people on the right path, how can it rid us of dirtiness?

Because if we ask ourselves what we are fighting for, we might very well answer that our struggle is to ensure that not one poor soul in Guinea or Cabo Verde has to live in squalor, that it's to eradicate filth and mess from our midst. When we achieve this, we'll have advanced a long way in our struggle. We have asked comrades to persuade our people to build latrines, for example. This does not mean that latrines are a sign of progress; no, latrines themselves are not progress, people that do their business in the bush may well be more advanced than people with latrines. But making latrines is a sign of us advancing in other areas, because putting distance between ourselves and where we do our business is a way of us avoiding diseases. Because we all know there are certain places where you have to hold your nose when you pass by or else . . . But it's the same in other African countries, even in cities you sometimes have to hold your nose when you pass by certain places. There's dirtiness everywhere. Those of us who are prepared to die for a cause, for our people's happiness and progress, must be prepared to clean, because it's easier to clean than die.

Of course, we have to remove everything from our schools that was put there by the colonialists, everything that shows a colonialist mentality. We've already started, we're publishing new books that speak of our Party, our struggle, our country, our people's present and future, our people's rights. There are some comrades who think that to educate our sons and daughters properly we should not speak of our Party. What nonsense! Any teacher who thinks like this is no teacher at all. The way we see it, a teacher is someone who educates our sons and daughters on our struggle, the rights of our people, our Party, our Party's anthem, our Party's worth, as well as the ABCs, the Cat and the Fox, the Wolf and the Little Goat etc. The Party should also be present, the leader of the Party, the leadership of the Party, the strength of our struggle, the strength of our people, the strength of our Party, the duty of our people.

When I went to school they taught us about the birth of Jesus Christ, that the Virgin Mary had a child as a virgin, and I even repeated this stuff back to them, it apparently made sense to me at the time. The miracle of the ascension—there were lots of miracles in the approved books of the time, the miracle of the roses and all the rest of it. Why then, if back then they taught children about miracles, can we not teach our people about the even greater miracle that is taking place in our country: men and women joining together and mobilizing the population to fight to end their suffering, to end poverty, to end misery, to end the beatings and kickings, to end forced labor, etc.? Is that so hard to understand? Any child can understand that.

And we should make every knowledgeable Party supervisor and Party militant a teacher. School teachers are not the only ones who have a duty to teach: every commander, every member of the Party leadership, our political commissars, security commissars, nurses—everyone has a duty to teach, to always be instructing, explaining, telling, clarifying, helping. Only by doing this can we move forward, comrades. We cannot leave the mission of educating to teachers alone. We have to make the most of every opportunity—and comrades who know me well, who deal with me a lot, know this is how I conduct myself—we have to turn every conversation we have, of no matter what nature, into a class, into a mini-lesson. Someone or other will learn from it. Every conversation we have should be a lesson, that way we save time, we advance. But if we just sit around telling tales about back in Pelon, Mansoa, and other places, without giving a thought to learning, we're just wasting time, comrades, we're not advancing.

We must avoid any kind of superiority complex on the part of those who know things and any kind of inferiority complex on the part of those who do not. A person with the capacity to teach must not distance themselves from anyone, especially not now, and especially not from our people. On the contrary, they should go deeper, immerse themselves in our people. I have explained this to comrades, for example, to comrades who go away to study. So far there have been two tendencies when people come back: one is for them to mix with our people, but to blend in so well that they make the same mistakes our people make; the other is for them to come back as trained engineers and immediately want to become Party leaders. Isn't Bôbô Keita in charge? Bôbô doesn't have my level of studies, I'm an engineer and he barely went to school, he should be out, he gets so many things wrong, he's holding back the work of our Party, he's ruining everything, etc., etc. These are two extremes that we don't want. What we want is for those who go away and study and acquire more knowledge to come back and show respect for our leaders, because they are our leaders whether they went to school or not. But when they notice some flaw in our operations, we want them to join their comrades and help improve things, help make sure we raise our standards by the day. "This advice comes from someone who knows more than we do, who's had the opportunity to learn things we haven't and who's here to help us." Mix, blend in, but don't forget you have to help improve things, raise standards day by day.

The Importance of the Portuguese Language

We must clamp down on opportunism of every kind, even in culture. For example, some comrades think that when it comes to education in our land it is imperative that we start teaching in Crioulo right away. Then there are others who think it would be better to teach in Fula, in Mandiga, in Balanta. This is a nice thing to hear, any Balanta person would be happy hearing it, but it just isn't possible right now. How are we going to write in Balanta? Who knows the phonetics of Balanta? People don't understand that these things have to be studied first, even Crioulo. For example, I might write *n'ca na bai*. Someone else might write *n'ka na bai*. It's the same thing. You can't teach like this. To teach a written language you need to have a certain way of writing, so that everyone writes in the same way, otherwise we'll be bedeviled in confusion.

But many comrades, with a sense of opportunism, want to forge ahead with Crioulo. We will teach in Crioulo, but only after studying it properly. Right now, the language we use for writing is Portuguese. This is why you can speak either at this seminar, Portuguese is as valid as Crioulo. We are not somehow more sons and daughters of our land if we speak Crioulo, that's just not true. We are more sons and daughters of our land if we follow our Party's rules, our Party's Guidelines, and serve our people well.

Nobody should have a complex because they don't speak Balanta, Mandinga, Pepel, Fula, or Mancanha. If they speak them, all the better, but if they don't, they can still make themselves understood, even if it's through hand gestures. If you're doing good work for the Party, you move forward. Because who speaks better Manjaco than Joaquim Batican, the traitor? Do any comrades know more Fula than the traitor Sene Sané, more of the Fula "doctrine" than the traitor Tcherno Rachid? Who speaks better Balanta than the traitor Fuab? We need to have the courage to put things to comrades straight. Our values, yes sir, but with no opportunism.

We need to have a real sense of our culture. The Portuguese language is one of the best things the Tugas gave us because a language doesn't prove anything, it's just a tool humans use to relate to one another, a tool, a means of speaking so that we can express the facts of life and the world. Just as mankind invented the radio so that we can talk over great distances, without speaking a particular language, using signals, so too did mankind, at a particular time in our development, invent speech; we felt the need to communicate and did so through talking. We developed our vocal cords, etc., until finally we spoke. And because language depends on the environment we live in, different people created their own languages.

We might notice, for example, that people who live close to the sea have lots of words related to the sea in their languages, people who live in the bush have lots of words related to the forest. People who live in the bush don't know how to say motorboat, for example, they don't know what a motorboat is because they don't live near water. There are lots of things to do with the sea and navigation in the languages of certain European people, like the Portuguese, for example, because the Portuguese live by the sea. Such things are the way they are for a reason.

Language is a tool that mankind created, through hard work and struggle, in order to communicate with others. And this gave humans a tremendous new power, because then nobody was stuck on their own, they started to communicate with others, societies with other societies, one people to another, one country to another, one continent to another. How wonderful! It was the first natural means of communication, through language. But the world has advanced a lot since then. We haven't advanced that much, not as much as the rest of the world, so our language only got so far, as far as we reached as a society, the world we lived in, whereas the Tugas, despite them being colonialists, lived in Europe, so their language advanced a lot more than ours, allowing them to express certain truths, for example in relation to science. They might say this, for example: the moon is a natural satellite of the earth. "Natural satellite"; say that in Balanta; say it in Macanha. You have to do quite a lot of talking to say it; it's possible to say, but you have to talk a lot to explain that a satellite is something that rotates around something else. Whereas in Portuguese one word is enough, and said in such a way that people anywhere in the world can understand. And mathematics, we want to learn mathematics, don't we? Let us say, for example, the square root of thirty-six. How do you say "square root" in Balanta? We have to speak the truth if we want to understand ourselves properly. I might say, for example: an object's weight is a product of mass times gravitational acceleration. How are we going to say that? How do you say "gravitational acceleration" in our language? You can't say it in Crioulo, you have to say it in Portuguese.

But if our country is to advance, in a few years' time every child of this land will need to know what gravitational acceleration is. I'm not going to explain it now, because there isn't time, we've got a lot of work to do. But comrades, to really advance, not only our leaders but every child of nine must know what gravitational acceleration is tomorrow. In Germany, for example, every kid knows. There are so many things we cannot say in our language, yet some people want us to ditch the Portuguese language because we are Africans and we must reject the foreigners' tongue. What these people really want is to advance themselves, not advance their people. We, as a Party, if we want to lead our people for a long time yet, if we want to advance as a people in science and in writing, we have to use the Portuguese tongue. And it's an honor to do so. It's the one thing we have to thank the Tugas for, the fact that they left us their language after robbing us of so many other things. When the day comes that we've completed an in-depth study of Crioulo, found out all the appropriate phonetic rules for Crioulo, then we can switch and start writing in Crioulo. Still, we're not forbidding anyone from writing in Crioulo, if someone wants to write a letter to Tchutcho in Crioulo, they should go ahead and write it. When he replies, he'll write in a different way, but it'll be understood, that's fine. But Crioulo is no good for science. Even in Balanta—I remember a comrade of ours, Ongo, who unfortunately died. Ongo and I wrote to each other in Portuguese, changing into Crioulo now and then, and he wrote in Balanta too. Because it is possible to write in Balanta, anyone who knows enough Portuguese will be able to write in Balanta. You might say for example *Watna* or else *n'calossa*. I know how to write these things, but in my own way. Another person will write them their way. Even *"djarama"*[3] in Fula can be written with a "d" and a "j" or it can be written just with a "j," but it reads as *djarama* because a "j" at the start of a word is the same as "dj." But we have to establish rules, like in Mandinga and other languages, we need to establish rules first. This is the way it has to be, comrades, because we need to take as much as we possibly can from other peoples' experiences, not just rely on our own experience. But if

---

3	Thank you

we want to use other peoples' experiences and apply them to our own land, then we have to use expressions from other peoples' languages. Now, if we already have a language with which we can do this, let's use it, there's no harm in that whatsoever.

It's all the same to us if we use Portuguese or Russian or French or English, so long as it serves our purpose, the same way that it doesn't make any difference if the tractors we use are Russian, English, American, etc., so long as they lead us towards our independence, so long as they enable us to work the land. Because language is a tool, and it just so happens we already have a language that serves our purpose and that everyone understands. So, we're not going to make everyone learn Russian, that would be pointless, especially not when we have our own language, Crioulo, that is so similar to Portuguese. If our schools teach students how Crioulo was derived from Portuguese and African languages, people will be able to learn Portuguese much quicker. Crioulo hinders people learning Portuguese because they don't know what the link between Portuguese and Crioulo is, but if they understand that link then it can help them learn Portuguese.

We must end our people's general indifference towards matters of culture by making conscious decisions and showing determination in what we do. We have already made inroads in this regard, and we must do away with the idea that if something comes from abroad it must be good and we should accept it, or else that because it's foreign it's worthless and we should reject it. This isn't culture, it's an obsession, it's a complex, either of inferiority or stupidity. We must be able to look at things from abroad, accept what's acceptable and reject what's useless. We must be capable of making a critical evaluation. And if we look carefully at our struggle, we'll see that part of what we've been doing has involved the constant application of the principle of critical assimilation, that's to say, making the most of what others have already done by determining, through our own critique, what serves our country's needs and what doesn't. Creating based on accumulated experience.

4. ARMED RESISTANCE

Comrades, over yesterday and today we've sought to clarify the nature of our resistance in general terms, as a response to Portuguese colonial oppression, and to define, albeit briefly, the various forms of resistance our struggle takes, each form being a response to a form of Portuguese repression: political oppression met with political resistance; economic oppression met with economic resistance; cultural oppression met with cultural resistance. It remains for us to talk about our armed resistance, which is how we meet armed oppression, colonialist aggression. This is a form of resistance that comrades already know a fair bit about, of course, because it is more visible than the other forms of resistance.

We have already spoken about the beginning of our armed resistance: comrades have heard about how our armed resistance is a political act on the one hand, because we are engaged in a war in our land in response to the Tugas engaging in war, but above all else, because we could find no other way for us to claim our political right to rule over ourselves, for our people to determine their own destiny and for us to advance, like other peoples of the world, down the path of progress. Earlier today, I reminded you that our armed resistance is also an expression of our cultural resistance, because by mounting armed resistance and risking our lives every day, we are rejecting the condition of being second-class Portuguese, or in fact third-class Portuguese, or even lapdog status, which the foreign Portuguese colonialists wish to impose on us. We have, through our Party's work, become conscious that we are part of the African people, that we belong to the continent known as Africa, that our destiny, in that we are human beings like any other human beings, deeply connected to the rest of humanity, is connected, in the first instance, to Africa and, as Africans and as humans, that we have just as much right to lead free and dignified lives as do the people of Portugal or of any other place in the world. Without disrespecting the Tugas, our personality is not the same as theirs, though some of us may be the sons and daughters of Tugas or the descendants of Tugas mixed with Africans. We want our dignity back, our own personality, in order to stand up for our rights and for everything that forms the legitimate basis of our people's culture.

We have also shown comrades that our armed resistance can, ultimately, be seen as the continuation of the resistance our people showed—in Guinea in particular, because Guinea was conquered by the Tugas—during the war of colonial conquest that the Tugas waged in our land for almost fifty years. Today we take up arms again, continuing our ancestors' fight, those who refused to give up the right to determine their own lives. In regards to Cabo Verde, our struggle, which remains political today but may become armed tomorrow, can be seen as the continuation of the resistance shown by those Africans, sons and daughters of Guinea and the surrounding areas, who were taken to Cabo Verde as slaves, who resisted as slaves, who suffered, rejected and fought the Tuga slavers who dominated them and sold them to America, to Brazil and to other parts of the world, as if they were beasts.

We must, therefore, conclude that our armed resistance is, in the first instance, the continuation of a longer struggle in defense of our dignity as Africans. We have a tradition of fighting, of defending our liberty and our right, as a society, to our own history and to taking our own path towards progress, just like any other people anywhere in the world.

We know who we are, we've already spoken about this a lot, we have clearly defined our position geographically, economically, culturally, and socially, both before and after the Tugas came to our land. Before the colonial situation and after the colonial situation.

We are part of a multitude of different peoples on the African continent who came into contact with Europeans after the European route to Asia, to the Far East, via the Mediterranean was shut off by the Turkish empire, which had conquered Southern Europe, Eastern

Europe, and Asia Minor. Hemmed in by the Turkish, the Europeans needed to find new routes to access the riches of Asia, which they'd become accustomed to buying, trading and exploiting. From that moment on, the Europeans, and the Portuguese in particular, because they were located on the tip of Europe, by the sea, began a series of navigations, which have come to be known as "the discoveries." The Tugas are obsessed with thinking that God revealed the sea route to them so that they could discover new countries, discover new worlds. This is a lie. The Tugas took to the seas firstly because they lived at the sea edge, and secondly because Portugal was very poor and had lots of people it could employ as sailors, unlike other countries in Europe that had fewer people prepared to spend a life away at sea. But thirdly, and most importantly, because Europe had no choice but to take to the sea to find a new route to the Indies. No God revealed the sea route to the Tugas. This is quite obvious when you consider that the Tugas soon went back to being poor and wretched, to boasting the smallest navy of any country in the world that has a navy. This needs to be made very clear, the events that led to our coming into contact with the Tugas.

The Tugas initially established relationships with different African peoples based on equality and, in a few cases, inferiority on Portugal's part, because some countries in Africa were much more developed than Portugal was at the time. I can tell you that the king of Ghana, for example, and the king of Mombasa and Melinde, on the East African coast, and the king of Congo, were all a bit shocked by the Tugas' poverty and the gifts the king of Portugal sent them, compared to what they might have sent to the king of Portugal. Portuguese kings wrote lovely letters to African kings requesting good relations, praising them, inviting them to trade, with due respect, etc., but it's been proven that the Portuguese kings were always giving secret orders too, instructing their people to find ways to trick, and to steal. So the Tugas established relationships with us: we Africans, trade relations along the coasts of our African lands, initially based on equality and respect. Even after a long time had passed there were still signed trade accords, in Guinea, for example, between the Pepel and Portuguese kings. And the Tugas, in order to trade with our land and with other parts of Africa, paid taxes, as did other European countries besides, countries that later turned into colonialist and imperialist countries.

Europe gradually transformed, becoming advanced in commercial terms and industrially developed, especially England. As capitalism developed at great pace, new needs arose in Europe. The accumulation of capital brought the need for new raw materials, in order to develop Europe further, as a response to European poverty, but so too the need for new markets to sell European products to. Before this, because of warring in Africa, wars fought among Africans themselves (the area our country lies in now saw lots of wars, for example, especially inwards from Fouta-Djalon, where various African military aristocracies fought with each other to conquer land for pasture, for farming, etc.), there were a lot of prisoners of war in Africa who were used as slaves. In Africa itself, economic and social systems were built around slavery, albeit a slavery with its own characteristics, different to slavery on other continents.

Systems of slavery still exist in Africa today. Indeed, when you stop and think about it, a *régulo*'s errand boys are really no more than slaves, comrades. Some of our "elders" have boys, here in our land, in the bush, who are like slaves. They're given food, they have children, but all those children are raised to serve the same "elder." Their children's children's children remain servants. This is called slavery. So we Africans, with our own concept of slavery, were open to the idea of arranging slaves for others.

America was discovered around this time and began to be colonized shortly thereafter. Brazil in South America, islands like Cuba, Jamaica, the so-called West Indies, some Latin American countries, especially in Central America, and what's known as North America, colonized by the English. In Brazil and the southern part of North America where the climate was harsher, in areas that were a bit behind, agriculture went down the hard labor route and the Europeans who'd left Europe to colonize it were somewhat well-to-do, for they'd been expelled from Europe, persecuted because of their religion, because of their politics, because of the class struggle in Europe. These kinds of people weren't about to pick up a hoe and start working the land, so they went out into the world to find people to do this work for them. Africa made for easy pickings in this sense, because there was slavery in Africa, Africans were used to buying and selling slaves. And so, the Tugas, who regularly navigated the Atlantic Ocean, and others like the French, the Dutch, etc., who knew the crossing from piracy voyages, stopped being pirates and instead of robbing at ports and at sea, they bought or hunted slaves in Africa to sell in America or the New World. A new type of trade began: slave trading.

The slave trade went on for a long time, long enough for more than a hundred million Africans to be sold around the world. Many of them died at sea, researchers have learned, through debilities or shipwrecks. African men and women were taken to various parts of the world, but especially to America.

Time passed and disputes started between the English on one side, along with a few other European countries, and America on the other, disputes over economic competition. Because America's rise had basically been facilitated by slave work, whereas in England, for example, there were no slaves and wages had to be paid. So there emerged in England, not out of humanitarian feeling, but out of economic necessity, out of the need to halt the march of American development, the idea of ending slavery.

Great theories were advanced about how slavery was a crime against humanity. Which is true, it is a crime, but it had been a crime for a very long time.

Slavery must end, [there was] great propaganda and international summits, etc., until there came a point when slavery was eventually outlawed. But the Tugas, already quite stubborn back then, carried on slave trading for a good while yet, with their fine slaving warehouse on the Cabo Verde islands, out in the Atlantic Ocean. Other slaves were taken to Portugal. In Portugal, there are still places that have "negro" in their name, because there were so many slaves there. Poço dos Negros, for example, because there were lots of Black people there who were kept as slaves and then, after the end of slavery, when they became free, they remained in Portugal. Even in the Alentejo there is a village where there are a lot of mixed-race people, descendants of Africans who the Marquês de Pombal sent to populate the Alentejo.

With slavery ending in Europe, the idea of giving slaves their freedom spread through America too and slavery was outlawed throughout the world. The North of America was industrialized while the South produced raw materials, based on slave labor. The idea emerged, in order to protect the industrial and economic interests of the North, to end slavery in America. The idea was to take away the advantage the great proprietors of the South, the owners of vast swathes of land and slaves, had over the industrialists in the North. So Lincoln, the American president, decided to end slavery. There was a war because of this. The South immediately declared that it was no longer part of the United States, that it wanted no part in any kind of federation, that it would be an independent state, and keep its slaves. War broke out, a harsh war, between Americans and other Americans, supposedly about the slaves, because the North wanted to free the slaves. A lie. The North wanted to end the advantage the South had because it had slaves and the North did not.

And if we study this further, we'll see that the Europeans who settled in America were of a different origin in the North and South. Place names in the North have certain roots, while those in the South have others. There are a lot of French names in the South, for example, and names from other countries besides. Because Americans, as you all know, are not from America. The real Americans are the Indians, almost all of whom were killed by Europeans. But the so-called Indians of North America are not Indians at all, of course, they're redskins who got called Indians because when Christopher Columbus discovered America, he thought he'd reached India, so when he saw people he called them Indians and they got stuck with that name, though they're not Indian at all.

A new era began, comrades, a world in which slavery had ended. The world was transformed by this. But in the meantime, capitalism in Europe had developed a lot, vast accumulations of capital, industrial development, the need for raw materials, the need, as I said, for new markets, until the most developed European states decided to do the following: to actually take control of Africa, to end the historical tradition of small-scale trading, small-scale contracts and respect for Africans. The European states, England, Germany, France and Belgium, for example, started to argue over who would take control of Africa. They determined to share Africa out, first through the companies they created, then through the states themselves, through colonial wars of occupation. It's a long chapter in history and I'm not going to recount it all now, but that's basically how our lands became colonies, occupied by colonialists.

And from that moment on, regardless of whether we were developed or not, or whether we were as advanced as the Europeans, our own history stopped. We were dragged into the history of the Europeans. Our history, our freedom and the freedom of our productive forces were taken away from us, seized by the colonialists. Of course, they were facilitated in this by the fact that we ourselves were forever divided. You'll know that in Guinea, for example, the Tugas fought against us one by one, defeating us one by one, race by race, and by using some races against others. It might be said that had certain Manjacos not helped the Tugas fight other Manjacos, it's hard to see how the Tugas could have ever defeated the Manjacos. It might also be said that had the Fula not helped the Tugas fight the Pepels, and especially had Honório Barreto not tricked the Pepels of Bissau into serving the Tugas, then the Tugas may well never have established themselves in our country.

A lot of people are not aware of the role Honório Barreto played in the Tugas' conquest of Guinea. Honório Barreto, son of Nha Rosa de Cacheu, a *badiu*[1] from the island of Santiago in Cabo Verde, and João Barreto, who was a sergeant in the Portuguese army, a Black man, born in Guinea and a descendant of Caboverdeans, a mixture of Caboverdeans and Manjacos, as Nha Rosa was also said to be, the daughter of a Caboverdean man and Manjaco woman who was taken to Cabo Verde. So Nha Rosa, Dona Rosa de Cacheu, was related to indigenous Africans from the region of Teixeira Pinto,[2] Cacheu, etc., as far as Casamansa, in other words as far as the river, which was called the Rio São Domingos back then and is known as the Casamansa river today. She was so liked among Africans that they agreed to whatever she said. She practically ran the economy. Honório Barreto, her son, was educated first in Cabo Verde and later in Portugal. He was a student of mathematics in Portugal, though he never finished his studies. He was a good guitar player and a bit of a reveler, and he returned to Guinea to take over his parents' business affairs. João Barreto had earlier been taken prisoner for rebelling against the ruling government, because he was a democrat, not one in favor of independence, but in favor of other Portuguese people who were democrats.

---

1 Comes from the Portuguese *vadio* meaning "vagrant," which was what the Portuguese colonists called slaves who escaped into the interior of the islands. Eventually, comes to refer to all residents of Santiago, due to the pervasiveness of African culture throughout, owing to the *badius* of the interior.
2 Teixiera Pinto is the colonial name of the region Canchungo.

After his father died, Honório Barreto took over the family's business affairs and became the richest man in Guinea. When faced with the Pepel revolt—there was only one governor on the ground among the Pepel people in Guinea and Cabo Verde at the time, and he reported to Praia—the governor general of Cabo Verde and Guinea sent a proposal to the Portuguese crown, queen Dona Maria at the time, saying that if she wanted Guinea to remain at peace, to end the wars there and for Portugal to genuinely take control of Guinea, then she should install Honório Barreto as governor. I read the letter the governor wrote to Dona Maria in the colonial archives in Lisbon. It said: "I have the honor of proposing to the queen that she choose as governor of Guinea, albeit acting under my command, an illustrious and intelligent young man by the name of Honório Barreto, who attended such and such a school, etc., etc. and who is as Portuguese as any of us. And I advise her to do this because, as the richest man in Guinea, no one has a greater interest in maintaining the Portuguese presence in Guinea than he does."

The queen understood this and Honório Barreto was named governor of Guinea. Honório Barreto established a plan of action for the Tugas to conquer Guinea: if he took proper control of Cacheu, Geba and Bissau for the Tugas, no one else would be capable of taking Guinea and they could put down any indigenous revolts. His plan was very well thought out, very intelligent.

But when, for example, the Tugas became angry with him later, because he was Black and in charge, he pulled off a great trick, giving everything up, returning to Cacheu and shutting himself away in his property there. When the Portuguese subsequently had difficulties with indigenous populations, they called for him, to avoid having the Pepels rise up against them. He returned. At one point, for example, the king of Intim, who was called N'Dongo and was one of the strongest of the Pepel kings, surrounded Amura, the fort of São Jose in Bissau, with his men, and he did it so well that the Portuguese died of starvation, unable to get out. Their ships never reached Bissau. Honório Barreto was in Cacheu and the Portuguese sent for him. People came from Cabo Verde, Tugas who were in Cabo Verde, and called for him. He agreed to come and he went to talk to the Pepel king and promised him that Pepel rights would be respected, that Portugal would not take their land in any way whatsoever, and that they would be paid taxes. He even made out a written contract. Meanwhile, the Tugas arranged for a large force to be sent from Portugal, departing Lisbon for Guinea, and when they arrived, they massacred the Pepels.

Another time, Honório Barreto made a contract with the *régulo* of Djeu de Rei, the island across from Bissau, in which the *régulo* and the Tugas agreed to the following: Djeu de Rei would leave the Tugas alone and not make war with them, and the Tugas would give the *régulo* a certain amount of firearms, a certain number of iron bars and so many liters of sugarcane rum every year. This is written on a signed contract, archived in Lisbon, which I've also read. I'm trying to give you an idea of how Honório Barreto knew exactly what to do to serve Portugal's interests.

His plan in fact enabled him to take control of Guinea himself and cede it to the Tugas as he pleased. Guinea's future lay in his hands at a time when the English and the French came along, wanting Guinea for themselves: the English wanted Bolama, the French wanted everything from Casamansa down. Honório Barreto proved himself a great Portuguese "patriot" in that he put up a strong resistance, accepting none of the promises or offers the French and English made him, keeping Guinea exclusively for the Tugas. The Tugas are right to build a statue of Honório Barreto in our land. The Tugas wouldn't have Guinea if it weren't for Honório Barreto. That's the truth of it. But we, too, should have some respect for Honório Barreto.

We can be critical of his attitude, but he was a brave man. At that time, with the prevailing mentality, as an individual who emerged from among our people but who was educated by the Portuguese, among the Portuguese, speaking good Portuguese, playing the guitar, singing fados, etc., there wasn't anything else he could really do, comrades. He was given a job and he did it well, for he was a brave man. Today we might not understand how the descendants of Honório Barreto, for example the Alvarengas (because Nha Rosa was called Rosa Alvarenga; João Barreto and Rosa Alvarenga became the Carvalhos, Alvarengas, etc. Barreto, an entire family, two entire families joining together in our land and producing fine people, such as Comrade Barreto, who's seated over there), how these descendants of Honório Barreto can still side with the Tugas, given the new phenomenon, given our people's struggle and independence in Africa, given the liberation struggles taking place everywhere. That Honório Barreto might serve the Tugas, okay, any one of us might have chosen to do that, if we'd had his education and lived in the same moment of history as he did. But that the descendants of Honório Barreto, whether they went to school or not, still choose the Tugas today is not only difficult to understand, it's unforgivable.

So comrades can now see where we emerged from, how we fell into the hands of the Tugas in the first place.

As for Cabo Verde, as comrades will know, there was no conquest of Cabo Verde. Cabo Verde is a group of islands that the Tugas "discovered" around that time. They came upon the western tip of Africa, where Dakar is today, and because of its greenness, for at the time they discovered it the place was very green, and because it was a cape—that's to say a bit of land that sticks out into the ocean—they called it *Cabo Verde* ("Green Cape"). A few days later, advancing out into the ocean, they came across some islands and because they were near the "green cape," they called them the *Cabo Verde* islands. Then each island got a name. The one they discovered in the month of May became *Maio* island, the one they discovered on Saint Tiago's feast day became *Santiago* island, the one covered in salt became *Sal* island, the one that looked pretty in the distance became *Boa Vista* island, etc. Names based on the Tugas' Christianity and their particular way of seeing things. But as you'll know, the area where Dakar is located today is called *Région du Cap Vert*. In Dakar you see a lot of things with Cap Vert written on and people think that's where Cabo Verde is, which is why I've given you this explanation.

There was no one living on the Cabo Verde islands at the time they were discovered. But there are theories that people had been there before, particularly people from the African coast, Manjacos as well as Lebus. Lebu fisherman from the Senegalese coast could have got as far as the Cabo Verde islands in their canoes, for it has recently been proven that some of their canoes, *nhomincas* canoes, for example, were capable of covering those kinds of distances. Besides this, there is the historical theory that the Phoenicians, who were an ancient people who inhabited what is now Lebanon, in Asia Minor, people we tend to call Syrians, navigated around Africa back in ancient times. It's said they completed what's known as the circumnavigation of Africa over a thousand years ago, and that they passed through the Cabo Verde islands and lived there.

Nevertheless, the fact is that, when the Tugas came across the Cabo Verde islands out in the middle of the ocean, they found no one living there. And when the slave trade started to develop, they decided to take slaves there and turn the Cabo Verde islands into a slaving warehouse. When the slave trade started to come to an end, each island passed into the hands of an important white man, a Dom whatever, to whom it was donated. These men turned the slaves into "workers" but exploited them like slaves, or made them servants in the landowner's house. This is our point of departure, the situation the Tugas created in Africa.

Now that we fully understand our point of departure, we need to understand where we're going to with our armed struggle. Our armed struggle, as we've said, is a form of political struggle that seeks to liberate our country from colonial and imperial economic exploitation. This is what our fundamental aim is. Liberate the productive forces of our country, from oppression, from colonial imperialist domination. But here's a question: Are we doing all this just to go back to where we were, back to a Cabo Verde of slaves, of serfs, of people raised to be servants? Are we doing all this to go back to a time when Manjacos and Pepels were forever fighting and when Mandingas and Balanta could never get along? This is the hard part. No, we are liberating our country in order to advance, like other people in the world; to progress, to lead lives of dignity, for there to be unity in our country, nationwide; to help raise a new and better Africa. This is what the objective of our struggle is, within the context of the wider world and the whole of humanity, a humanity we belong to as human beings.

When it comes to our struggle, every shot we fire at the Buba barrack or at a Tuga on the road or in an ambush is, therefore, a political act of the highest order. We are serving humanity, comrades, we are serving our people, our country, Africa, humanity. This is the sense of responsibility we bear when we fire our guns, when we wage war in our land in order to free our people.

That is why we must coordinate our armed struggle in the best way possible according to our reality on the ground, and according to other peoples' experience of struggle, when that experience is relevant to ours. This is why we must avoid doing anything in our struggle that denigrates human dignity. Our Party forbids any criminal act, anything done in the name of our struggle that is hateful or blood-thirsty. We do feel hatred and we do shed the blood of the colonialists who dominate us, but we do so knowing exactly what we are doing and why. Comrades, we mustn't confuse things. That's why we're having trouble getting our Felupe brothers to join us, because they think that when you kill someone in war you have to chop their heads off and cut off their ears. We have difficulty accepting this. But it comes easy to the Tugas. That's why our war is quite different to many other wars in Africa, comrades. And our enemy—who are criminals of the worst kind, barbaric, the very worst kind of people, among the worst people to ever walk the earth—are ashamed in the face of our purity of purpose, and the high-mindedness of our struggle for national liberation.

Our Party understood the need to mobilize the masses to fight, to organize the masses to fight, and so we mobilized the masses, we knew this had to be the first stage of our struggle, comrades, and we did a good job of it. And if we want to continue with the job, and we must continue, then we need to be continuously mobilizing and orga-nizing the masses. We created armed groups almost naturally, rooted in our people's environment, supported by our people. Groups that developed bit by bit. We carried out actions against the enemy, devel-oped our struggle step by step, created new types of fighting groups, improved our weapons, always with the support of our people. We've done our utmost to extend the war into every area of our land and today all that remains, more or less, is to take the armed struggle to the islands: Bissau island, Bolama island, the Bijagós archipelago, and the Cabo Verde archipelago. We've engaged in armed struggle in every other part of our country. We've even carried out attacks in Bissau, and on Bolama too. We attacked Bolama just a few days ago, the Tugas announced it on their radio.

We have to be able, through our armed struggle, our armed resis-tance, to maintain our strength—to preserve our strength but also build it up by the day. A people that takes up arms but isn't able to pre-serve and build up its strength ends up losing, because an armed upris-ing either gains in strength and advances or else it disappears. And the best way to build up our strength is to remain constantly active.

Carrying out an armed struggle, our armed resistance, is like being a gymnast in a way, for the more actions you perform, the more movements you make, the more gymnastic you become. A lot of comrades sadly do not understand this and are capable of spending hours on end doing nothing, or in fact destroying our strength, because the less active a soldier is, the harder it is for them to perform the next action.

We managed to lead our people into taking up arms, step by step, in three stages: first stage, the sons and daughters of our land, people of the bush and the towns, became guerrillas. Not many people, but we gradually increased the number of guerrillas, and we transformed our guerrilla forces into a regular army. But right after that, we gave people in the villages arms, creating militias. And now, bit by bit, we are providing arms to everyone, our entire population, in the liberated areas at least. An armed people. For this is the defining feature of an armed resistance, a people fighting for its liberty.

What is our objective? To destroy enemy forces; to destroy, by any means necessary, every sign of life in the enemy. War is hard, it's not nice, it's difficult, but nobody goes to war for fun, only criminals kill for the fun of killing. Nevertheless, war is killing, comrades. Whoever kills the most, and commits the fewest mistakes, wins the war. That's why our objective, in terms of our armed resistance, is to eliminate every last sign of life in the enemy. We are obliged to eliminate the colonialist Tugas; any Tuga who wields a weapon against us, against the freedom of our people, must be eliminated.

And within our struggle, we must coordinate our work in such a way so that we lose as few of our own fighters as possible. Indeed, as a Party we have sought to coordinate our fighting tactics, as well as our overall strategy, in such a way so as to minimize the number of comrades who die in the war. We must fight our war, do everything possible at every stage, but prepare today to fight tomorrow's stage better. This has been our Party's guiding principle. We have recommended that our comrades act with the utmost caution, that we carry out actions against the enemy only when it's the right moment to act, but that we do act, for the land is ours. We must remain constantly active because it's constantly possible to act, given the right circumstances, circumstances we ourselves can create.

We have sought to preserve life, to protect the lives of our comrades to the maximum. And it's fair to say that many of the comrades we've lost in the fight have been lost due to mistakes they themselves have made. Mistakes in terms of vigilance, mistakes in terms of security, mistakes of calculation, even mistakes in disobeying Party Guidelines. A lack of care taken on paths that might be mined, a lack of care taken crossing rivers that might be patrolled by enemy boats. How many times have comrades reached rivers to cross and, instead of establishing communications with the other side, where comrades are well placed to monitor the enemy's movements, they've just jumped in their canoes and set off? They get halfway across and encounter the Tugas. It happened to me crossing the Rio Farim on my way back from the north of our country. Before we'd reached the other side, an enemy boat appeared at the bend in the river. It was coming up right behind us when we made land, in the middle of a mangrove. And we all know that Comrade Luís Cabral, for example, had to throw himself into the water with other comrades, they very nearly died, because an enemy boat was right on top of them. How many comrades have died like this? It's just a lack of care, a lack of attention to detail, a lack of appreciation that doing a thing well means thinking it through properly. Too much trust in luck!

Comrades have died, for example, in bombings through lack of attention, not taking proper care with planes, not following the Party rules—make shelters, leave the base. People die at war, it's normal to die at war, anyone who goes to war knows that they may live or they may die, but whether they die or not is to a large degree dependent on the mistakes they make, dependent on whether they do or do not follow instructions issued by the Party, issued by whoever's leading you, on how best to preserve your life. And preserving your life doesn't mean cowardice, it doesn't mean refusing to fight the war. How many comrades have died outside the combat zones, how many comrades have died outside the country even! Had they been inside our land they might not have died. Sometimes comrades are on the front line for years, then one day they leave and go back to their village, and the Tugas kill them as soon as they get there. So we shouldn't be afraid to die at war, but to die for a reason, to die usefully, not at random just because you trusted your luck.

We are proud that, compared to other wars, be they in Africa or outside Africa, few people have died in our war relative to how many might have done, given our particular circumstances. Our Party has understood how to coordinate the struggle so as to keep loss of life among comrades to a minimum. And for comrades who are wounded, we've done our utmost to aid their recovery. This is one of the strengths of our struggle. Therefore, not only must we defend ourselves, with constant action, because the best form of defense in an armed struggle like ours is action, the best form of defense is attack, but also defend the conquests we've made. That said, this shouldn't be confused with tying ourselves down just to defend a liberated area, rather than going to the front to attack the Tugas in their barracks. We have to find ways of defending the liberated areas, but defending the liberated areas must not stop us from advancing on the enemy and hitting them with ever more strikes.

As the war has advanced, our Party has managed to adapt our combat structures. Comrades will remember well what the struggle was like at the start. Bit by bit we modified our guerrilla groups, we created our army corps and our army units, we created commands, we started to coordinate our fight in terms of zones, different regions. Before, for example, our army command was our Party's central committee, but as our Armed Forces grew and the war advanced, we had to separate local leadership of the Party from leadership of the Armed Forces, although the leaders of the Armed Forces were also Party leaders. We created war fronts, army corps, different sectors of the struggle, etc., all of which shows comrades how dynamic our struggle has been. And one of the great strengths of our struggle is the following: we have never let our struggle crystallize, that's to say become frozen in a given state of evolution. On the contrary, we have made sure it has constantly evolved, forever adapting to changing circumstances. We were able to transition from pistol to mortar, but through a process of modification, adjusting our entire structure until we arrived at the mortar. We have been able to change the nature of our fight, open up new fronts in the struggle, open up new fronts at the right moment to do so. Sometimes, of course, given our circumstances, there's been a bit of a delay. And sometimes we have made mistakes, such as, for example, when we created units called sections that had too many people in, we had to reduce them in size afterwards. You'll remember the Pidjiguiti section, the Vitorino section, etc., which we later had to divide up because there were too many people for the command to coordinate at the time. It was too much, so we ended up with bi-groups.

For it should be said that in a war like ours, in a terrain like ours, the best way to fight is in reduced numbers, with people divided into small groups. Look at the attack a few days ago in Pitche, after the meeting we held with comrades in Gabú. We were happy with comrade Baro Seidi in the end, with the attack he led, but we told him he could still do better. He basically acted on a whim, he and Buonte Na Sansa, his political commissar. After that meeting, he went back with his soldiers and attacked Pitche with two groups of eighteen, entering the Tugas' barrack, catching the Tugas unawares in their shelters, demolishing a number of houses, etc., etc. In other words, we remain convinced that the best way to fight this war is with small groups and lots of courage, making the most of our weapons, our light weapons especially, comrades.

Unfortunately, ever since we've had mortars, and I've said this before, our comrades in the infantry have gotten a bit lax and left *"Patchanga"*[3] bullets rusting in their chambers. But we're fighting this, the leadership of the Party is fighting this, I'm fighting this, you'll be aware, for example, that I'm taking people out of the infantry and placing them in other army corps and sending them to other places. And our comrade commanders, our leaders, thankfully have a clear understanding of this and are helping us a lot in this sense. There's no point in having five bi-groups to get the Tugas out of the Buba area or the Cubucaré area when if you join two bi-groups from one side and three from the other, to make five, we might take them north to reinforce our offensive in Chão dos Manjacos or in Nhaera, for example, both of them extremely important to us.

We must, therefore, with every step we take, yesterday, today and for as long as our struggle lasts, coordinate our struggle, have total control of our struggle, know exactly what's happening where. And we must do everything we can to ensure that relations between our Armed Forces and our people are as good as they possibly can be. We must convince our people, through our gestures, through our actions, through our words, that our troops are their own sons and daughters, that they're fighting to defend them, that our soldiers come from their bosoms, from their bellies, and are here to defend them, not to harm them.

3　*"Patchanga"* is how PAIGC members would pronounce the PKP "Pecheneg" machine gun in creole.

Several comrades in the Armed Forces, even some supervisors, have hindered our Party's efforts, seriously hindered our struggle, by wrecking the relationship between our Armed Forces and the local population. As I've already said, this is a crime of betrayal, it serves the Tugas. We have to clamp down very hard on this, really clamp down on it. And I will say to comrades the following: no matter how strong the Party is, if we do not maintain a good relationship with our people, day in and day out, if we do not reinforce and grow this relationship every single day, through political work and through the concrete actions of our Armed Forces, our struggle will be doomed to failure.

In order to recruit new people to the Armed Forces, in order to ensure that we have the local population's support, even to justify the sacrifices we're asking everyone to make, it is essential, comrades, that we develop, on a daily basis, good relations between the Armed Forces and the population of our country. Does this mean that we must avoid causing any harm in places where we must cause harm to advance? Easy now, comrades, we'll do what we have to do. But we will not cause harm out of individual interest, because someone is obsessed with beating people up, kicking out or whatever. We do it only in the interest of our people.

As I've already said, it's good for us to be clear, at every moment of our armed struggle, about where we're heading, about how our struggle is progressing at every given moment. Our objective is to get the Portuguese colonialists out of our country, out of Guinea and Cabo Verde. The idea, the aim isn't to just lash out at the Tugas, to throw them to the ground like we would in one of our land's wrestling bouts. Our objective is to get the colonialist Tugas out of our land.

Look at the case of the Vietnam War, which led to the independence of the Republic of North Vietnam. When the war ended, with triumph for the Vietnamese at Dien Bien Phu, where they surrounded and defeated around thirty thousand French, the French had five hundred thousand soldiers in Vietnam, well-positioned, in all areas. But because of the defeat at Dien Bien Phu, which was an enemy camp, and because of the political pressure in the international sphere, France was obliged to concede. Some army officials were furious at the time, such as General Salan and others. Why? Because the French were still strong, stronger than ever. Take the specific case of Algeria. When Algeria gained independence through negotiations at Evian, the French presence had never been stronger in Algeria, with French troops everywhere, all ganged together, hundreds of thousands of French troops as well as a million French civilians, many of them armed. But it was because of political work, political pressure exerted within the country, and because of the courage of the Algerian people, tremendous courage, comrades, the great sacrifices made by people in the cities. When, for example, the French outlawed protests in Algiers (saying that anyone who took to the streets would be killed), the Algerians, men, women and children, went out into the streets one Sunday waving their flag. The French killed over six hundred Algerians in a single day, on the streets of Algiers. But the next Sunday the Algerians took to the streets again. Courage is required, comrades. We should appreciate that in our war, compared to the wars for independence in Vietnam or Algeria, we've had it okay, hardly anyone has died.

And while we wage war, our people in Bissau bask in our victories. My goodness, people are being invited to all kinds of places they never used to go, permits to go to Portugal, Mr. Mamadú Djassi has appeared in the newspaper, esteemed Mrs. Dona Mariama Camará in Bissau, reaping the rewards of our struggle already. In Algeria, while soldiers were fighting in the crags, the bush and the mountains, people in the city rose up in force, in protest and unarmed, to show the French that they simply had to leave. And because this prompted assassinations and massacres, world opinion, public opinion even in France, turned against the French government. It can be said that one of the major forces that helped win the war in Algeria was public opinion in France itself, and those sons and daughters of Algeria who lived in France, numbering more than five hundred thousand, who committed acts of sabotage in France itself. But as you know, many others sided with the French, so there were Algerians killing other Algerians, in Algeria and in France. But the force of global public opinion won out, along with the courage of the Algerian people and the sacrifices they agreed to make, because more than a million and a half people died in Algeria, died for their independence, comrades. That means twice the entire population of Guinea died in the war in Algeria during seven and a half years of struggle.

But the objective of a war of liberation is not just to get the enemy to ask for mercy, to admit that they've lost. That's not it. It's for them to sit down and admit that we're right, that we should take control of our own country. That's why we must understand where we're going with this war. And the more we beat the enemy the better, in every little battle and confrontation, because then the sooner the day will come when they decide to leave because things have gotten so bad. Thankfully the Tugas already know they've lost here, but they haven't left yet, don't forget, so we haven't defeated them yet. They know they have to hold on because Angola and Mozambique are holding on and so they have to be strong and hold on a bit longer, provided we don't advance on Cabo Verde. The day the struggle starts for real in Cabo Verde, further down the line, the day we take up arms there, the war will end here for certain. That doesn't mean it can't end without war breaking out in Cabo Verde, because it can. But it's true that when we launch the war in Cabo Verde, the Tugas will be afflicted on all fronts

Comrades, it's worth forever repeating that the essential objective of our armed resistance is to achieve something we've been unable to achieve through politics alone. It is to open up new prospects for our people, prospects of independence, peace, work and justice, the prospect of progress. We are convinced that our Party can achieve this.

In accordance with our people's destiny, a destiny we ourselves are now shaping, and in accordance with the historical demands of our time, our Party's mission is to, through our political, economic, and cultural resistance, and through the hard but necessary actions of our armed resistance, open up a new path to our people, give them the security they require, and assure them that tomorrow their lives will progress. This is our mission, comrades—everyone's, but especially those new comrades who are gaining ever more responsibility within our Party.